GOING GAGA

For Miko, Kasia and Coky

MEL GIEDROYC
GOING GAGA

EBURY
PRESS

1 3 5 7 9 10 8 6 4 2

Published in 2006 by Ebury Press, an imprint of Ebury Publishing
This edition published in 2007

Ebury Publishing is a division of the Random House Group

The Random House Group Limited Reg. No. 954009

Addresses for companies within the Random House Group
can be found at www.randomhouse.co.uk

A CIP catalogue record for this book is available from the British Library

The Random House Group Limited makes every effort to ensure that the
papers used in our books are made from trees that have been legally
sourced from well-managed and credibly certified forests. Our paper
procurement policy can be found on www.randomhouse.co.uk

Printed and bound in Great Britain by
Cox & Wyman Ltd, Reading, Berkshire

9780091905927

Going Ga Ga is a lightly fictionalized account of my own experiences as a
first-time mother. Names, people, places and dates have been changed to
protect the privacy of others. Otherwise, except in minor respects not
affecting the overall accuracy of the book, the contents are true.

ACKNOWLEDGEMENTS

With love and thanks to Andrew Goodfellow at Ebury for his long fuse and gentle persistence. To Alex Hazle, Emma Harrow and Mari Roberts for their patience, hard work and great haircuts. To Simon Trewin at PFD for his eagle eye and continual support. To Samira, Lucy, Deborah and Susan at ICM for their all-round good vibes and advice. To Mum, Dad and the family for their love and excellent gags. To Ben for putting up with me on a daily basis. And to the younger generation who have provided me with babysitting work over the years: to Mary, Jo, Frank, Ant, Charlie, Lily, Jack, Hannah, Chip and Fred. To Sos, Simon Bowie, Jan and Melchi. To Ziggy, Cas and Rosebud. And most of all Flossie and Vita, who are my constant inspiration.

Prologue

'I think we're going to have to throw away some of these photos,' said Dan.

'Baby photos?' I asked incredulously, as he held a fistful over the wastepaper basket. I lunged to grab them. 'No way, Dan. Those are moments, timeless moments, never-to-be-repeated-again living snapshots of our baby's precious life.'

'We're not actually throwing her in the bin,' he said, lifting the photos just slightly out of my reach.

'Give me those, you callous man,' I said, tears pricking at my eyes.

'It's getting ridiculous,' said Dan, warming to his theme. 'She's five months old and we've got maybe upward of four hundred photos of her. I mean, look at this lot. What the hell is the point of these?'

He handed me a packet and I smiled fondly as I leafed through them. They were photos of her clothes. I'd laid them all out on the sofa – two woollen bonnets, a little pair of shoes, a mini poncho, six different vests, a tiny coat, a summer dress – and photographed each and every item.

'They're a testament to Jo's clothes,' I explained.

Dan raised one eyebrow.

'So that we don't ever forget them.'

'Wouldn't a testament to her clothes be more interesting with a testament to her, i.e., her own body, inside them?'

'Don't you see, Dan? The photos are mementoes of everything she's ever worn.'

'Yes. Why on earth have the real clothes a mere few feet away upstairs when you can sit and look at these mementoes of them.'

I let this thought flit briefly across my brain, and then realized it was preposterous.

'But don't you see, these are the memories of the clothes. Memories are timeless. Ageless. Can't you see how much more important they are than the clothes themselves?'

A pause.

'No.'

'God, you're so male.'

'When we're old and dusty,' he said, 'call me old-fashioned but I'd like to be reminded of things like birthdays, her on horseback, skiing, maybe her wedding.'

'Hang on, Dan,' I said. 'Skiing? Horses? Who do you think we're bringing up here? Fergie?'

'Well, I don't want to be sitting in Happy Villas Nursing Home leafing through this ridiculous half-baked version of a Mini Boden catalogue, for God's sake. I mean, look at these pictures – you can't even make out the cow print on these bootees, the lighting's atrocious.'

'Well, all right, David Bailey, what about these then?'

I'd spotted some of Dan's work and thrust them in front of his face. Twenty photos featuring Jo lying beside a different piece of DIY equipment – one next to a pair of pliers, another beside an angle grinder, one beside a lathe, a vice, jigsaw, and so on. Dan grabbed them protectively to his chest.

'I wanted to juxtapose her vulnerability and frailness with the hardness and potential danger that these objects symbolize.'

I rolled my eyes.

2

'Well, at least mine have actually got Jo in them,' said Dan sulkily.

'They're still boring,' I mumbled.

'They're creative,' he mumbled back.

'I hate black and whites anyway,' I said, barely audibly.

'Philistine,' mouthed Dan.

Dan's love of all things DIY tends to frustrate me a bit. Much as I appreciate his practical side, I do wish we could sometimes paint our nails together in front of a Judith Krantz weepy. Dan doesn't much care for telly – he'd rather be stuck behind it tinkering with the scart leads. I cry in front of it once a day. Dan only allows himself to brim once a year, when he gets the garden furniture out of the shed. He's so proud of the way the teak shines after all that work he put into the linseed oiling.

I know it's useful to have one person in the partnership who can grout, put together a shelving unit and build a wormery, but does his hand always have to be hovering over the extendable tape measure attached permanently to his belt? Does he have to be up at six in the morning constructing a birdfeeder outside when he could be feeding his own bird upstairs in bed? I long for slivers of buttered toast and a shoeful of tea served to me in bed on a tray. Since our daughter arrived five months ago, all that's gone. I can't even remember the colour of Dan's eyes. I know they're blue, but are they azure with a hint of green or cornflower with flecks of grey? I simply don't know – it's been so long since I gazed into them for any length of time.

His eyes happened to be down at this point, shaking his head at the sea of photos around him.

Our living room was getting a bit cramped. A lot of the floor space was now taken up with Jo's baby-gym. I'd love to go to a gym where all you do is lie and dribble underneath some large primary-coloured blobs. The only thing that gets a workout is your optical nerve as your eyes swivel between giraffe, snail and seahorse. Elsewhere in the room Dan's guitar and amp had given way to a baby-walker, and our pseudo-grown-up coffee table had been brushed aside for the baby-swing, day crib and changing-mat area. And of course there was the bouncy chair nestling comfortably where my CD collection had once been, plus an inflatable seesaw, activity mat, rotating dandler and huge sheepskin fleece so that Baby can recognize its mother's smell. (Surely its mother has to be a sheep for that to work?) The room had also officially become a No Fly Zone. All available airspace was taken up with mobiles: sheep flying over fluffy clouds, a zany butterfly family with stripy legs and ridiculous hobnail boots – and the pièce de résistance? A beauty constructed out of the heads of some twentieth-century feminists. My friend Pen made it and presented it to Jo saying, 'I don't want her surrounded by all those macho toys that babies get bombarded with.'

'What, like fluffy animals?' I asked.

'If they're lions with manes, then yes,' she said adamantly.

'Right,' I said.

'And that twat who drives the red van,' she said.

'Postman Pat?'

'That's the one. Why does it have to be a man who drives the car?'

'Well, Dan always drives us. I'm scared of fourth gear now I've had a child.'

Pen continued: 'And as for Barbie, if I ever see one in this flat I'll shave her head and put a pair of Doctor Martens on her feet.'

'Come on, Pen.'

'I'm serious, Mel. It's really important for Jo to have proper feminist role models, right from Day One.'

I thought about this for a moment.

'What about me? Aren't I a good feminist role model?'

Pen didn't answer, and seemed suddenly engrossed by a piece of fluff on her sleeve. I felt annoyed at her implication that my principles had gone soft just because I'd had a baby.

'Would you like to try some of my home-baked macaroons, Pen? Wait a jiff while I fetch my hand-crocheted doilies. I'll set them out for us on a table. Oh, is that the time? I'll need to get down to the hairdresser's for my daily set. Doesn't time fly when you've got the hoovering to do!' And I flounced out of the room leaving her to hang the heads of Andrea Dworkin, Naomi Wolf, Angela Neustatter and Camille Paglia above Jo's bouncing chair.

Basically our daughter had slowly taken over the whole flat, which wasn't bad going for somebody the size of a small bag of compost. What was once a rather civilized bathroom with candles, white fluffy towels and his 'n' hers dressing gowns now resembled the changing room of a desperately run-down swimming pool. Sponge bags spilled pads everywhere, limp grey towels hung miserably on racks and an array of garish plastic toys and yet more gadgetry littered every surface. Adult bathing was made virtually impossible because of the baby's bathing throne erected right at the centre of the tub. It was a present from my friend Amanda who'd scribbled on the gift-tag: 'I picked this up in New York for you. Courteney Cox was in the shop buying one too.'

Typical Amanda. I dreaded to think what gigantic amounts of gear her eight-month-old son had collected since his birth – a mini fur coat and some cufflinks, no doubt. Who'd have thought you needed all this gubbins for one tiny person who was no bigger than the pack of nappies used to keep their bottom dry?

Most confusing of all, where had the landing gone? Our pristine little space at the top of the stairs had been replaced by a nappy-bin that on a bad day stank as badly as medieval England.

The whole of the upstairs was covered in bumpers and buffers, sleeping sacs with zips, fleeces and spongy bedspreads, not forgetting the travel cot, which was forced to go by the doorway of our bedroom. It was the bane of Dan's life.

'BLOODY travel cot,' he'd shout.

'Don't swear in front of the baby.'

His temper was flaring with the photo albums now. He was trying to stick the photos individually into those fiddly little corners.

'BLOODY corners.'

'Don't swear in front of the baby.'

'EFFING corners.'

'The only thing missing there is "uck", Dan.'

'BLINKING corners.'

'Your tone is aggressive, which is as bad as the swearing itself. Come here, I'll do them,' I snapped.

I sensed a bicker hovering in the air. Bickering was our only form of communal recreation now. We didn't go out any more. I'd forgotten the name of our nearest pub. Was it the Merkin and Firkin or was it the Jerkin and Firkin? No idea. An evening's entertainment now consisted of two choices: either a reality TV show featuring wrestling celebs, or a darned good bicker. While it could be diverting to watch two people pummel each other into the dust, bickering was actually more fun and sometimes ended up with us pummelling each other anyway, so we felt like we were getting more value for our money that way.

On this occasion the bicker was averted by the vigorous gyrations of a five-month-old larynx. A pair of fists started to bob in and out of the basket in the corner of the room. Thank God for the distraction of our daughter. I ran towards the basket, tripping over photo albums on the way.

'There we go, my gorgeous. I'm going to give you a big fat kiss.'

'I didn't know you cared,' said Dan gloomily.

I plunged past him, scooped up our baby and planted an enormous smacker on her padded little neck.

'Didn't think so,' he mumbled, and shuffled off into the kitchen, tripping over the baby-springer as he went.

'BLOODY bouncer.'

'Stop swearing, and it's a springer, not a bouncer. And can you please get me a clean muslin square?' I added, sitting down with Jo in my lap.

'There aren't any,' Dan called. 'I had a really bad nose bleed and it was the nearest thing to hand. Sorry, but they're all buggered.'

'What? How ruddy dare you? You know I need them all the time. Winding, blotting, wiping, padding ...'

'My nose bleed was really heavy.'

'You are so selfish.'

'I must have lost a pint of blood,' he called out mournfully.

'Poor Jo will have nothing to be sick on.'

'Don't worry about me.'

'You are the pits, Dan.'

Now I was secretly pleased – here was our elusive bicker rearing its head once more. I continued where I'd left off.

'A nose bleed? Who gets nose bleeds? That's a useless thing to get. I want you to place every bloody muslin square into a soaker bucket – and that wasn't a swear word, I was describing the blood – and add a non-biological detergent, Dan. And then put the machine on to pre-wash ...'

I heard the kitchen door slam.

'Dan ... Dan?'

I looked down at Jo, and the minx raised her little gingery caterpillar eyebrows at me just like her father. In a slightly ironic way. My bad mood melted with pride and I couldn't help smiling.

Here was yet another shining example of how unbelievably advanced our daughter was. I was tempted to phone the UCAS clearing system straight away to see if there were any university places left for October. Not only could she drink milk extremely skilfully out of a bottle, and take a toy with one hand and then brilliantly transfer it to the other hand, she could now add facial expressions to her repertoire.

I stroked her head as she drank from her bottle. Her jaw moving gustily over the teat quite suddenly brought Nora to mind. Nora. That had only been five months ago. It felt like a lifetime.

Chapter One

Nora was one of the midwives on night duty just after Jo had been born, a very matter-of-fact Irish woman with glasses and freckles.

'If you need any help getting Baby to feed, then just give me a shout. My name's Nora.'

How I'd chuckled when she'd first told me her name. Nora. Apt for somebody who shows you how to clamp a gnawing mouth onto your norks. Maybe her surname was Titoff?

I thought it unlikely I'd need the good Nora's help as I looked over into Jo's plastic cot, where she was sleeping as soundly as a little woodchuck. She was an angel-baby, this one. Still euphoric having given birth only six hours before, I was totally convinced that everything about her, me, our lives was just perfect.

'Oh my God look, Dan! Look at that AMAZING jug!'

Dan looked around him, saw three mothers breastfeeding and said, 'Er ... which jug?'

'The one on the windowsill.'

'Oh. That jug.'

'Yes. The clear one. The one with the carnations in. Isn't it amazing? Isn't it so clear-cut and beautiful?'

'You mean that plastic one?' He was pointing to a hospital water-jug.

'Yes! Look at the way the light just sort of arcs through it, and then bounces off that heart monitor. Isn't that just the most beautiful thing you've ever seen? God I feel amazing. I just want to take a walk through this amazing hospital, with the jug and the flowers, and stand outside it for a bit and feel the sun on my face and just breathe it all in!'

I leant forward in my bed as if to get out, before Dan gently manoeuvred me back in.

'Remember the pads, Mel.'

Ah yes, the pads. I did feel a bit like an old boiler that has just been lagged for winter. Or is the word 'cladded'? I didn't want to ask Dan what the right terminology was and risk the hour-long monologue about boiler servicing. Whatever the word was, I felt like an astronaut who'd just landed on earth with a year's worth of space-poop in his trousers.

'I don't care – I'll just glide! I want to meet everyone in this wonderful place. There are so many lovely babies to see and get to know. So many potential friends for Jo. I've got so much to share, so much to find out, so much to give! Oh aren't maternity units just amazing?'

And then I burst into tears while Dan scouted round for something to mop up with. His life was becoming one long trip to the Noah's Ark Experience theme park. All he could find were some panty-pads. They did the job.

'Oh I love you, Dan. I love you so much, and Jo, and us. I just love us all so much.'

The lady in the next-door bed was emerging from her sleep and opened one tortoise-like eye very slowly. Dan looked at her slightly apologetically. She looked careworn, and her upper arms spilled out of a nightie that had seen better days. She took one look at us and said, 'Must be your first.'

'Yes!' I said breathlessly, beaming towards our cot.

'Thought so,' she said, and heaved herself up into a sitting position, wincing slightly. 'My sixth,' she said, barely nodding towards her cot. There were no flowers, no cards, nothing around it to suggest a celebration of any kind. 'My old man hasn't even been in yet.'

Dan looked genuinely shocked. 'Didn't he want to be there to cut the cord?'

'Nah. He was down Crystal Palace, wasn't he? They told him over the tannoy at half-time that I'd dropped.' She gave a wheezing laugh. 'He missed the second goal and all, he was right pissed off.'

'So you were on your own?' I said, wide-eyed.

'Oh yeah. Only took twenty minutes, didn't it?'

'Boy or girl?' I enquired dutifully.

'Boy. Our sixth. We keep trying for a girl' – a moment of boredom passed over her face – 'but keep getting these. We'll have another, maybe we'll strike lucky next time.'

'Well done, anyway,' I said, sounding like the captain of the lacrosse team.

She gave me a blank look.

'I'm Mel by the way,' I said.

'You're that lady used to be on the telly, aren't you?'

'Yes, that's right,' I said, trying to sound suitably abashed.

'You used to do that thing, didn't you? Never saw it.'

Dan coughed slightly.

'I'm Dan. What's your name?'

'Fran,' she replied.

At this point a gangly teenager with very baggy trousers appeared in the ward. A small boy was at his side, no bigger than four years old. They approached her bedside.

'Here's that lady used to be on the telly, didn't she?'

The boys shrugged their shoulders blankly.

'Did you get my lemonade?' she asked.

'Forgot,' said the teenager. 'Bought you these though.'

He handed her a packet of cigarettes.

'Ta, darling.'

'That's exactly what you'll get in your lungs if you smoke those. Tar, I mean,' murmured Dan. Fran rolled her eyes.

I shot Dan a look.

'Here he is, then,' Fran announced to her sons.

'Boy, is it?' asked the teenager. At which point he looked into the cot and tilted his head slightly backwards in acknowledgement. He couldn't hide a tiny smile though, and touched his new brother's cheek with a finger.

'Let's have a look,' said the four-year-old, who was lifted up to see into the cot.

'These are my sons,' said Fran. 'Say hello, Dylan and Shane.'

'All right?' said Dylan, looking at the floor.

Shane didn't respond, but had started running a little plastic car up and down the cot.

'Congratulations on your new brother,' I gushed. 'Six brothers. Wow!'

'Have one more brother and you'll have a musical on your hands!' quipped Dan. They looked blankly at us. '*Seven Brides For Seven Brothers*.' Dan's voice trailed off into nothingness. He coughed lightly and tweaked Jo's blanket.

Dylan turned on his personal stereo, his mother picked up a magazine, Shane was engrossed with his car and their new arrival slept on. That was that. No fuss, no gush. I suddenly felt self-conscious about the flowers, cards and presents that we'd placed all around our little curtained area.

Jo started to stir in her cot. This put us onto immediate red alert.

'Do you think she's hungry?' I asked immediately, ready to lower the flaps on my gigantic nursing bra.

'Maybe. She might be cold. Shall I ask for another blanket?'

'Do you think she's still tired?'

'Shall we wake her?'

'Maybe pull the curtain over a bit, Dan. I think she may be getting too much light.'

'No, it's good for her to have light. Especially if she's a bit jaundiced.'

'Jaundice? Do you think so? Let's press the Attention Button. We'd better get the consultant involved. Jaundice can be dangerous if not treated properly.'

And so we fuss-budgeted several hours away while the family next to us remained silent and calm, chewing the occasional toffee.

'Oh my God! What's the time?' I asked Dan. 'They're running a pelvic-floor workshop at twelve. I'd better go!' Again I tried to get out of the bed.

'Are you sure that's a good idea?' said Dan.

'I must,' I said heroically. 'I'll take the baby in case she needs a feed.'

There then followed a very intricate set of manoeuvres to get the baby out of her cot. Dan scooped her up while I held her head, then he transferred her to me, taking over charge of her head. Then I had to somehow cover her feet with the blanket and at the same time get the blanket out from under my armpit while helping Dan to hold her head. Meanwhile the teenage Dylan had flicked his own baby brother onto one shoulder like a pet rat.

'Hang on,' I said. 'I need the loo.'

Then the whole process had to be repeated backwards to get Jo back into her cot so that I could go to the bathroom. By the time I'd shuffled back and we'd got Jo out of the cot for the second time, it was twenty past twelve and I was knackered.

'Oh stuff the pelvic floor muscles. I'm sure they're in there somewhere.'

'You'd better get some kip,' Dan warned. 'You're going to get seriously overtired.'

'Sleep? Sleep at a time like this? How can I? Our daughter is barely ten hours old and you want me to sleep? I don't want to sleep again ever. I mustn't miss a moment of her. I want to touch her, know her, imbibe her ...'

I was suddenly aware of three pairs of eyes on me, and looked round to see Fran and her boys staring at me.

And so I spent a lovely afternoon with my first-born. Dan snoozed in the chair a bit, but I stayed awake, hugging myself, checking her, sighing deeply, then shuffling round the ward smiling at other mothers, and then going back into our little nest again.

As the afternoon wore on into evening, and still she slept, I began to feel slightly weary. I had a bath and contemplated the still enormous girth of my stomach. The baby had come out, but strangely there seemed to be no obvious change in size of pregnancy bump. Interesting. I'd have to ask Nora about that. I got back into bed, shut my eyes and was immediately in a dream where I was at a banquet. I was just opening my jaws round an enormous side of ham when an alien sound jabbed at my ears. An insistent little barking, like a fox-cub. I woke up and saw Jo's eyes actually open for the first time since the birth. They looked angry. And her mouth was open and formed into an 'O', meaning 'O get on with it, you silly woman.'

I fumbled around and did a reasonable job of marrying her mouth with a strange veined balloon that had once fitted snugly into a lacy B-cupped bustier. Oh dear. She kept going for a little while as I felt an increasing shaft of pain go straight from bosom to brain. Time to call Nora.

'Why don't you try a bit of skin-on-skin?' she suggested.

This rather sinister turn of phrase had been imprinted on our minds throughout the antenatal classes as a way of bonding with offspring. Apparently they like nothing better than to press their naked bodies into your slightly tired folds of flesh.

All the other mothers in our ward were beginning to settle down with their infants for the night, mostly well fed and ready to kip. Contented adult snores were starting to mingle with the babies' snuffling as I rustled round in our curtained-off booth, desperate to get our little one off to sleep. There really wasn't room with Dan there too. His big frame was starting to annoy me, and he smelled of Scotch eggs. Two months ago I would have murdered someone for a Scotch egg, but now they just reminded me of dodgy petrol stations.

'Do you think she's still hungry?' said Dan.

His very presence was starting to grate, and he was also yawning incessantly.

'Look, why don't you go home and sleep?' I said sharply. 'No point in both of us getting no sleep.'

'Yeah, OK,' he said a little too quickly for my liking. 'I might meet up with my brother for a quick pint before going home.' He started to put his jacket on. 'I don't want to go though,' he added hastily, and planted a kiss on my mouth that smelt of Monster Munch.

'Just go,' I said grumpily.

I had a sudden desire to be him. To be a man. A flat-chested, no-breasted man, with an easy stride and no cladding down the gusset. His back was straight as he receded down the corridor – that's because he didn't have bosoms distended to the size of two large beer-guts bumping around in front of him.

Jo was starting to bark again, and Fran was starting to tut-tut. I'd woken her up. Jo's bark started to rise in volume and pitch, and I knew that I was going to have to get her out of there to avoid a lynching. I didn't fancy my chances of surviving suffocation by ten hormonal mothers.

'So sorry. It's her. Just been born,' I whispered in the general direction of the room as I bundled my yelping baby into the corridor. Now what? Where was Nora? Oh God, maybe Jo was ill?

Nora took me to an empty delivery room down the corridor and settled me into a rocking chair.

'Wide awake, that one!' she said, smiling.

'Why? It's nine in the evening, for Pete's sake!'

'Her clock's back to front, probably.'

'I did stay up rather late sometimes when I was pregnant. Up to eleven on occasion.'

'Oh goodness, it's nothing to do with that – it's just her. You'll have to wait till she adjusts, that's all.'

I spent the next four hours trying to help her adjust. Gentle rocking, shuffling up and down the corridor and then going through my entire repertoire of hits from my youth. She loved Duran Duran, but wasn't so keen on Bauhaus. 'Damn. I was looking forward to singing "Bela Lugosi's Dead",' I said to her crumpled little face. And I shuffled off down the corridor again, singing 'Rio' for the nth time.

As I saw the ward clock reach 2 a.m., I realized that I hadn't slept for thirty hours. I also realized, rather neatly, that I hadn't done that since the last time I was shuffling down a corridor singing 'Rio', although then it was in a students' hall of residence and I was drunk and wearing a bin-liner, as opposed to a winceyette nightie in a maternity ward.

Where was Nora? She was probably helping some other mother out. God, the other mothers were so demanding. I decided to go in search of her. Down the corridor again, past the thank-you cards pinned onto the wall.

'To all in the Edith Dare Ward – you've been brilliant. Love from Baby Jo-Lee.'

I thought that was bloody ridiculous. Imagine that. A card from a twelve-hour-old baby.

'To all the midwives, thank you for delivering me, love Millie.'

Silly Millie and her even sillier parents. Oh dear, the rose tints were falling away from my eyes pretty fast. I looked over at the window where the jugs were kept. Yes, they were ordinary, rather ugly plastic jugs. No mistaking those.

I found Nora with another mother, whose baby was lost inside her fecund folds.

'Well done, Joanna. You're doing absolutely brilliantly. Look at how content your little one is!' cooed Nora. And then she turned to the writhing purple mess in my arms.

'Oh,' she said, 'still not asleep? Did you try a bit of skin-on-skin?'

Of course. I'd forgotten the skin-on-skin thing. I got myself back to the rocking chair and decided to give it a go.

At 5 a.m. there was a light tapping on the door, and I answered, half laughing, half crying.

'Welcome to Club Tropicana. Fun and sunshine, there's enough for everyone,' I sang loudly.

'It's Nora. Can I come in?'

'Nora! Come on in and join the fun. Order of the night is crying, a bit more crying, and then crying with some additional screaming. It's great!'

'Oh dear,' was her muted response. She looked at me, blushing slightly. 'Mel,' she said quietly, 'I assume you've been doing skin-on-skin with your baby?'

'Abso-ruddy-lutely,' I said wildly. 'For the past three hours, and it's had absolutely no effect whatsoever. Doctor Spock can go and beam himself up to Planet Nob-Jockey as far as I'm concerned because he got it SO WRONG.'

'OK. Can I suggest one thing?' she said gently.

'That we leave here and go and start a new life together in Malaga, Nora? I'm in,' I said, starting to hit the crest of hysteria.

'No.' Her tone was firm now. 'That you put some clothes on yourself and your baby. You'll both get chilly.'

I looked down at my butt-naked form, squashed rather unphotogenically into the rocking chair, with my little daughter, also nude, tucked into one of my many crevices.

'But what about the skin-on-skin?' I protested.

'It can be any part of your skin. Like her tummy against your neck or your breast. It doesn't have to be ... all of your skin.'

'Ah,' I said sheepishly, 'OK,' and crossed my legs. 'Would you mind awfully passing me that hand towel over there, Nora? Actually, make that a large bath towel. Thank you so much.'

I got a few snatched moments of sleep before Jo finally settled into a log-like slumber at about ten to nine in the morning. She was totally serene, her features at rest and her skin no longer the colour of a blueberry. I, on the other hand, caught sight of my reflection and thought that my old pottery teacher, Mrs McCulloch, had broken into the ward. Mrs McCulloch, with her tangled mess of lank hair and sandblasted wrinkled face due to too many years at the kiln. I shuffled over to the bathroom. Yes, my fears were confirmed – Mrs McCulloch had actually morphed into me. God I was tired.

I went back to my bed and lay down with my dressing gown splayed rather unbecomingly over my hairy legs. I didn't care. It was 9 a.m., and this was going to be the first sleep I'd had since the birth of my baby.

* * *

I looked at the clock. 9.19 a.m. I must have slept for a whole twenty-four hours. I felt fantastic. And good old Jo – what a star. I didn't realize that babies could sleep for twenty-four hours when they were still so tiny.

'Thanks for looking after Jo,' I said to Nora, who was doing a ward round.

'Oh that's OK; you've only been out a few minutes.'

'What? I thought that this was tomorrow?'

'No, it's still today.'

'But I've only had nineteen minutes' sleep!' I said.

'Welcome to motherhood,' she said as she left.

I looked around me. All I could see were zombified forms of hollow-eyed women shuffling round in nighties. I was so tired I'd gone through to the other side and felt wired again. I needed activity. I sat up on the bed. What's there to do in hospital? I could go and browse around the metallic helium balloon collection. Or maybe go and get some tokens for the yellow telephone trolley.

As I was pondering this, I heard the familiar dulcet tones of my mother ringing down the corridor. She was chatting to somebody, presumably my dad, and humming something at the same time. It sounded like Gilbert & Sullivan. Oh no. That would confirm my status as the geek of the ward.

Mum peeked her headscarved head around the curtain. Dad followed soon after. They gave me the most cursory of greetings before hunching immediately over my daughter's cot. They were pleased as punch with her.

'Look at that profile, dear. That's definitely the Parkinson side of the family. Although let's not hope that she takes after Great Aunt Emily. She drowned in a well aged three.'

'Isn't she gorgeous?' I said, brimming.

'Gosh you look tired.'

'Yes, Mum, that's probably because I had nineteen minutes' sleep last night.'

Dad pulled back the bedcovers and very tenderly helped me into bed. Mum sat herself down in the chair and drew breath, which is always a bad sign.

'It really is ridiculous. When you were born I simply wasn't allowed to leave the hospital until you were practically sleeping through the night. I expect they'll turf you out today, won't they?'

'I don't know,' I said. I felt like my eyeballs had been taken out and rolled in gravel.

'Well, maybe I should speak to someone,' she said. 'Who's in charge of this place? In my day it used to be matron. Who's in charge of the ward now? It's probably some wanker in a suit and a clipboard ticking off those awful hospital targets, or whatever they're called ...'

'Mum, am I dreaming or did you just say the word "wanker"?'

'Wanker. Yes, I did. Your father taught it to me. Didn't you, dear?'

'Er, yes, I did indeed.'

'He told me that it means fool.'

Dad looked at me with a crafty glint in his eye.

'That's right,' he said. 'Now, where is that coffee machine?' and off he went to find it, his shoulders rising and falling with laughter.

'Now' – Mum had started fishing around in a National Trust bag – 'I've brought provisions. You're probably feeling like your lower cupboards have been somewhat rummaged around in ... if you know what I mean. Don't let them try to give you silly pills and cream. This is what you need,' and she plonked an enormous bag of something white and granular on the bedside table. For a moment I thought my mum had become a coke dealer.

'Salt,' she said. 'It's the only thing. Every time you wash, do tinies or just need a freshen-up – salt. Oodles of it. With hot water.

Stings like Hades, but it's worth it. Now, what else? I've knitted bootees, bonnet and gloves for Littly and I fished out that macintosh mattress that you used to sleep on. Honestly, all this talk these days about the danger of mattresses. Absolute rubbish. You slept on horse-hair and macintosh and look at you!'

Whereupon she turned to look at me with a smile, which quickly slid off her face like a Dalí clock.

'Oh. Dear, may I suggest you run a comb through your hair and put a little bit of powder on your nose? You look like something out of a Turkish prison.'

'Mum. I've just given birth, for Pete's sake.'

'Yes, but it's no excuse. You don't want Dan's eyes to start wandering, do you? Especially after he's seen you in your altogether huffing and puffing to get Littly out. You know, I do think it's a shame that husbands have to see their wives in that … rather indiscreet way. It was wonderful for your father to come into the hospital and find me washed and brushed, and Littly just there, care of the stork's first-class cabin. No mess, no fuss. No ruderies on display. Honestly, is it any wonder that so many marriages break up after the husband has been forced to look at all that down there?'

Before I could summon up the energy to say something withering or launch a plastic jug at my mother's head, I was saved by Nora poking her friendly face round the curtain again.

'Do you need any painkillers?' she asked.

'She doesn't need painkillers, dear,' Mum chipped in straight away, 'she needs a good hairdresser and three Valium. Are you in charge here?'

'I'm one of the senior midwives. I'm sure I can be of some help,' she answered, amazingly cordially for somebody probably as sleepless as me.

'Well, where do I begin?'

'Mum, please.' I could feel my cheeks hotting up.

'Now. I really think that my daughter and granddaughter should not be discharged until Littly is sleeping through the night. That's what happened to every mother of my generation, and I believe they still practise the same in France' – her expression soured – 'which is one of the very few advantages of being French. That and béchamel sauce. Anyway, can this be arranged?'

Nora looked weary. 'We usually let Mum and Baby go within two days, unless there are complications. Then the community midwife takes over with home visits.'

'Hospital policy, eh? Look at my daughter. She looks like a heroin addict. Are you honestly going to let her leave your hospital looking like that?'

'Mum, I'm fine, and it's not really Nora's problem—'

But there was no stopping her.

'Now, Nora dear. I cut these crysanths in the garden this morn-ing. They're rather prone to wilting if they don't get a nice drink. I don't want to be a wanker, but would you mind awfully getting me a vase for them? Glass rather than plastic. Thank you so much.'

A stream of people passed through that day, and I was so tired I'd developed three separate twitches in my face. Oh, for the stern broad-beamed matron of yesteryear to come and shoo away the visitors. Dan arrived soon after Mum and Dad had left, and fell asleep almost immediately in the chair. His breath was beery, the wretch. Little Jo was blissfully unaware of everything and slept as soundly as a snail. Man I was jealous. I'd have given anything to coil myself up in the cot with her.

I was just drifting off when my friend Pen turned up with a girl from Berlin. Great. I had to make conversation with a German girl in PVC trousers who sneered gothically into Jo's cot and then kept kissing Pen dramatically on the lips. Drinking a cup of tea in a maternity ward was obviously not her idea of the London Experience. She was probably itching to get to Spitalfields Market, or wherever it is that posers go. Bloody German. They stayed for two hours. They even ordered in a takeaway. I was livid, and Dan was absolutely no use. He joined in, talking merrily away in German and dropping big gobbets of plum sauce all over the sheets. I was desperate to get my head down. Like my daughter seemed to be doing so easily. She didn't even move a muscle when Dan accidentally spat out a piece of cashew nut on her head. We shut up hospitality at around seven in the evening and I was just drifting off when Jo woke up, and suddenly the night stretched in front of us once again.

She stayed very calm for about five minutes, gripping onto my shoulder like a little koala. And then she ripped into her barking mode.

It was another night of hollering and knockering. Holler, knockers, holler, knockers.

Hospital policy won out, and we left the following day, after another glorious night of about twelve minutes' sleep. I was now concerned that my eyes were never going to emerge from my face again. There was precious little sign of them – they were like little currants in an ever-expanding bowl of greying dough. We left a card for the ward staff.

'To everyone on the Edith Dare Ward. Ha ha ha ha! My plan to crush my parents is going well. I shall have annihilated them before the winter is finished. Ha ha ha! The Demon Baby Jo.'

I noticed the midwives looking rather puzzled as they passed the card around. This was definitely one that wouldn't be pinned up on the wall.

Chapter Two

It was good to get back home, a family at last.

I made sure I spent a lot of time getting from the car into the flat, just to make sure that as many neighbours as possible got the chance to ogle the supreme gorgeousness wrapped up in my arms. Our neighbour Irene poked a gnarled finger rather too strongly into her chest for my liking.

'Look at the little thing. He's gorgeous.'

'Thanks, Irene. It's a girl.'

'What's his name?'

'She's called Jo.'

'Jo? For Joseph? Nice name Joseph. Nice man too. Good with wood, God bless him.'

'Irene, she's actually a girl.'

And then she addressed the baby.

'You make sure your mammy gives you enough to eat. Boys need a lot of food, you know. I've got three meself and they still eat me out of house and home. Goodbye, darling,' with which she chucked Jo's cheek and went off in search of fags.

Dan had decked the flat out with all the cards, presents and flowers we'd received. There was one bunch of television flowers, easily the most expensive – wrapped in swathes of tissue paper and tied with an entire bed of bulrushes. It was from a TV company I'd worked with not long before giving birth. They'd made a documentary about overweight dogs, and I'd recorded the voiceover for it. Sweet of them to send flowers, but I didn't want to be reminded of the world of work just now, so I put them on a shelf in the downstairs loo.

I had a couple of hours of truly blackout sleep while Dan minded the baby, and woke up feeling fresh as a daisy.

Sitting down on the sofa with Jo in her basket at my feet, one hand wrapped round a nice mug of builder's tea while the other dipped in and out of a tin of custard creams, it seemed to me the world was a beautiful place.

I looked down at her sleeping, her absurdly small body as compact as a loaf of bread in its little white sleeping suit. Her fists were still clenched and defensive, as if putting up a fight against these strange people she'd only been introduced to so recently. I crouched down beside the basket to stroke her, and then lay on my back and stared at the ceiling. I suddenly saw myself lying in an open coffin. There I was in a white shroud, lying next to her tiny breathing body. It had never crossed my mind before, in any real sense, that one day I would be dead. Oh my God, I'd have a funeral and everything. And there'd be no Mum to make the flap-jacks, because chances are she'd be dead too. We'd all be dead! But what if I died first, then Dan, and Mum outlived us both? She'd take over our baby. Jo would be sent to boarding school and would end up either as a show-jumper or a drug-addled wreck. Oh no. This was terrible. I spotted a brown patch on the ceiling. I looked around the living room. All I could see were dust, cobwebs, death and destruction. I felt a huge lump fill my throat, like a hard-boiled egg that was swallowed too fast. My bottom lip started to judder and I felt every muscle in my face collapse as I started to cry. I had no control over my lips at all. Endless tears gushed out, on and on they came, hotter and hotter. I'd turned into a geyser. And not through any gender-realignment surgery.

Dan came into the room with more tea, and took in the sight of his sodden wife on the floor. He braced himself subtly, almost imperceptibly. His eyes refocused, and there was the merest suggestion that his top lip had pulled itself over his teeth.

'Come on, sweetheart,' he said gently, helping me back up onto the sofa. 'Would you like another custard cream?'

'I'm ... going ... to ... die,' I said, my voice strangely strangulated and about three octaves higher than normal.

'No you won't. The sell-by date's 2008,' he said. 'Custard creams have got so much sugar in them they'll outlive us all.'

'That's what I mean. I'm going ... to ... d ... d ... die.'

Dan pondered this moment of existential angst. Stroking my hair, he crooned: 'We are born to die. It's the only certainty in all of our lives.'

'I ... don't ... want ... to ... die.' Every word was punctuated with a gasp.

He thought for a few moments.

'I don't want you to either. I really don't fancy trying to breastfeed.'

'I've ... only ... just ... begun ... to ... to ...' I was finding it hard to get any words out at all.

'Enjoy yourself?' suggested Dan.

'N ... n ... no.'

'Realize what a flaming gorgeous hunk you're married to?'

'N ... n ... no.'

'Finally appreciate that Fairport Convention are the greatest band ever that ever lived?' Poor Dan was trying to cheer me up.

I tried to get my breath back.

'I've only just begun to l ... l ... l ... live.' And there followed twenty minutes of hot waterworks. Dan looked as if he'd been sitting in one of those 'Sponge-A-Teacher' stalls that you get at school fêtes. The guy was drenched.

'Can I go and put a new shirt on, sweetheart?' he whispered gently during a lull.

'Yes,' I said, amazingly squawk-free.

Dan stood up.

'No. No, Dan! Don't go. Don't leave me here. Not when I'm going to … to … to … DIE SOON!'

Dan was eventually released from my grip later that evening.

The sofa is what immediately comes to mind when I think about those first couple of months having Jo at home with us. My old brown velvet friend, my island, my home. I was in it, on it or astride it, pretty much all day and all night. Its shape had actually become the inverse of my large body. I should probably have entered it for the Turner Prize.

I could only have certain cushions on it in a particular formation, and woe betide Dan if he tried any funny business like sitting on it without asking my permission first. There was a perfectly sized gap between bottom cushion and arm which I'd created for the biscuit barrel, another for a large jar of Celebrations and a third for the baby, when she wasn't clamped onto my norks. The sofa arms were used for cups of tea, muslin squares and custard creams, but their prime function was to act as holding bay for my beautiful array of remote controls. They became like my other children. I even had names for them. Siobhan operated the video, Norman the TV and Bernard the DVD. God, I loved them as my own. I could whisk between them and press their buttons faster than any Wild West shooter.

The TV viewing schedule became my obsession. It was my specialist subject. From learning Chinese at three in the morning with the Open University through to celebrity plastic surgery in the small hours, I was devoted to it all. It was the first time I'd ever watched soap operas. I watched each and every one of them. Sometimes I watched an episode again on another digital channel on the same day. I knew all the characters more intimately than my own family, and I preferred their company over real friends.

'Helen's really going to have to watch how she treats John, you know,' I said to Dan one morning.

'Helen that you used to work with? I thought her husband's name was Mark.'

'No, Helen Bates, landlady of the Anchor. She used to be with Deb's ex David, but she slept around a hell of a lot after her illness – kind of a delayed reaction to the horror of it all, or something, at least that's what Nelly thinks. I don't know myself, but I really think that John's bad news for her. Well, he's damaged goods. Especially with the alcoholism after his business went down and everything. What do you reckon, Dan? Dan? Dan, are you there?'

Dan had left the room.

The odd live friend managed to make it through to the sofa. My so-called friend Amanda, for instance. I'm convinced she only keeps in touch because I'm occasionally on the telly, but Dan says I'm being harsh. Our mums knew each other when we were babies in Leatherhead. So you could say that she was my oldest friend, although I probably have more in common with Irene our neighbour than I do with Amanda. Like my on-and-off cystitis, she remains an annoying feature of my life.

Anyway, I managed to keep the telly on very quietly in the background throughout her visit. Even if I couldn't hear it, I still needed to see if the young lad from *Hollyoaks* managed to get over the grief of losing his boyfriend.

Amanda looked around the rather dog-eared surroundings with a mixture of pity and disdain. It was 5 p.m. and I was wearing a Snoopy pyjama top with terrible breast-milk stains, and tracksuit trousers.

I allowed Amanda to perch on the arm of the sofa; she wasn't friend enough to be allowed access to the sacred cushion area. She made her perching look like it was part of some Pilates routine – Amanda always does that. She is a personal trainer and is always exercising. Even if she lifts something out of a cupboard, she manages to make it look aerobic. When she sleeps she's probably exercising her nostrils. She didn't stop jangling her Jeep keys in carefully manicured fingers either, a very positive sign that she wasn't intending to stay long.

'So are you going out much?' she asked.

'I went to the newsagents ... oh ... about five days ago, I think. All the way to the top of the road. It was great. Everybody was there – Irene, Brendan the drunk, several school kids and the newsagent's wife.'

Amanda let a brief smile flash over her mouth, but not her eyes. She's not renowned for her sense of humour.

'You should get out, Mel. A week after I'd had Balthazar I was in my Jimmy Choos down at China Whites.'

'That's great, Amanda. And a week after I'd had Jo I was in my Garfield slippers down at Threshers.'

Oh God I wanted her to go. *Hollyoaks* looked like it was getting exciting. Something was about to kick off in the restaurant. I yawned a bit too hugely.

'Well, I'd better make tracks,' said Amanda. 'I'm training some-body at six. I'll give you a call really soon. Oh yeah, do you fancy coming to a bit of a do?'

I stared into the middle distance. 'What, with people and stuff?'

'A lovely girl I train, who's become a really really close friend …'

Here we go – did I have a crash mat to hand? One would surely be needed for this clanger of a name drop that was about to thump onto my living-room floor.

'Tania Bryant,' she announced proudly.

The name meant less to me than the name of the current regional manager of the Connex train network.

'Tania Bryant's so fab,' enthused Amanda, 'a real girl's girl. I play golf with her quite a lot. She hosts these brilliant parties for her kids and invites loads of celebs along. Last year she did one in the Hilton and there was a pirate-ship theme. Balthazar wore some really fabby Dolce and Gabbana stripy trousers. Apparently all the kids loved it. I didn't actually go into the room where all the kids were, but my nanny said it was a riot. It's wicked, you can chat to lots of people you haven't seen for ages, and you don't get disturbed by the kids at all.'

I felt a chill sweep round the sofa. I couldn't think of anything worse than a kids' party hosted by a dodgy celeb for other dodgy celebs, in honour of kids that were actually hidden away. Who was this Tania Bryant? She sounded like the baroness in *Chitty Chitty Bang Bang*, for God's sake, who banned all children from her kingdom.

'She's throwing a Middle-Eastern-themed bash for her seven-year-old twins in a couple of weeks. Fancy coming?' said Amanda.

I was going to have to come up with something convincing.

'Ooh, now, the next couple of weeks are kind of busy. We've got the wedding in *Emmerdale*, the funeral in *Coronation Street*, and the Mitchell brothers are returning to Albert Square. So, no, I'm afraid I'm busy.'

Amanda continued, oblivious.

'Shane Richie's kids were at the last one. There was a photo of them in *OK!* magazine, and you can see me in the background! And she'll have a do for her daughter Amethyst later in the year.'

She was still jangling those keys. Desperate measures were required to get rid of her now. Of course. My new weapons of mass distraction. I unbelted the enormous hooks on the cantilever jumbo-bra and let the flaps down. With the cabin doors now at manual, I prepared to release the beasts. A look of pure fear crossed Amanda's face.

'Oh God. I didn't realize you were into all that. Babes, I'll give you a call nearer the time,' and she brushed my cheek with a kiss that smelled overpoweringly musky and slightly cheap, like an air-hostess.

'Cutie,' said Amanda in the direction of my daughter, whom she'd barely glanced at.

Phew, she was gone.

The sensible TV doctor's book was of course effusive about the positive benefits of breastfeeding. The main draw seems to be that you magically get thinner every time you do it. Looking down at the several spare tyres flopping over my tracksuit trousers, I couldn't help feeling that I'd been sold a lie. It even went on to describe a sort of tugging feeling in one's core while you feed your baby as the uterus is magically retracted to its former taut glory, leaving only a flat stomach in its wake, as if nothing untoward had ever taken place there. Every time Jo fed, I waited with bated breath to feel the tugging thing. How glorious to get all thin just by sitting on my arse with my boobs out! The slight problem with the whole theory was that it didn't seem to work. I'd fully expected to jump back into my pre-pregnancy jeans a couple of months after giving birth, but I'd barely managed to get one leg over the knee. What the hell was going on? I was still in drawstring trousers and my back breasts were seriously competing with my frontals for size and weight.

Maybe I just had to wait a bit and then suddenly I'd get skinny. It was early days. Breastfeeding seemed to be all I did during those first couple of months. I'd started to look like one of those women in pictures by Hogarth. Those drunken fallen women with bed-head, random babies falling out of their arms because they're too busy holding gin bottles. I'd had an image of us all having lots of day trips, showing our baby the world. The only worlds the baby saw were those which Siobhan, Norman and Bernard let her see. Only when the room started to stink of hot TV did I switch it off, and then I got bored. My mother gave some tips about all the useful things you can do while breastfeeding your baby.

'You can crochet with one hand. You can probably even make a good fist of some embroidery. I used to read. I read hundreds of books when I was feeding. Got through the whole of Dickens. Goodness, imagine Charles Dickens looking down on me, with my bosoms showing, reading *Great Expectations*!'

'I'm sure he's seen it all before, Mum, and his expectations probably weren't very great.'

My mother laughed before looking briefly confused.

'You should stop watching that ghastly television,' she added. 'How will Dan be able to discuss literature with his wife if she's turned into a vegetable?'

'Listen, Mum, I can barely follow the narrative thread of the instructions on the back of a microwave meal, let alone the three-act structure of a Pushkin novel. I can't even watch *When Harry Met Sally* any more without asking Dan two hundred times what's going on.'

'Well, in my day you put up and shut up. I did your father's accounts when I was feeding you, you know.'

I blocked her out and flicked through yet another celebrity magazine I'd now become addicted to. I could just about follow the articles, although there was one about Mariah Carey's sarong that was a bit tricky for me.

There were occasions in those first few months when I simply wanted to get a small grip-bag, go to Gatwick airport and just get on the first flight out. Haifa, Magaluf, Manchester – I didn't care where it was going, as long as the destination had a darkened room with stout walls, a bed and a pair of ear-plugs. Just somewhere, anywhere, that I could be on my own, recover my sense of humour and the feeling in my nipples.

Of course, coupled with these feelings were times of the purest most ecstatic happiness I'd ever known in my life – even better than seeing ABC live at the Hammersmith Apollo in '84. We were deeply in love with our daughter, that's for sure.

'Oh look at her face! She looks like Cherie Blair when she's straining her mouth like that.'

'She sneered! I swear to God she just sneered!'

There was the endless analysis.

'Do you think it's possible to get MRSA in a domestic environment? I'm going to sterilize the phones, door handles and kitchen chairs just in case,' and then later: 'What about the levels of dust in the flat? Can dust be sterilized? I'm going to sterilize the hoover just in case.'

Seeing Dan in yellow rubber gloves was no longer a rare treat; he was in them more than my mother was these days.

And of course we revelled in sheer wonder at the all-round brilliance of our daughter.

'She picked up that toy. Did you see that? She saw it, moved her hand and just picked it up. Judged it perfectly. Deftly. Confidently. She's amazing.'

And then for the other twenty hours of the day there was a bizarre feeling of being ground methodically by an enormous mincing machine. Like one of those ones you see in cartoons, where the legs of the person are still kicking about while their head is being slowly converted into strings of fatty beef.

Night-time was still a bit Elm Street. We'd got her sleeping in her own room, which we were a bit smug about. Her night-time feed made me feel like Ernest Shackleton as I trudged across the wasteland of the landing, a freezing, tortuous, lonely journey over to her bedroom. I listened to a lot of radio at 2 a.m. and hope that my daughter hasn't been too disturbed by discussions on incest, the gay clergy and penis worship. Which doesn't just take place in Papua New Guinea apparently. There are instances of it in Solihull.

I have semi-blocked out certain of the truly terrible times, like the month when she developed the habit of screaming at three in the morning for an hour, for no apparent reason. My mother attributed it to my father's side of the family.

'She's a quarter Polish, darling. They're all emotion and passion. It's nothing to do with the Parkinsons. We never raise our voices. Have you tried her in a salt bath?'

Dan was pretty admirable and took on a fair share of the screaming watch. That was all you could do really – watch.

One night, I was lying in bed about as relaxed as an ironing board. The screaming had gone on for forty minutes, and I felt it was time to relieve my husband. Not in that way – sexual antics between Dan and me were rare to say the least.

I went downstairs and found him holding Jo like you would a dumb-bell in a gym. He had her in one hand and was performing some kind of bicep-curl in front of the window, so that he could analyze the reflection of his muscle pumping each time she was lifted up.

'Dan! For God's sake! What are you doing to her?'

'Getting her off to sleep,' he puffed.

'Well, re-enacting an early Arnold Schwarzenegger film is not the way to go about it. How about some lullabies?'

'I'm killing two birds with one stone here,' he gasped. 'Don't want to get out of shape.'

I was beginning to lose my rag with him.

'It's all about you, isn't it? Just give her to me, get back into bed and do what you do best.'

'Well, thank you so much, Mel. Who's been up since five yesterday morning so that you could have a lie-in?'

'I don't care, Dan. Who's had her breasts emptied six times today, leaving nothing behind but two flapping haversacks? Who has sacrificed a flattish stomach for a stretched, wrinkled sack that now has the consistency of old porridge?'

'Well, who's got the agonizing cold sore around here?' said Dan, self-pityingly.

'Cold sore? Cold sore?' I laughed. 'A cold sore would be a pleasant distraction for me right now! You want to compare pain with me, buddy, and I'm happy to.'

I'd never called Dan 'buddy' before, and I must say I found it rather refreshing.

'Oh here we go,' he said, 'the old you-don't-understand-pain-because-you've-never-given-birth routine. Well, change the record, sunshine, because the needle's stuck and it's boring.'

What was going on here? Dan had never in his life called anyone 'sunshine' before, but again I found it strangely appealing.

He left the room with a bang of the door, which briefly quashed the screaming. For a minute, and then she was off again.

I settled down with her on my brown velvet beauty. It was a very windy night. Through the windows, the trees on the street looked like they were about to de-root themselves and be tossed into orbit, and the sky was a sort of red-black. I can't vouch for that exact colour. Near-exhaustion does strange things to the brain. I was convinced one day that our car had stripes all over it, and Dan took an hour to convince me that it was still the same boring navy that it'd always been.

The baby just wouldn't stop screaming. She didn't even pause for breath.

Clever girl, I found myself thinking, a natural rolling breather. 'You might take that skill to stage school with you when you're older,' I said to her.

I was too tired to walk round the room, rock her or dandle her, so I simply sat with her facing me on my knees, and let her go for it. I started to find her face almost mesmerizing. Her voice was actually getting hoarse, and the little veins were all up on her fuzzy head. Her face was bathed in a liverish light, a reflection from the stormy night outside. Her eyes were as black as liquorice drops, and on and on went the screaming. Grinding, relentless, useless noise. And then things got seriously weird. Her tongue started to morph in front of my eyes, and got blacker and visibly pointy. The room felt noticeably hotter, as the fireplace seemed to blaze with flames. Strange, considering we have a three-bar electric heater in our living room. What was happening? Was I possessed?

I looked around me. Shadows seemed more elongated, the window was swimming with small dots. I looked down at Jo and saw something truly terrible. In my lap was not my darling baby, pink and soft, but something swarthy from another world. She'd turned into the devil. She didn't have horns, but she had the face of purest evil. My heart was thumping as fast as a baby gerbil's. I thought I was going to faint. I was hot, I was cold, I tried to call for Dan, but all that emerged was a croak. I shut my eyes and put her, still screaming, into her basket. I went like a sleepwalker into the kitchen and tried to calm myself down with a cup of tea and a trusty custard cream. She was still screaming. Oh God, what was I going to tell the community midwife?

'So, any problems this week with Mum or Baby?'

'Oh nothing really. She's got a bit of cradle cap and a touch of nappy rash. Oh, and she's turned into Beelzebub. Anything you can give me for that?'

I calmed myself down by the kettle, and then crept back into the living room. The wind howled as I approached the basket. I would take one peep. One little peep. If she was still the devil then I'd have to wake Dan up and we'd all have to go to casualty. I felt nauseous as I bent down.

'Please don't still be the devil,' I said under my breath.

I took a deep breath and peeked in. Thank God in Heaven above. The devil had gone and she was normal again. Still screaming her head off, mind, but who was complaining now that she'd stopped being Satan?

There was only one thing for it – some music. I plumped for Kajagoogoo, and it was soon blaring out of the stereo. She stopped screaming and was fast asleep within two minutes. Thank you, Limahl. You did go on to do something useful after the band broke up after all.

Chapter Three

Dan eventually got his own way with the photos, and left a huge bag of them outside a couple of weeks later. Something about it worried me. What if somebody from Social Services happened to be passing our flat and a gust of wind sent the photos flying around their feet? Wouldn't they look at them and be suspicious? Wouldn't they think there was some kind of abuse going on in the house, with parents so heartless that they could discard such precious mementoes?

Our spending was getting out of control. Jo was being taken out for walks in a brand new buggy, which converted rather cunningly into a car seat, carry cot and probably a filing cabinet, hostess trolley and tandem if I could just find the right lever. It looked like something from NASA and had cost us the best part of three hundred quid. I just couldn't help buying things for the baby. A T-shirt saying: 'You think I'm cute? You should see my dad!' A babygro with 'Milk Addict' on the front, and a vest embroidered with the words 'Baby Bitch'. This last item was worn only the once. Too many old ladies on the bus looked daggers at me so I'd thrown it away. Oh God, another piece of incriminating evidence for Social Services to get their hands on.

I would regularly go out to the shops for a pint of milk and come back with bags stuffed with baby booty – a variflo beaker with ten adjustable lids, Winnie the Pooh teething ring with accompanying Tigger bib and rattle, fourteen pairs of little Ninja Turtle socks, factor 87 sun cream, two windmills, plastic stacking cups and a set of baby books made out of sponge. I had to use my womanly wiles to smuggle the baby booty past Dan, who had taken to analyzing our receipts as if they were long-lost pieces of holy scripture.

'Now, Mel. There's a receipt here for £17.85 from yesterday.'

I hummed gently, trying to make light of the matter.

'Oh. Yes. That must be the hardware I got. Hinges, screws and stuff.'

'The shop appears to be called "Sunny Bunny". I don't remember a hardware shop called Sunny Bunny.'

'Hmmm,' I said, as I turned to immerse myself in a box of teabags.

'We've just got to curb our spending, Mel. Someone round here's got to keep an eye on it. I can't believe you paid £17.85 for some old pieces of sponge, anyway.'

'Those pieces of sponge, Dan, are actually essential learning tools for our daughter. They are supposed to stimulate hand-eye coordination as well as colour awareness, touch therapy and numeracy skills. Do you want her to grow up understimulated?'

'But haven't we got enough sponge in here? The flat's like a bouncy castle – we might as well open up the front door and tell kids to take their shoes off, for God's sake.'

'Stop swearing.'

'Everywhere I look there's some piece of bloody developmental learning toy-thing that we've spent good money on. And does she develop? No, she either pukes over it, chews it or tosses it away.'

'If you had your way, Dan, she'd have no toys and stimuli.'

'It would certainly solve the space issue.'

There was a silence as both of us looked round. Dan did have a point. You could barely see out into the garden any more because of a large hammock strung across the back door, filled with her soft-toy collection.

'I think we should move,' I announced.

'What?'

'Move house. Get a bigger place.'

Dan thought about this and then said, 'How about we just set fire to 90 per cent of our belongings?'

'Come on, Dan. We'll get loads for this flat – up and coming area and all that. And then we just move a bit further out, somewhere a bit untrendy, into a little house. I'd love a proper garden for Jo. There's not even room for a sandpit out there.'

'Let alone the tree house, paddling pool, swings, slides, roundabout and seesaw, petting zoo and bandstand that you've got planned,' he said wryly.

'Let's at least think about it. We could talk to the bank.'

'I guess so.' I could see he was coming round to the idea. 'Yes. I've always really fancied a proper kind of workshop space at the end of the garden where I could tinker round with a few ideas, invent something, you know.'

'And how about a playroom for the kids?'

'Did you just say "kids"?' said Dan, suddenly looking terrified.

So we set up an appointment with our bank.

We were sitting in the waiting area to see the personal banker, and Dan and I got chatting with each other.

'Ah-boom. Ah-boom. Ah-BOOM!'

'Oddle diddle oddle diddle.'

'Ah-boom. Ah-boom!'

'Oddle diddle oddle diddle!'

This seemed to be the way a lot of our conversations were going. More and more we talked to each other through the medium of our daughter.

A neat young man approached us, clicking a biro in one hand, and asked us to follow him into his little booth. He introduced himself to us as Robin Jones, our 'Relationship Manager'.

Robin looked like he might be in a barber-shop group in his spare time. He was what my mother would call 'nippet'. Everything about him was chipper, smoothed and combed.

'OK, so we're thinking about moving some time soon, are we?' asked Robin, with the trace of a wink.

'Yes. It's becoming a bit like The Old Woman Who Lived In A Shoe,' I replied.

'You know what, people probably would live in a shoe, the way the housing market's going,' said Robin knowingly. 'Put some cornice work on a flip-flop and you could probably sell it as a studio flat.'

'Unbelievable.' I nodded.

'Hokey cokey.' Robin was getting our financial details up on the computer screen. 'So we'll be looking to get a larger mortgage, will we?'

'Yes,' said Dan.

'OK. Let's just look at what we've got up on the screen here. This is money going out of the account here – ' Robin pointed to a large forest of numbers on the screen – 'and this is money coming in here,' he said, pointing to a small copse of numbers. 'And the income drops off from around here.' He pointed to a blank space.

'December. That's when I had Jo,' I said. 'But Dan's work's going great though,' I added enthusiastically, 'because he works for a subtitling company. The work's really regular, isn't it, Dan?'

'You write subtitles for those foreign films?' asked Robin.

'That's right,' sighed Dan.

'So *vous parlez le Français*, no doubt?'

'A little. German and Spanish are my strongest languages.'

'I like a nice foreign film. I suppose you had to do the subtitles for *Trainspotting* too!' And Robin laughed and laughed until I thought he would roll off his chair.

'So. Our mortgage,' I said, trying to rein Robin back in.

'Okey dokey. Well, it all looks positive – you're likely to make a bit on your flat, your credit rating's good. We'll obviously need to see some steady income in that account of yours. Are you planning to work any time soon?' said Robin, looking at me jovially.

'Yes. Absolutely. I'm sure that I've got some TV things in the pipeline. Dan?'

'What? Oh yes, work's good, it's a solid company and goo-jee goo-jee goo-jee goo!'

Robin looked quizzical. Jo had just put her head onto one shoulder and was looking up at us unbearably cutely.

'Ah-boom. Ah-boom. Ah-BOOM!' was Dan's response.

It was his default response to most things she did.

'Hello you!' said Robin in a falsetto voice, waving at Jo. She responded brilliantly by putting her head coquettishly onto her other shoulder.

'Ah-boom. Ah-BOOM!' said Dan.

'How old is she?'

'Six months, two days,' I replied at speed.

'And do you want a liddle mortgagey-wortagey then?' said Robin in a rather alarming way, directly to Jo. 'You'll need a mortgage for your Wendy house, won't you?' Jo gurgled at him. 'Yes! You will!'

'Yes,' I laughed politely.

Robin laughed long and loud, so that his neck turned quite pink.

'Oh dear!' he said, lightly wiping one eye. 'A mortgage on a Wendy house, what am I like? Right, let's have a look at these figures in more detail. Yes, you'll definitely want to start saving for that Wendy house right away!'

The sad thing is we laughed along with Robin. That's the way with bank managers. They have you over the financial barrel and so you are forced to laugh at their gags.

Jo had stopped the head-on-shoulder business and was now giving Robin a rather frosty look. It's a technique that comes directly from my dad's side of the family and is known as the Baltic glare. It comes at you all of a sudden, like two icicles. Even Jo's six-month-old version of the Baltic glare was uncompromising, and with her it meant only one thing – a meltdown was on the way.

'Okey dokey,' said Robin brightly, 'let's get down to some details.'

'Ah-boom. Ah-BOOM!' said Dan.

'So is your flat on the market?'

'Yes, we're just … aba-ba! Aba-ba! Aba-ba!'

Jo started to make a curdling noise in her throat.

'Ah-boom. Ah-BOOM!'

'Aba-ba! Aba-ba!'

'And have you found a property yet that you wish to purchase?'

Jo's mouth turned dangerously downwards. She was warming up for a good one.

'Bottle, Dan.'

'Found a property?' asked Robin.

'No, Dan, not in the bag. It's in the little pocket at the back of the buggy.'

'No, it's not.'

'Back pocket. No. On the back. Look, you take her. I'll look for the bottle.'

'Ah-boom. Ah-BOOM!' Dan took her wriggling form into his arms.

'So. The property?' said Robin, with a light note of urgency creeping into his voice.

'It's not here, Dan. I put it in this pocket just before we left this morning.'

'Are you sure you didn't just put it in the bag?'

'No. I put it in the pocket, Dan.'

'Well, I'm sorry, but you obviously didn't.'

'Look. I distinctly remember putting it in the back pocket of the buggy.'

The Baltic glare was now fully glacial, and Jo started to growl unnervingly.

'Hello?' said Robin with a jaunty little wave. 'Can I just butt in? Have we found a property that we might be interested in—'

And then she let rip. Her eyes scrunched up into mean little mouse droppings, coupled with a sudden and blotchy rash over her forehead. She started to bellow. Dan had to raise his voice to be heard above the noise.

'I thought we had a good system going whereby the bottle goes in the bag, Mel, and I don't see why you knowingly had to just buck that system.'

'Buck the system? It isn't my system, Dan! And who decided that it was a system in the first place?'

'Ah-boom. Ah-BOOM! Ah-BOOM!' he shouted.

'Perhaps we should wrap things up here and reconvene some other time?' said Robin speaking through cupped hands.

'Just a minute, Robin' – and I put my hand out to block his face – 'when you decide you want to put the bottle in the bag it's a "system" all of a sudden. What about flexibility, Dan? What if I suddenly decide that I actually want the bottle in the back pocket of the buggy?'

Poor Jo was starting to go stiff with anger, her little legs as rigid as rolling pins in her trousers.

'You just don't want to admit that my system is right, Mel, and that it works. Ah-boom! Ah-boom!'

'My system. MY system. What about OUR system, Dan? It's like some bloody totalitarian state or something. Ja wohl, mein husband. Ve vill put ze bottle in ze bag!' And I clicked my heels together.

'You're being completely immature, Mel, it's just embarrassing ...'

Robin put up his hand and coughed politely. Then he stood up. His voice was loud and surprisingly firm.

'Might I suggest something that might align itself quite nicely with Dan's system, but that might also take into account Mel's queries about that aforementioned system?'

We were shocked into silence. Even Jo dipped the volume of her shouts to listen to Robin's words of wisdom. He cleared his throat.

'I think we should end this meeting forthwith, and that you should go home and find another bottle of milk to give your baby.'

A sudden shaft of light hit Robin's sandy eyebrows, giving him the air of an early Celtic leader. Dan and I looked at each other and nodded grudgingly.

'Fair play, Robin,' mumbled Dan.

'Of course, that's absolutely right,' I agreed.

Jo put her head onto one shoulder and actually cooed at Robin, the little tart. I looked at him with a new respect. His title of 'Relationship Manager' wasn't so far off the mark after all.

We marched home like a pair of Siberian peasants – heads down, shoulders hunched and feet shuffling. There was no extreme cold to block out – in fact, it was rather a pleasant summer morning – just extreme noise emanating from the buggy. Man, how do humans so tiny summon up the calories to create so much devastating noise on such a regular basis? If only it were a skill that could be carried through into adult life. It would certainly solve the obesity crisis in this country.

As we trudged homeward it struck me that we had said good-bye forever to the lingering stroll of the childless couple – that directionless meander that could take you anywhere – a pub, a stolen cinema trip in the middle of the morning, a quick nap under a tree in a park.

We had joined the millions of other parents on the military buggy march. Our eyes glazed, our teeth set, shoulders hunched and arms outstretched in front of us like zombies, we all gripped the handles of our buggies and marched, marched, marched. We knew where we were going and had the co-ordinates in our heads to get us there as quickly as possible. Our time frame for the journey was completely determined by the contents of the buggy – how many minutes do we have before the nappy implodes? How long before the next hunger tantrum?

I used to laugh at the amount of parents I saw jogging along with their buggies. I always wanted to approach them, put a comforting hand on their shoulders and say, 'Come on, guys! Chill out, can't you? It's a beautiful day and your baby probably just wants to shoot the breeze a bit in there.'

Of course, what I didn't know then was that the baby's nappy was filled with a sludge-green substance marked 'Hazchem', which was swiftly creeping up his back. His lunch was also fifteen minutes late and his sleepless mum was desperately running home to the loo before her poor incontinent bladder released another unexpected puddle into her trousers. I'm glad I never approached those parents. If someone had approached me now with the advice 'chill out', I would have floored them with one single punch to the face.

Thankfully Jo had nodded off, so we decided to take a detour through the park. It was a beautiful day, the snapdragons were out and the bees were buzzing round the flower beds. Toddlers were splashing in the big municipal paddling pool, which was full of dirt and floating plasters, but they didn't care. This was Toddler Riviera. OK, Dirk Bogarde was unlikely to stroll past in a panama hat, but for them it was heaven.

Dan and I sat on a bench. He put his arm round me and sighed contentedly. It was amazing – as soon as the baby was asleep we could both feel our shoulders drop back down to their default position.

'I'm sorry if I get a bit bossy sometimes,' said Dan.

'You are bossy. I'm sorry if I nag,' I replied.

'Yes, you do nag.'

Dan lowered his arm so that his hand was resting on the enormous girdle of flesh where the side of my waist had once been. I gently shifted his hand away. He placed it rather self-consciously in his lap and shut his eyes.

Something about warm weather always makes me feel fat. Every year I vow will be the summer where I emerge from winter like a sort of reborn colt, suddenly bronzed and skinny. Fat chance.

I looked down at my legs on the bench. My thighs were splayed across a whole half it. They were even larger than Dan's, who has the thighs of a rugby player. I felt ashamed that I was still wearing a pair of drawstring maternity trousers. The contents of my pre-pregnancy wardrobe remained so far untouched. Maybe I would never go there again. It can happen.

There was a girl in my class called Ann Gwynn whose mother had had four children and she was not only as large as the back end of a bus, she was as large as the terminus. Her hormones had gone into free-fall after her first child, and she'd never been able to lose any baby-weight. With each child that came she just got larger and larger. Poor Mrs Gwynn. We'd laughed at her in her gigantic flapping tent-dresses, pouring sweat at the school gates and mopping her forehead with supersize fingers of bratwurst proportions. She looked like she needed a set of castors to transport her home, rather than the wobbling puffed-up soufflés that had once been her ankles. Mother Nature was an old cow sometimes. She allowed some to come through motherhood almost physically unscathed, but random others had to pay a price. Especially if you were one of the ones who'd lived off Cheddar cheese, deep-fried waffles and Double Deckers for nine months.

I felt suddenly bleak. The heat was oppressing me, the sun highlighting all of my contours, which felt so misshapen compared to what they'd been a year ago. Most of my flesh now seemed to be residing outside of my clothes – strange bits of it squirted out in different places, as if piped through an icing-bag.

My eye was caught by a group of mums by the swings. They were taking it in turns to put each of their babies, who didn't look much older than Jo, into swings, and then pushed them energetically so that their defined biceps glinted in the sun. All of them were chatting, white-teethed and smiley. There wasn't a love handle, jowl or double chin to swing between them. All seemed animated and lithe. One even had a pair of shorts and a halter-neck top on, for Pete's sake. I felt large and lonely. To be fair, I'd made no effort whatsoever to get out and meet other mums. Half a year had passed on the sofa, and bar a few mates with children who'd been round to visit, Jo had been denied any social interaction.

Right. Things had to change, and this seemed like a good enough place to start. With Dan asleep, I would stroll over to the swings and engage the mums in chatty conversation. My mission was not to leave the swings until I had one of their phone numbers.

I was sure I could fit into their gang. With a bit of a diet and a detox, a haircut and a shave, I'd soon be shinning over climbing frames in my hot-pants with the best of them. I suddenly saw all of us in a big gaggle having a picnic here in the park. I'd be at the centre of the chat and everyone would be laughing at some clever quip I'd made. Meanwhile, Jo would be playing happily, clapping and cooing with her three new best baby friends.

I wandered over to the swings with Jo still asleep in the buggy. They were taking their kids out of the swings and setting up some snacks on a nearby table.

'She's asleep!' I addressed all of them with a laugh. They smiled back politely. 'She always goes down at around this hour, but we've been stuck in a bank for most of the morning, so it's not surprising that she's dropped off like this. Lovely weather, isn't it? Thank goodness! Makes it so much easier with the little ones, doesn't it? Yours look about the same age as mine, actually. My daughter's six months and nine days but she is quite tall for her age. Well, my husband's snoozing over there and you can see that he's not exactly vertically challenged, is he! Anyway, it's so nice to meet other mums with kids of the same age, isn't it? I mean, it's what it's all about. Getting them interacting and all that. Anyway, my number's 8443 5626. So do call if you'd like, and we can arrange something and all hook up really soon.'

All I could hear were the bees buzzing round the snapdragons. I could feel beads of sweat pricking the back of my neck. That monologue was the most strenuous exercise I'd done in over a year. And it wasn't quite over.

'So,' I said plunging ever further into the abyss, 'that's 8443 5626. I, er, don't have a pen, I'm afraid.'

The mums all looked at each other rather blankly. I could see one of Jo's feet stirring in the buggy.

'Please?' said one of the mums. 'We no speak very good English. Can you repeat?'

Jo's foot was starting to kick. Suddenly it all became clear. Of course. How would a mum have the energy to push a swing and show off a defined bicep at the same time? These were au pairs. How could I have been so stupid?

I laughed.

'You are au pairs?' I said very slowly and loudly, like my mother does when talking to foreigners.

'Yes, au pair. I'm from Slovenia and my friend from Sweden. And from Italia.'

'How do you do?' I said to all three, with my best Henry Higgins pronunciation. Jo had now fully woken up. The legs were both kicking. The poor lamb was starving.

'Well, you're probably half my age and I don't think we'd have a lot in common, do you?'

Blank stares all round.

'But maybe you could pass on my number to the mums of all this lot. It's 8443 5626. Tell them to get in touch.'

Even if they knew what I was on about, I don't think they heard the number over Jo's screams.

I felt pretty chuffed with my first foray into the world of new friends. Dan and I sat at the kitchen table, and for the first time I could see a plan formulating. I was keen to share it with my husband.

'Basically, Dan, my plan for the next couple of months is to lose the baby-weight, make about five friends for Jo, get some work, earn some money, sell this flat and move into a really nice house. Oh, and cover up the wings of grey hair you've been so sweet not to mention. I know they're there. Saw them this morning – there are about fifty of them over each ear.'

Dan looked slightly worried.

'Er … yes. Sounds great.'

He offered me a piece of his doughnut, I bit into it and felt the jam burst gloriously into the back of my throat.

'So,' I carried on full of verve, sugar coating my lips and glorious doughnut appearing out of both corners of my mouth, 'weight loss starts today. I intend to lose a stone a month.'

Dan just looked at me with a weak smile.

Basically the world was full of mums. They were everywhere. I calculated that on an average journey to the bank I'd probably cross paths with about four mums. So there and back was eight mums a day! Fantastic – I'd cross paths with over two thousand mums a year. It would therefore be likely that I'd make at least a hundred new mum-friends within a year period. Whenever I left the house now, I would be extra vigilant. I'd smile in a friendly way and look for any opportunity to chat up a mum and try to make contact. A local network, that's what I needed. A posse of like-minded, fun, up-for-it mums, all of us within half a mile of each other. Easy.

One day I had an appointment for Jo in the baby clinic down at Dr Sweeting's surgery, and set out, pen in pocket, just in case a new local contact should emerge from the outing. I'd applied some makeup – just a little bit of fake tan on my chops and a whiff of mascara. This was potentially an exciting venture, and I wanted to try to look my best. Jo was looking really sweet. She now had enough hair to scrape together into a little fountain on the top of her head. I'd toyed with the idea of giving myself the same hairdo as a jaunty little conversation piece, but decided that it might be over-egging it.

I entered the surgery waiting room full of smiles. Jo was gurgling, and I could tell from people's reactions that she was making a pretty good impression. I'd bought a rather trendy new top too, the first item of clothing I'd managed to buy since Jo's arrival. It was retro-1980s, lemon yellow, off the shoulder with a few pieces of urban scrawl written down one side. I felt pretty cool. Sadly my bottom half was still housed in the drawstring trousers, but I was being much better about snacking. I'd eaten only two custard creams so far that morning, which was a massive improvement.

I looked around the waiting room. Lots of mums, and one dad, with their kids ranging from the freshest newborn to fully walking toddlers. Here was a whole cocktail party of future friends! I smiled broadly and sat down in the only available space, next to a comfort-able-looking woman with a very erect baby sitting on her knees. From his baseball cap down to his moulded leather shoes, every available piece of flesh was covered in baby blue.

'I bet he never gets mistaken for a girl in all that blue!' I said, laughing.

His mum looked at me over her glasses and smiled back.

'No, I never do!' she answered back in a high-pitched voice.

I was rather confused by this.

'Hello there, you,' I addressed the baby, slightly self-consciously. And then asked Mum dutifully: 'So, how old is he?'

Mum looked at Baby and then at me, and then said in the same high-pitched voice: 'I'm seven months and I'm a very big boy, aren't I?'

Her baby remained silent.

'Yes, you are,' said his mum in what I supposed to be her

normal voice – average female register and possibly slightly northern.

'Is it your first?' I endeavoured, slightly worrying about which voice was going to answer me back.

'Yes,' said the high-pitched baby voice. 'I'm all on my own until my mummy and daddy give me a brother or sister to play with.'

The penny dropped. What was happening here was a sort of sinister mother/baby ventriloquist act.

The receptionist called out a name. 'Matthew Chambers.'

'Ooh, Matthew,' said the mum. 'That's you, isn't it?'

'Come on, Mum! It's time to see the doctor – we'd better not be late,' she replied to herself, in the dreadful squeaky falsetto.

'All right, Little Man, now you let Mummy get you all snuggly and cosy in your buggy and then we'll go and see the nice doctor,' she said, as Mummy once again. I was entranced by this act being played out before me, and looked around to see if anyone else was finding it similarly weird. No, everyone looked fine with it; a couple of mums even seemed to be smiling encouragingly towards them.

'Thank you, Mummy,' she said in the baby voice, once the baby-blue crocheted blanket was safely tucked round the little boy. 'You're a very good mummy. I am nicely tucked in, aren't I?' she squawked.

And they made their way to the door of the waiting room. I manipulated Jo's hand into the waving position and waggled it round, and said, rather too loudly: 'Bye-bye, Matthew.'

The ventriloquist mum did the same with Matthew, and he was forced to wave back at us. 'Bye-bye!'

And then I said very loudly and squeakily: 'See you soon, Matthew! My name's Jo.'

This waiting room was getting claustrophobic. I looked at the little slide in the corner, getting slidier by the minute as three babies dribbled down it. The toy box looked like it was home to many Petri dishes of germs, and the dog-eared books were probably dripping with tuberculosis. I was starting to feel itchy. These mothers didn't look in the least interested in either me or my daughter, who was quite obviously the prettiest, most engaging, entertaining and advanced baby in the room. When another patient's name was called out, Jo did her ironic eyebrow routine, with perfect comic timing. I laughed and looked around the room expectantly to see if anyone else had noticed. Nobody seemed to have seen a thing. Extraordinary.

We saw Dr Sweeting, who pronounced the all-clear on Jo's little rash. She couldn't comment on whether raising one's eyebrows at Jo's age would push up her developmental percentile.

On the way out, I picked up a leaflet in reception, advertising a parent and baby group, held in a nearby church hall. 'Angie's Action Kids. All Babies from Six Months welcome. Bring a mug and a smile!'

I pushed the buggy home despondently. I felt tired. In the baby-free era, I'd have gone home right now and put my feet up in front of a nice bit of daytime telly, possibly had a kip, or maybe even gone for a swim or a trip to the hairdresser's. No chance of that now. This was Jo's liveliest time of day, and I was mentally donning my motley costume and hat covered with bells for my forthcoming role as jester to my daughter. I glanced in the hall mirror. I looked like a fool already – fake tan was streaking down my neck. I pondered the morning's events. The only mum I'd had any sort of connection with spoke like a baby. Could I strike up a friendship with her? She might be embarrassing in a dinner-party situation, but if I just restricted her to me and our kids, then it might be possible. It might even be quite fun to talk like babies all day. I looked at myself in the mirror again and shook my head.

'You are losing your grip. This is a woman with a helmet hair-cut and mushroom-coloured comfortable shoes who talks like a baby. GET A GRIP.'

That told me.

I played our answering machine messages. One from my mum about tips for good begonia potting. And then a ream of messages from the estate agent Gary telling us there was a queue of people wanting to see our flat, and then yet more estate agents – Steve, Andrew and Brian – telling us how many wonderful houses there were out there and how they were dying to show them to us. I made a mental note to start house-hunting. Oh and hallelujah, praise Him above, there was actually a message from my agent.

'Darling, it's me.'

A tingle of excitement went up my spine. An audition? A little job offer? And then her clipped voice again: 'Nothing to report. Byee.'

I reached for the custard creams. I ate nine.

Right, it was seriously time to take control. I was going to have to get back into the work mindset. I would also start to think about possibly phoning the local gym to find out their opening hours. All good. I would phone my agent and remind her again that I was available for all work. And I would go to Angie's Action Kids. Tomorrow. Excellent.

Dan phoned from our local caff and asked if we wanted to go and join him for a cup of tea.

'There's loads of interest in the flat. I thought you were at work,' I said.

Jo and I trundled round the corner. It was good to be out of the confines of the flat. It was always a relief to see Dan, because it meant that I could hand the baby over to him. It was nice to have the full use of one's two hands and lap for a bit. I tinkered with both sugar pot and spoon at the same time, just because I could. I regaled Dan with our morning's encounters.

'All I want to do, Dan, is meet some mums with a similar outlook to me. Look – there's a mum just come in with the double-buggy. Hang on a sec, I think I'll go over and—'

'Relax. These things have got to happen organically.'

Annoyingly, he was right.

'We've got to make some friends for Jo. She's a total Nobby-No-Mates.'

'She's only six months old.'

'I know, but it's not good for her, love. She won't be able to relate to anyone but us. We'll end up educating her at home with a chemistry lab in the garden, that sort of thing. Her friends will be the birds. She'll only communicate in birdsong. Oh, Dan, we're terrible parents.'

'Come on, Mel, everything's OK.' Dan stroked my hand. 'You're probably tired – and look at that. I think Jo's just made a friend.'

Dan pointed to Jerome, the cafe owner, who was bouncing Jo up and down in his lap, causing her to scream with merriment. Everyone in the cafe had turned round to watch and laugh.

'Yeah, but he's seventy and he's got no teeth,' I whispered to Dan.

'So they've got one thing in common,' he replied.

'Well, it's OK for you, I'm in all day looking after Jo. At least you're at work, in the company of other adults and everything. I long to go back to work and have a bit of normal interaction for God's sake.'

There was a pause.

'Mel,' said Dan.

'Yes?' I said.

'About work.'
'Yes.'
'I don't go to work any more.'
'What?'
'I resigned.'

Chapter Four

News of my husband's resignation went down like a carafe of cold sick. I just couldn't believe he'd had the gall to do it when we had a nipper in tow and were supposed to be moving house.

'You resigned?' I kept saying to him back at home. 'How could you?'

'Being a dad's made me think about my position in the world a lot more. Who am I? How am I defined? What am I doing?'

'I'll tell you who you are,' I replied. 'You're a twat. How are you defined? Er. Hang on, oh yes – twat. And what are you doing? Acting like a twat.'

'Don't swear,' said Dan smugly, covering up our daughter's ears.

'It's time for her to learn a bit about life, Dan. Listen, Jo' – I was starting to shout now – 'your father is an arsing twat!'

'Look, I can see you're angry,' said Dan, trying to hold his temper.

'Too right I'm bloody angry, Dan. Your resignation is the act of a supremely selfish man. Why the hell couldn't you have waited till we moved house?'

'I've got all the contacts I need. I know everyone in subtitling. They're not going to suddenly turn round and not employ me just because I work for myself. It's time for me to stand up and be my own man.'

'What about the mortgage, Dan?'

'We can't let our lives be ruled by the mortgage, Mel. It's

eunuchs like that Robin Jones with his silly corporate tie who have got us by the short and curlies.'

'Robin's all man,' I cut in.

'Look at what we've become!' said Dan, standing up passionately. 'Remember when we were younger? We wanted big important things like world peace and an end to the arms race.'

'We went on a few marches, Dan. We were there at the Womad festival with our Che Guevara T-shirts. But we were hardly going to change the world, were we?'

'We can't stop trying, though. Our world's become so bloody small, Mel, can't you see? All we think about now is minutiae.'

'And you think your daughter's just a bit of minutiae, do you, Dan?'

'No. She's very very big. She's the biggest thing we've got.'

Jo looked up at this and spat a big bit of dribble and then laughed. Dan sat down and put his head in his hands.

'Your job was crucial for us being able to move.'

'Well, why don't you do some work, Mel?'

He'd hit a raw nerve.

'I can't. I've just had a baby.'

'Over six months ago, Mel,' he said gently.

'Yeah, well, you don't know what it's like, Dan, to bear a child.'

Dan rolled his eyes. 'Here we go,' he said.

'Juggling work and motherhood is like juggling knives with a blindfold on. Or fire. That's right, it's like juggling fire and knives and a baby all at the same time.'

'I could do with some support,' said Dan, looking at me.

I remained silent.

'I'm off,' said Dan, heading for the kitchen door.

'That's right, you just go off and plane your stupid piece of wood.'

All Dan had been able to do since breaking the news of his resignation was spend time in the little shed. He left with a slam of the door.

Several minutes later I heard him clanking around. Whenever Dan is stressed he seeks solace in the bosom of his mistress – DIY. In the far distant past, before Jo was a mere quiver in her father's scrotal sack, I had been known to get a bit jealous of this time-consuming passion of his.

'But what do you do in there?' I'd badger him.

'I've got something on the go,' he'd say elusively.

And when he was out, I'd scour the shed for any signs of girly mags or sinister implements of a possible sexual nature. I found screws, nuts, a piece of hose, his beloved Black and Decker jigsaw. Hmmm. Anything was possible. If Dan came to bed wearing his tool belt, I'd be worried.

At the moment, however, I was glad for him to be out from under my feet. The flat was feeling really small with the three of us in it all the time.

'Right. It said on the spec, don't judge a book by its cover, and you know what? I think they were damn right,' said Steve brightly, as he unlocked yet another property for my perusal. Between us we'd seen about fifteen already, and nothing had really bowled us over.

'After you,' said Steve.

Jo had nodded off in her buggy, thank goodness, and was now saved from further inane chat about original features, additional loft space and off-street parking.

We were looking at an area about three miles from our flat. Only ten minutes' drive away in good traffic, but it felt like another world. There were lots of tree-lined streets with neat little red roofs and double-glazing everywhere. Quite a bit of pebble-dashing and stone-cladding too, I noticed. It was the sort of area that I'd been taken to when I was learning to drive. Slightly away from the urban madness – much more space to do a three-point turn without getting mown down by some crackhead joyrider. It was pleasant. Quiet. Possibly quite boring.

'Here we are,' said Steve, ushering me into the house. He was wearing a suit that made him look as if it was his first day at Big School. He had traces of acne round his jawline and his hair was spiked with gel. He looked about fourteen. This was part of a trend I'd noticed since I'd had a baby: how young people in positions of authority looked. I'd been prescribed antibiotics by a girl doctor who looked like she should have been at home watching *Blue Peter*.

'It does need a bit of tarting up,' said Steve, pulling his arms from his sleeves to reveal an expensive-looking watch. Like his outfit, it was too big for his puny body.

Maybe I just wasn't in the right frame of mind for this, but my heart sank at the sight of yet another pine kitchen, magnolia-walled living room with fitted shagpile, and walk-in wardrobe in the master bedroom. Maybe Dan was right. Our world did seem very small.

'Look at that black marble surface. Beautiful,' said Steve, running his hand over the morgue-like chopping area in the kitchen.

'Hmmm.'

'Nice spotlights,' said Steve, twiddling the dimmer switch.

'Great.'

'And look at that view from the sink,' he said, his suit crackling as he strode towards the window.

I surveyed the lawn and decking with a sigh.

'It's nice for ladies like you to have a bit of a view from the sink, isn't it?'

I felt like boxing his ears and sending him to the headmaster.

My mood was thawing towards Dan. I was starting to think that maybe we shouldn't move after all. We were bulging at the seams in our flat, but it was urban, it was exciting. I'd even started to suggest business plans to Dan.

'How about starting a picture-framing business from home? An old Latin teacher of mine did that. He made a real success of it. He just loved to work with wood. He became a Quaker.'

'Mel, just because I'm doing a bit of woodwork in the shed does not mean that I'm planning on joining the Amish community sometime soon.'

'I'm trying to be supportive, Dan.'

'I know, but please stop bombarding me with craft ideas. Magazine racks, children's wooden flutes, toys on wheels. I've gone freelance, not care-in-the-community.'

'All right,' I grumbled. 'I was only trying to help.'

'You know what would really help? You spend some time getting some work done, and I'll look after Jo.'

'What, for more than an hour?'

'Mel, I am perfectly capable of taking on the role of prime carer.'

Nanny Dan. It was surely a good thing, but I couldn't help feeling a niggling worry. Dan was really good with Jo, there was no doubt about that. She loved him absolutely, and bar the odd incident like the one when she'd almost lost her cheek to an electric sander, I felt completely happy about him looking after her. He did try feeding her curious things sometimes, though, which worried me a bit. There was the time when he gave her fried pig's heart and beetroot for lunch. All chopped up very safely, of course. He said that he was trying to stretch her taste buds.

To be honest I'd be glad to have a bit of a break. Jo had started waking up in the night again, out of nowhere. I tried to be good and not lift her out of her cot, but of course I woke up every time she cried and found it really hard to get back to sleep. My mouth felt constantly gritty. I'd taken to brushing my teeth about five times a day to try to strip the sandy sensation away, but it didn't seem to work. My eyes now had permanent bags. And not fashionable little clutch bags that said, 'Look at me, I was out for a few drinks last night.' These were big old grip-bags strapped to my lower lids, face luggage that was going to be with me for the rest of my life. I'd given up wearing under-eye concealer. It just made me look as if I was wearing goggles.

Dan agreed to look after the baby for three hours the next morning so that I could do some e-mailing, make some calls, and just generally try and get a bit of work off the ground.

I phoned my agent.

'Hiya, honey. How are you, my sweet?' she said with a larynx that sounded like it had been gargling in bleach.

'I'm fine,' I said. 'Has everyone forgotten I exist now that I've had a baby?'

'Oh honey! Of course not!' I could hear her tapping away on her computer in the background. 'We've just got to get your profile up a bit, that's all, and then the work'll come flooding in, you'll see.'

'Well, we're moving house, so it's got to,' I said in a rather surly way.

'Oh honey, that's great.' I could hear her opening some kind of snack in the background. 'Just one minute, honey, can I put you on hold?'

I imagined her chunking into an overpriced titbit she'd bought to stave off the hangover. Fair enough. I'd choose an overpriced bit of sushi over someone else's whinge any day of the week.

Two minutes later she was back, suddenly brimful of energy and big-talk.

'Now, something did come through for you, which I think sounds really exciting.'

'Oh great,' I said gushingly.

It's amazing how quickly you can think your agent is the best in the world.

'Right, bear with me, honey.' I could hear the inviting rustle of paper in the background. 'What have we got? Oh yes, Living TV have commissioned a thirteen-part series they'd like you to consider.'

My pecker was up. I was in demand. OK, it was a cable channel, but who cared? My mind raced – would it be a live show? I suddenly yearned for the buzz of a live telly job. I saw myself in rather tight jeans, with an earpiece in, saying something pithy – I smelled a sudden chink of freedom.

'Right, here we are,' she said tantalizingly. 'Yes, it's a series about women losing their baby-weight. A kind of reality contest show where you'd follow the women and weigh them in every week. They want you as a sort of figure the women can relate to, I think. So whaddya reckon, hon?'

I couldn't think of a worse job than following a load of mums round with baby-weight issues. I was doing that in the privacy of my own flat every day, thank you very much.

'Er …' was all I could muster. 'Can I think about it?'

'Of course, hon. And we must meet up soon. I'm dying to see the piccies.'

'Well, I can come by the office and show you some. We've got some really sweet ones of her taking her first bath.'

'Yes. OK, sweets, must dash. I've got to go to a screening. Big kiss.'

And with that she was gone. A screening. Of what? Something glamorous and exciting. How I longed to go to a screening.

Right. Time to get proactive. I would compose an e-mail and send it to everyone I'd ever worked with in TV. I mulled it over in my head: 'Hi there. My name's Mel and I'd love a really cushy TV job for maybe two to three hours a day that comes with a luxury crèche and pays really really well. I'll need a rest built into that time as well.'

I'd started staring out of the window, fantasizing about Robin Jones dressed as King Arthur and myself as Guinevere, when I heard Dan's cry.

'Mel! Mel! Quick! Can you come down?'

It sounded urgent. It sounded like there'd been some kind of accident. He'd had that electric jigsaw out earlier on – my mind raced to casualty, me holding Jo's dismembered fingers in a matchbox. I raced down, two stairs at a time, and appeared before them, breathless. There was no blood. All seemed normal. Jo was in her highchair, gurgling. Gas. Was there a slight whiff of gas?

'Is the house about to explode?' I demanded. 'For God's sake, let's get out of here. What the hell's going on?'

Dan looked calm. I managed to get my breath back.

'Dan, I thought there'd been a terrible accident.'

'Well, there's about to be. Look, I'm desperate for a crap – can you mind Jo for ten minutes?'

Ten minutes? Mothers never allow themselves ten minutes for

that sort of activity. Ten minutes? I could get a wash on, feed the baby, sweep the floor, get something in the oven for supper and apply some fake tan in under ten minutes these days. Time seemed to have compressed since having a baby. But for Dan, not even a full-scale biological terrorist attack on London would stand in the way of his ten-minute crap.

Fifteen minutes later and I was back on the computer upstairs composing another gushingly insincere e-mail, this time to the company who'd made the documentary about the overweight dogs. Man, I'd really hit the skids. I started the e-mail with: 'Darling all.'

Now what kind of a sad tosser had I become? I'd met these people for about two hours, thought they were all prats, and now had reduced myself to their level by pretending to actually like them. I put my head in my hands and was bewailing the ghastliness of a freelance life in the media, when I heard Dan's voice again.

'Mel! Quick! I need you!'

What, again? What was the matter with Dan's bowels, for goodness' sake?

'What's going on?' I was really quite cross now. And pretty breathless. God I needed to get down to the gym.

'It's Jo.'

Oh no. She looked peaceful enough in her highchair but there was obviously something very wrong. Maybe her heart had stopped. Was she choking silently? Maybe she'd gone blind?

'Dan, what the hell's wrong with her? Why is she so pale? So silent? Is she breathing? What have you done to her? Dan, talk to me!'

My heart was racing. I thought I was going to pass out.

'She's fine. I just can't find any bibs.'

'Bibs? Dan, they're in a pile beside the tea towels.'

'I know that, but there aren't any there.'

'Well, try the airing cupboard.'

'Ditto.'

'Well, improvize.'

'With what?'

'A tea towel, I dunno. Anything. Use your own pants for all I care. Look, I'm trying to work up there, you know. Some of us round here are actually worried about the financial implications of both of us being freelance and taking on a larger mortgage.'

And with that rather pompous barb, I swept back upstairs.

I settled down to the computer. Five minutes later I heard the front door go and the sound of voices in the hall. Now what was going on? Maybe it was Social Services wanting to follow up those baby photos. Maybe it was the supermarket online delivery people. Surely not: I was still placing the order. It was up on the screen in front of me:

Multi pack baby wipes × 4: £5.80

Organic porridge baby jars × 12: £6.25

And there were a few extra things I hadn't been able to resist. Really useful things like:

Barbecue: £59.99

Mister Snakey's Swing 'n' Sandpit Set: £30.99

Jungle Tree Babyseat: £12.99

Kiddy Ice-cream and Lolly Maker: £8.99

The door opened, and I swung round to see Dan holding Jo, with a professional-looking man and woman smiling round the door. Very Social Services. I smiled at them politely enough, but my jaw was clenched.

'Hi,' I said.

'Sorry to disturb you,' the woman said.

'Oh no, that's fine. I'm just working. Mouths to feed. Don't mind me.'

She scanned the room as if looking for dirt. I didn't like her; she was wearing a matching olive-green jacket and skirt and court shoes. I bet she didn't even have any children of her own.

'Is this where the baby sleeps?' the man asked.

'No,' said Dan, 'she sleeps downstairs, although there would be room for her up in here, as you can see.'

'The window's quite small in here, isn't it?' said the lady.

My goat had been trotting around freely up to this point, but now it was well and truly got.

'You have a problem with the window in here? I can assure you it's regulation size for the use of the room.'

'How's it for a baby, though?'

'Our baby doesn't sleep in this room. Maybe you'd like to check and see where she is sleeping. It's easy to find, it's the room with the breathable mattress, smoke alarm, carbon monoxide gauge and thermometer hanging on the wall.'

'We'll see it in a minute, I'm sure.'

I stood up.

'Oh will you? Look, can I see some ID? I feel rather uncomfortable with you two just barging into our house like this.'

I took Jo from Dan and hugged her protectively to me. Dan looked uncomfortable.

'Mel, this is Roger and Indrani—'

'I don't care what their names are, I just want to know which department they come from and who gave them the authority to come in here and tell us that we're bad parents. I knew it was a mistake to throw those photos away, Dan, and I blame you for that.'

Jo was totally silent in my arms, obviously deeply impressed by my tigress display. She knew that Mummy was in control here. Total control.

'Mel, Roger and Indrani are interested in the flat.'

'So it seems,' I said. 'That's right. Come round and judge us. Snoop around and then go and write your foul little report on us.'

'Mel, they've come via the estate agent. They're looking round the flat because they might be interested in buying it.'

There was a pause that felt like a million years. A whole species of dinosaurs had re-evolved and roamed the earth again.

'So you're not from the Social Services?' I asked quietly.

'No,' said Roger, 'and I'm sorry to be nosy about your baby arrangements. We were just wondering if this office space could be used as a nursery.'

Indrani shot me a filthy look. 'I think we should go, Roger. Judging by the enormous amounts of work going on here,' and she looked pointedly at the big supermarket logo still up on the screen. She turned on her heel and was gone, her husband following down the stairs behind her.

I could hear Dan trying to persuade them to stay.

'I must show you the shed. It's full of possibilities. And the stucco work on the ceiling in the front room is absolutely—'

The front door banged.

I sat down heavily at the computer. I could hear Dan coming back up the stairs.

'Well done, our first prospective buyers have been turned away by the mad wife in the attic. Bloody brilliant. They seemed really interested as well.'

'I thought they'd come to take Jo away.'

'You were so rude, and—' His eye was caught by the computer

screen. 'What the hell is Mister Snakey's Swing 'n' Sandpit Set? And a barbecue? £59.99? Have you bought this stuff?'

If I'd had a full coat of wool and a dingleberry-covered backside, I couldn't have looked more sheepish than I did at that precise moment.

'Yes,' I said quietly.

'That's over a hundred quid you've spent on tat for a garden we don't even possess! And we aren't ever likely to, because you shout at people who want to buy our flat, which would have given us the chance to possess a bigger garden. A jungle tree babyseat? What's the point in having one of those when you don't even have a tree to attach it to?' He was bright red now.

'The ice-cream maker looks good, though. It does the nozzly ones like you get from ice-cream vans.'

Dan groaned. 'I don't want a nozzly ice cream.'

'I thought you didn't want to move house,' I said.

'I thought we'd decided to,' said Dan.

'I don't know what we're doing,' I said.

Jo lunged for the bottle of milk in Dan's hand. At least someone in the family knew what they wanted. Dan took her in his arms.

'We need a night out,' I said.

'We need twenty grand.'

'We mustn't get so money-obsessed. What about love?'

'What about it?' he grumbled. 'We never have sex any more.'

'That is so untrue. We did ... er ... three weeks ago.'

'It was four.'

'Is this what all this is basically about, Dan? This is all about sex, isn't it? That's so typical of you. You're not getting your oats at the moment and suddenly everything's my fault, is it?'

'I'm a bloke, Mel. You can't blame me.'

'I feel so sorry for you, Dan,' I said, rearing up. 'You seem to have forgotten that I had to carry the weight of a boulder inside me for nine months, and at the end of it I had to push that boulder through what used to be the size of a constrictive aeroplane sock. The results of which have left my face ravaged, my brain set in aspic and my hair as grey as Blake Carrington's. I have been sliced up, patched up, and what was once a taut little cul-de-sac of love now resembles the Blackwall Tunnel. So I'm so sorry if it's not on tap for you – you'll simply have to make do with a five-knuckle shuffle when you've stopped planing that wood.'

And with that I slammed the door behind me and stomped downstairs. Quite cunningly, I had left Jo in the room with Dan, so he would have to look after her until the argument blew over, which by my reckoning would be at least twenty minutes. Excellent. Enough time for me to put my feet up, have a cup of tea and possibly catch the tail end of *Dancing On Ice*.

I was waiting for the kettle to boil when the phone rang.

'Hello, Mel. It's Robin Jones here at the bank.'

'Oh hi there, Robin, how are you?' I could imagine him in his neat little booth with his life all serene and organized. He was probably just about to take his lunch break, which wouldn't involve mushed-up butternut squash, the lucky thing. How I longed for a lunch break on my own, just a neat little sandwich with no mess.

'Good news, Mel.'

'What's that, Robin? Have I inherited a fortune from a long-lost Swiss uncle?'

Robin chuckled. 'Not quite, but the bank have OK'd your mortgage.'

'What?'

'Well, going on your TV earnings from *Ex Maniac* they've agreed to lend you what we've asked for, meaning that you can look for exactly the sort of property you were wanting to.'

71

'Oh, Robin, that's amazing.'

'All in a day's work.'

'Wow. You're brilliant.'

'I'm just doing my job.'

'I must tell Dan. Actually, I can't tell Dan. We've had a terrible row, Robin.'

There was a light cough at the other end of the line.

'It's tough at the moment,' I continued, 'we're just so tired with the baby and everything, and then Dan resigning and going freelance just added to the whole stress of everything. And you start to blow everything out of proportion, don't you? You just see red and then you're rowing and nothing gets achieved. And it doesn't help that our … physical relationship is a bit … unphysical at the moment. That can put a terrible wedge between couples, and you don't want it to go on too long, do you? It's better to jump on the pony again as soon as possible and get cantering, don't you think?'

There was a silence, and then Robin said, 'Okey dokey, I'll put the forms for you in the post by end of play today. They should be with you in the morning.'

'Thanks, Robin, speak really soon.'

'Goodbye.'

'Bye and thank you so so much for everything. And for listening.'

He coughed again. What an amazing Relationship Manager he was turning out to be.

Six more people came to look round the flat that week, and I behaved impeccably each time. Dan thought I was overcooking it a bit.

'Do you really think they need to see how the loo seat goes up and down, Mel?'

'It's a brilliant loo seat. The action is so smooth.'

'And what about the cupboard under the stairs? I'm not sure if they actually need to get inside it to appreciate it.'

'I disagree with you, Dan. You have to get into the cupboard to realize its potential. You could probably get a small games room in there.'

'Solitaire at a push,' he replied, 'as long as you kept your legs wrapped round your earholes.'

The mood had lifted since our little contretemps. We had started to laugh about the Social Services incident, which was a good sign that things were getting back on track. I would have to start thinking about ways of getting our sex life back into gear. The gym would have to be tackled. Just not today. I had other plans. The leaflet for Angie's Action Kids still lay crumpled at the bottom of the buggy. It started at ten, and I didn't want to be a minute late for it. I'd missed the last one because it had taken me so long to get out of the house.

I'd been putting Jo's coat on, which always takes a good three minutes in itself. I opened the front door while Jo grunted and turned scarlet red in the buggy. Time to go straight back in and change the nappy. The nappy had exploded all the way up her back, so I needed to give her an entire change of clothes. I'd got her wiped and changed when I caught sight of a tiny piece of poo hanging from the back of her hair. I got her out of her clothes again and into the bath for a hair wash. After I'd dried her, I got her dressed again and turned away from the changing mat to get her nappy. When I turned back to her I noticed that she'd done an enormous pee and it had actually travelled up the back of the vest. I took off the vest and had to wipe her down again, dry her off and get her dressed in new vest. Once dressed, I took her downstairs and back into the buggy by the front door. On leaving the house I realized I hadn't made her a bottle, so went back into the kitchen to do so. There was no pre-boiled water so I put the kettle on, waited for it to boil and then cool down to a tepid temperature. I was counting out the spoonfuls of formula aloud, but Jo started shouting with boredom in her buggy.

'Five … six … coming, darling! Six … or was that five? Oh bollocks, I'd better start again.'

I got it right on the third attempt. I was just leaving the house when the phone rang. It might be Robin. I looked forward to his daily phone calls. It wasn't. An unknown voice said: 'Is that Mrs Morris?'

'Yes, speaking.'

'Mrs Morris, I'm phoning you from the Telecom South company. Did you know that you can pay for your gas, electricity, water and phone all in one?'

'No. How amazing,' I replied, crouching down to give Jo her bottle. He then proceeded to tell me in enormous, fifteen-minute detail about the plus-points of changing all of our utilities to Telecom South, and could he send someone round tomorrow to bring the relevant forms?

'Er … yes, of course,' I said and put the phone down, eyes beginning to swivel in my head.

I was just going out the door when I realized I'd forgotten to put any snacks for Jo in the buggy. I raced back inside and grabbed a couple of biscuits.

Phew. Ready to go.

I was just leaving again when I realized that I was absolutely busting for a pee and had to run back inside and talk to Jo very loudly from the loo, to keep her occupied.

'THIS LITTLE PIGGY WENT TO MARKET,' I bellowed from the loo.

Trousers up, I finally managed to leave the house. We got to the end of the street and I looked at my watch. Five minutes past eleven. Action Kids well and truly over. And Jo had lunch at twelve, and if it wasn't in front of her at the stroke of twelve midday precisely, Jo turned back into the devil and I turned into a raving, purple-faced basket-case with boggling eyes and spittle pouring out of my mouth. Nobody had warned me about this kind of thing. They tell you about stretch-marks, sleep deprivation, the baby-blues and all that kind of thing, but nobody ever sat me down and said to me: 'It will take you on average two hours to leave the house. You will never get anything done. Answering the phone once a morning will become a major achievement. You will never have time to wipe your own bottom properly again.'

But this week was different. It was now eight in the morning, and I was determined that by ten on the dot I'd be outside the church hall, ready for a spot of Angie and her Action Kids.

Amazingly we rounded the corner at two minutes to. I'd even managed to put a bit of slap on. I was feeling something akin to human again. And the sun had just come out.

There was a small gaggle of women and buggies waiting to go inside, and they were all chatting animatedly among themselves. No sign of any ventriloquists at first sight, thank goodness. They looked pretty normal on the whole, and I was glad to see that at least half of them were in plimsolls, backless leather sandals or train-ers. This immediately put me at my ease. I always like to judge a demographic by the shoes, and I felt comforted by this array of footwear. I smiled at most of them and even mouthed the word 'Hello' to a couple. I also did a lot of smiling at the babies. This always goes down well with mums. I had remembered to take my address book with me. If I didn't leave this mum-and-toddler group with a new phone number inside it this morning, I would run round naked in my garden with a potty on my head singing the Chinese national anthem.

A few of them seemed to be waiting for someone. They were looking down the street and then looking at their watches.

'Has anyone spoken to her this morning?' said one mum in a poncho.

'I saw her last night at yoga,' said another in a big jumper. 'She said she was definitely coming.'

'You know Judy, she's always got a thousand and one things on the go.'

This Judy person sounded important. She sounded like a linch-pin to me. I found that I was waiting for her now myself.

'Have you got the time?' I asked Poncho Mum.

'Er ... it's just gone ten.'

'Great. What time does it normally finish?'

'Usually about quarter to— Oh, here she is!' She stopped chatting to me and started waving madly, along with a couple of the others.

'Come on, slow coach!' a rotund mum started yelling. Everyone laughed. I looked down the street and watched as a small woman with lots of curly blonde hair came puffing down the pavement, running behind her buggy. She had pink jeans on which were baggy and rolled up, trainers, a roll-neck sweater, and as she came closer I saw that she had a freckled face, red cheeks and green eyes.

'Oh my God!' she addressed the group. 'How scatty am I? I took Oliver to the doctor this morning and left his violin in the waiting room. I had to run all the way back to the surgery before dropping him at the childminder's.' She laughed and then brushed the hair out of her face.

'Hi, love,' she greeted a chosen woman in the group and then it was hugs all round. She looked over to me, saw that I was new blood, smiled and said, 'Hello, have you been here before?'

'No,' I said, suddenly a bit self-conscious.

'I know you from somewhere,' she said.

'Er ... ' I said, never quite sure what to do in these circumstances. People occasionally recognized me from the telly.

'I do know you from somewhere. It'll come to me,' she said, picking her baby girl out of her buggy with ease. 'Now, who's got the cakes this week?'

Everyone laughed. They all seemed to know her. I wished that I knew her. She seemed so relaxed with herself and her motherhood.

The door to the church hall opened and a woman in a bright yellow T-shirt bearing the legend 'Angie's Action Kids', coupled with a pair of vibrant cherry tracksuit trousers on the bottom and soft black jazz pumps, clapped her hands and announced: 'OK, Mums! In you come! No dawdling now!'

Everyone laughed and made their way inside. The room was filled with various pieces of primary-coloured play equipment. A big yellow triangle, a huge red spongy ladder and slide, a big blue circle with a hole in the middle. There was a floor laid out with crash mats. Everyone took their shoes off and we were ready to begin. I was positioned directly opposite Judy, either side of a big pool filled with balls. Jo was looking round her with interest. Why hadn't I done this kind of thing with her before? It all felt like really great fun.

Angie had a lot of gold jewellery on, which clinked as she clapped her red-nailed hands together. She smiled at the group and said 'Herro!' in a slightly alarming way, while waving her hand frantically at the babies. Her voice was notched up a good two octaves. Angie picked up a tambourine lying next to her and said, 'He-llo ba-bies!' while beating a rhythm on the tambourine, and all the mums responded in the same rhythm with: 'He-llo An-gie.'

'OK, Mums, now if you want to put Baby onto your knee, we'll start with a little song about ten little fingers. That's ten … little … fingers,' she repeated, again in time with the tambourine.

I wondered if she took the tambourine home with her at night, and at random moments, if the mood took her, would pull it out and repeat certain phrases.

'There's … fuck-all … on the … telly.'

I made a mental note of this. Maybe I'd try and collar Judy after the session and tell her about it too.

Angie ran a tight ship. There was no room for freestyling here. Every minute was taken up with her telling us mums what to do – making Baby do a forward roll, holding a ball above Baby's head to make it reach, giving Baby various sensory bags to hold and feel. All of which was accompanied by Angie on different instruments. She shook a large plastic tube with beads in it, which was supposed to sound like rain. Everyone's reaction was: 'Oooh! Listen. It's RAIN. Splish-splosh rain, on the window pane,' and other such rhymes.

I looked around me. I was the only mum not joining in. I decided to just mumble anything whenever the other mums opened their mouths. I didn't want to let Jo down. I kept my smile up so that my cheeks were starting to ache, and I found myself gurning into Jo's face a lot and going, 'Woooh!'

I think Jo was enjoying herself. She didn't seem in the least bit interested in making friends with any of the other babies, though.

Angie called out suddenly: 'Cuckoo! Cuckoo!'

'Who are you? Who are you?' responded the other mothers dutifully. Jo started to mither and Angie's avidly plucked and pencilled eyebrows were arched in our direction. She called to Jo across the circle.

'Join in, Baby! Join in, Baby! Don't say maybe – join in, Baby!'

Angie's voice sounded as if she'd had some training. It had a force that could throw it from one end of the room to the other.

Jo started crying and Angie responded by leapfrogging over to us and producing a metal whistle. She slid the whistle up and down the scale, which made all the mums shout in unison: 'Up the scale and down the scale. In and out of the water pail!'

'I am high!' shrieked Angie.

'I am low!' shouted the mums.

'I am high!'

'I am low!' went the mums.

And all I could do was smile at them inanely.

I felt a bit annoyed with my daughter. Why the hell couldn't she perform? She was just being a wet blanket. Why couldn't she sit erectly and jingle a finger bell like the little boy in the dungarees?

There was an amazing amount of ritual going on here. I felt like we were being initiated into the toddler-lodge of the Masons or something. Maybe Angie was on the verge of rolling up a cherry-red trouser leg, and exposing her left breast.

Jo growled on. Why couldn't she giggle and coo at Angie's impression of a rabbit or laugh as a triangle was beaten directly in front of her face?

All of the mums seemed so engrossed in it all. Even Judy. With her rolled-up trousers, I'd put her down as more of a laisser-faire character, somebody a bit subversive who might even enjoy a spliff once the kids had gone to bed. I wasn't so sure watching her on all fours, gurning fulsomely at her little girl and joining in with the crocodile rhyme.

'You're new, aren't you?'

Angie had come over to join us. We were sitting away from the group now, to give Jo a chance to cheer up.

'Yes, it's our first time. I only live nearby. This is great!' I added a bit over-enthusiastically.

'And who's this little monkey?' she said loudly into Jo's face.

'This is Jo.'

'Do you want to come with Angie, Jo?' she said. 'Come with Angie and join in the actions with all of the others?'

Jo quite clearly wanted no such thing and cried lustily when Angie tried to pick her up.

'I'm afraid she's rebelling against your rhymes,' I said with a little laugh.

'Well, everyone else seems to be happy enough with them,' she answered sharply, looking me directly in the eye. 'I've been doing Angie's Actions for over ten years in this area. Many children round here have grown up with my rhymes and actions.'

'Wow,' I said, finding the thought of that momentarily sinister.

'You'll have to concentrate hard if you're going to get anything out of the rhymes,' she said acidly.

'Oh I will,' I said, reddening.

'Do you play music to her at home? It's just that she doesn't seem very used to it.'

I was taken aback at this veiled criticism of Jo's upbringing.

'Yes … absolutely. We have music playing all the time in the house.'

'Really? Well, you might want to buy a selection of my tapes to add to your collection. That way you and she can get used to the songs we do here, and you won't feel so … out of your depth.'

And she gave me the broadest smile, so that every crow's foot round her eye was etched deep into her coppery face. She was back into the class, shaking a maraca in front of a toddler here, clicking a castanet there.

I spent the rest of the session trying to concentrate. Judy threw me the odd encouraging smile, which was nice. I was so looking forward to having a chat with her. I just knew we were going to get on.

At quarter to eleven, Angie rang a bell and sang: 'Bye-bye girls and bye-bye boys!'

'We're going home to find our toys!' responded the mums.

'You did sing and you did rhyme,' sang Angie.

'We will be back next time,' ended the mothers with a flourish, while I just mumbled.

I felt like pointing out to Angie that some of the scansion in her rhyming left a lot to be desired, but was interrupted by all of the mums chorusing 'Bye-bye, Angie! Bye-bye, Angie!' while waving their babies' hands vigorously.

We all made our way towards the hatch and Angie passed the biscuit box round. There were rich pickings, with several of them wrapped in foil, which is always a good sign. Angie passed the box last to me, and all that was left were plain ones – shorties, digestives, dismal wafers and the like.

'Have you paid for the session?' she asked me.

'No, I'm so sorry, I haven't.'

'People usually like to pay a whole term's worth in advance. See you next week, Moira.'

'Oh. Of course.'

'And try to make life a rhyme. That way your little one will appreciate this session a bit more than she has done today. Look at her. Grumpelstiltskin.'

Almost to prove her wrong and show that my daughter was in fact the most rhythmically gifted, musical, advanced girl of the whole group, I said without hesitation, 'I'd love to sign up for a term,' and wrote a cheque out there and then. I also bought two of her tapes, which were extremely overpriced at a fiver each.

'See you next week,' said Angie.

'Please don't think she's a freak,' I said and laughed. Angie looked totally confused. 'That was a rhyme,' I explained.

Once outside the hall, the mums hung around chatting. I made a beeline for Judy.

'Blimey,' I said. 'She's a bit hardcore.'

Judy looked at me, confused. 'Angie?'

'Yeah,' I said. 'What an old dragon.'

'Angie's lovely,' said Judy. 'I've known her for years. I did classes here with Oliver, my eldest, and she's done parties for me several times. She's great at doing parties.'

I was about to say that I'd rather have Ann Widdecombe doing children's entertainment at one of my parties, but managed to stop myself.

'The class was great, though,' I said. 'We'll definitely come back.'

'That's good,' said Judy.

'How old's yours?' I enquired politely of her.

'She's nearly nine months.'

'This is Jo,' I said. 'She's nearly seven months.'

'And this is Minnie,' she said, introducing her pretty, very petite, green-eyed girl. 'Is Jo your first?' she asked, crouching down and tickling Jo's stomach.

'Yes. Can you tell from the bags?'

Judy laughed. 'The sleep deprivation's a nightmare, isn't it?' she said.

'Tell me about it,' I said. 'I don't know what we're doing wrong, but recently she's started waking up again, just once, in the middle of the night, for no reason.'

'I must lend you the Tamsin Orr book. Have you read it? It's called *Oh Calm Little Child*. There's a whole series. The *Calm Little Weaning* book, *Calm Little Potty-training* … God I've got all of them. I'll bring them next session.'

This was a golden moment. It was perfect. Jo and Minnie were reaching out for each other's hands; I was here talking to Judy, my new friend. The sun had come out, I felt energetic for the first time in weeks. OK, so Angie and I hadn't exactly hit it off, but there was a whole term stretching ahead of us.

'Do you want to come for a coffee? I'm going with Bridget and Alison.' She gestured to Big Jumper Mum and Poncho Mum, who were waiting for her.

'That's really kind of you, Judy. I've got to get home actually. I'd love to next time.'

'Fine.'

'Angie's a real character. Great. Bye then.'

'Bye,' the three of them said together.

'Bye,' I said joyfully, before skipping home, yes actually skipping, behind my lovely gurgling daughter in her buggy.

Chapter Five

The shed was now Dan's work HQ. He'd take the cordless phone in there for hours and sit in a deckchair, trying to drum up work. I sat precariously on the edge of a wheelbarrow.

'Why don't you just work at the kitchen table?' I asked. 'It's much more comfy.'

'No, the distance between shed and house is key. I leave the house to go to work.'

'It's all draughty in here.'

'Won't be when I've put down the carpet.'

His mobile rang. Dan put on his serious work face to answer it. Time to leave.

Back inside there were two messages for me on the answering machine. One from Pen asking me to phone her back. And the other from my mother.

'Hello. This is a message for Melanie. It's her mother here, Mrs Parkinson. Could she please be so kind as to return this call? Thank you so much.'

Mum had never really got comfortable with the answering machine. She thought it new-fangled, and could only leave very formal messages on it that referred to me in the third person.

I owed them both a call. I'd been hopeless about keeping in touch with friends and family. Our social circle seemed to have diminished over the months – there never seemed to be enough time to speak to anyone. I was on the point of lifting the phone when it rang.

'Good morning, Robin Jones here.'

I smiled. 'Hi, Robin, how are you?'

'Fine thanks, Mrs—'

'Please call me Mel.'

'Yes, well, just thought I'd phone to see if you received those forms.'

'Yes we did, and I shall post them back to you this very afternoon.'

'If you would, then I can get the ball rolling ASAP. Okey dokey?'

'Oh, Robin. I wonder if I could order another chequebook?'

'That shouldn't be a problem.'

'I used the last one up today, paying for a term's worth of Angie's Action classes for my daughter. It was quite good fun actually, and I met some nice people. One in particular I think could become a real friend.'

'So if you just pop the forms in—'

'It's hard making friends when you're older, isn't it, Robin? I mean, you're settled. You have your friends in place. You know who you like. Yet I think it's so important to be open to new friendships, don't you?'

'Mm. Well, I'll sort that chequebook out.'

'Dan hasn't made a new friend for ages. But blokes are much more stuck in their ways. When did you last make a new friend, Robin?'

'I ... er ... the chequebook,' he stammered.

Dan appeared in the kitchen. He looked like he had something to say.

'Oops. He's here. Speak soon, Robin – maybe tomorrow?'

At the other end, Robin coughed and hung up.

Dan scooped me up into a hug, and kissed me. 'Mel. I've got some news.' He was smiling.

'What?'

'Good news. I've been offered my first bit of freelance stuff.'

'Brilliant,' I said, squeezing him.

'It's two months' work and the money's good.'

'You're so clever,' I said, stroking his hair. 'When does it start?'

'In a couple of weeks. There's a bit of a drawback.'

I stopped stroking his hair. 'Meaning?'

'It's in Germany.'

I withdrew from the hug. 'Germany?'

'Berlin. I'll be there for six weeks. But it's not so bad. I'll be able to come back for some weekends. I'm sure.'

I folded my arms across my chest. 'So what about all this child-care you were going to do?'

'I'll do as much as I can in the next couple of weeks.'

I had no work on the horizon, it was true, but Dan's sudden break for childless freedom made me feel a pang of jealousy. He was beam-ing from ear to ear, probably already imagining the endless nights of unbroken sleep on a technologically advanced German mattress, drinks in a bierkeller after work, endless late-night bratwurst.

'What the hell am I going to do about selling our flat, Dan?'

'You're perfectly capable of dealing with it while I'm away,' Dan said. 'I'm sure Robin will be there to offer advice,' he added with a little wink.

'What about finding a new house to live in, Dan?'

'Just keep looking. You'll see something we like, I'm sure.'

I hadn't seen Dan in such a good mood for ages. He even started to hum some Bob Dylan round the kitchen. The baby started to cry upstairs.

'You get her, Dan,' I said, plonking myself down at the table. 'I'm going to make the most of you being around.'

Several days later and Dan decided that he was going to do a full day looking after Jo on his own. He was adamant that he was going to do the whole thing by himself.

'You need a bit of Me Time,' he announced.

'What, so I spend the whole day devoted to you?' I said.

'No. Me Time meaning You Time. It's all about women empowering themselves and saying, "I'm not just a mum. I'm a woman too."'

'Dan, don't go all Sunday supplement on me.'

He was wearing muesli-coloured trousers and backless male mules with socks, which was making me feel slightly nervous.

'Look,' he said, rearranging his tackle in the muesli slacks, 'I want to be involved in my daughter's life too. I don't want to be some distant figure she just remembers as a shadowy guy hanging round in the background when she was young.'

'You're dressing to the left,' I said.

'Listen, we're two equal parts of a marriage here. At the altar we promised to have and to hold. And for my money that means having a baby and also holding it.'

More nut arranging. He squirmed, and thankfully everything went back to its normal place. I suddenly noticed that Dan had a lot of hair sprouting from his nostrils. Mother Nature's answer to stretch marks, I suppose.

'Right, I'm off!' he said, and practically threw Jo into the buggy. He made off towards the front door.

'Hang on!' I shouted. 'What about a coat for her, Dan?'

'She'll be fine. It's nice and bracing out there. Good for her circulation.'

'It's autumnal out there, Dan. I always take a jumper for her if it's sunny but chilly, a coat for her for when it clouds over, and a scarf and sun cream if it's dazzlingly fresh.'

'And what about flippers in case of a sudden flash flood?' mumbled Dan, unjumbling the necessary gear in the cupboard underneath the stairs.

'Now what about spares?' I asked.

'I think the buggy tyres can cope with London pavements, Mel.'

'No. Spare clothes. What if she has an explosion? I normally keep a change in the compartment under the seat. And what's the plan for lunch?'

'I'll wing it. We can just drop into the pub and I can mush up a bit of sandwich or something.'

'She's seven months old, Dan. What do you expect her to do? Sit there and flick beer-mats with you and discuss the football results? She's a baby. She needs to go somewhere that has a high-chair and a properly cleansed surface, where she can eat her daily vegetables, fruit and a bit of carb. A mushed-up sandwich? And what were you intending to mush this sandwich up with, pray? Half a lager shandy, I suppose.'

His face looked blank.

'There's food for her in the ice-cube trays in the freezer.'

He opened and shut his mouth and looked blankly at me.

'There are different ice-cube trays, which I've pre-prepared and frozen for Jo's trips out. One's filled with fish-pie cubes, the other's spag bol. And there's her favourite pudding, which is in the pink ice-cube tray, which is papaya, pear and apple purée. Take as many cubes as you need; I find six per meal sufficient. Pop them out into little freezer bags, which you'll find beside the fridge, and by the time it's lunchtime you'll find that the food cubes have all defrosted and as long as you're somewhere that has a microwave she'll be fine.'

Dan was looking at me with a regret in his eyes, which said: This is the same woman who used to be able to drink ten flaming sambucas but now prefers a milky beverage on a tray. I'd actually enjoyed that monologue. Just as I'd enjoyed colour-coding the ice-cube trays for savoury and sweet. Oh my God, what was happening to me? Next I'd be wearing a headscarf tucked under my chin like my mum.

Dan kept his eyes on me and backed away towards the freezer compartment. He looked like a trapped animal.

'Here are spare nappies and wipes,' I said, a bright sunny 1950s-housewife smile all over my face, glad that he'd forgotten everything and been so utterly male and useless. 'And where are you taking her this morning?'

'Playhut,' said Dan, still looking at me mournfully.

'Then you'll need the Playhut pass,' I said smugly. 'Also they ask you to contribute to snack time. So if I were you I'd put a couple of digestives into a freezer bag and give them to the play coordinator.'

'Mel, that's the second time you've said "freezer bag" in about ten seconds. You're scaring me.'

'I'm just thinking ahead. If it wasn't for me thinking of every-thing and preparing it all, she'd be eating jellied eels and rolling around in her own faeces.'

'All right, all right. Can we go now, please?'

The baby was starting to wriggle in her buggy.

'Have you got the homeopathic teething powders?'

'Yes. And I've got the leeches in case she gets a fever,' Dan mumbled.

'You'll thank me when you're the one stranded and she's poorly.'

'Stranded? Stranded? We're in London, for God's sake. I'm taking her to the Playhut, not the bloody Congo.'

I narrowed my eyes at Dan, which was shorthand for: Don't swear in front of her.

'And do you know what, Mel? I'm actually going to leave the house without my Pac-a-mac. Yes, I'm really going to play Russian roulette with the weather this morning. Ha!'

He whooshed the buggy out of the flat and was halfway down the steps when I called out: 'What about the phone number for Dr Sweeting's surgery? If she suddenly develops an allergy it could be life threatening!'

Dan muttered something about an allergy to nagging wives, and was off down the street.

'Do you know where the nearest hospital to Playhut is, Dan? What if she chokes on a developmental aid?'

He marched on regardless.

'Do you know her blood group, Dan? What if she had to have a transfusion? Would you know what to ask for, Dan?' I was really having to yell at him now.

'And, Dan!' My voice was cracking with stress now. 'Remember to wipe her bottom from front to back. If you do it back to front, the way you do on yours, she could get a really nasty infection! FRONT TO BACK, DAN! THAT'S THE WAY I LIKE IT DONE! SWEEP FROM VAGINA TO ANUS!'

At which precise moment our elderly Irish neighbour Irene rounded the corner, obligatory fag protruding out of corner of mouth.

'I never liked interference with my anus, so I didn't,' she said to me beadily. 'How's that little lad of yours keeping?'

I was completely red in the face and simply said, 'He's fine, thanks, Irene. He's doing great.'

No sign of Dan now. He'd crossed the big road. Damn. I'd meant to remind him to take the sterilized face-flannel.

Turning back up the steps and going into the house, I breathed deeply. Me Time. A whole day of it. How would I fill it? How about a six-hour kip followed by a bit of Miss Marple on UK Gold? Or I could head straight into town, see a film and then take in an exhibition? Bit too energetic. I could sit at the computer and do some work. I'd been asked to write an article about juggling work and motherhood for the female section of a newspaper. Maybe I'd start it later. I'd just quickly switch on the telly and have a peek at a re-run of *Midsomer Murders*.

The flat was so quiet. No squawking, no babbling from her Teletubbies video. There was her little gym, all empty and expectant. I wondered what she and Dan were doing now. Maybe it was song-time and they were all doing 'The Wheels On The Bus'? It was nearly ten. Nearly time for her snack juice bottle. I hoped Dan would remember. I resisted calling his mobile to remind him – he'd only get tetchy and think I was interfering. But Jo was likely to get very grouchy if she didn't have snack juice at ten. Maybe I'd call him. Hmmm. Playhut was only a few streets away – why not just pop round there and tell him in person? I could pretend that I was just passing anyway. That settled it. I tidied up the kitchen, put on a jacket and left the house.

Once outside Playhut I hesitated at the door. Dan had only left the house about twenty-five minutes ago. He'd think I was being totally paranoid if I were to go in now and tell him what to do. I had become a bit of a fishwife since Jo had been born. This was the perfect opportunity to address the issue and keep it in check. I'd spy on them instead. There was a slightly raised area of earth under a tree just by one of the windows, the perfect place to get a bird's-eye of everything that was going on inside Playhut.

I positioned myself under the tree and looked inside. It all looked promising. The cabin was newly built and the toys, beanbags and furniture were still bright and intact round the edges. There was a little book corner with several children immersed in reading; another part of the room had a big banner saying 'Messy Play' and several toddlers stripped to their nappies were rubbing flour and water onto a table. And there was a spongy area for the tiny ones called 'BabyZone', where four babies plus carers, including Dan and Jo, were grouped. Dan was stretched out on the floor with his back to me; Jo looked pretty happy propped up in a beanbag. She was looking cross-eyed at a fluorescent monkey. A young mum was tickling her baby on the tummy, another was changing her child's nappy, and there was a familiar-looking woman with a rather stodgy boy, squashed into a hideous baby-blue sailor suit. I'd definitely seen her somewhere before.

One look at her mouth grimaced into a tiny little hole told me – it was Ventriloquist Mum. The mother/baby act was clearly still in place. Her mouth was busying itself around the dual voices, and her unfortunate son, who looked as if he'd piled on about two stone, simply stared into the middle distance. He was surely a serial killer in the making. I suddenly saw him aged thirty-seven, still dressed head to toe in baby blue. Ventriloquist Boy would still be living in the same cul-de-sac where he'd been born, never allowed to leave his domineering mother. She still spoke for him, his own voice having been reduced to a series of grunts and mumbles. One day he would take a sawn-off shotgun from his wardrobe and blast around the cul-de-sac before finally turning the gun on his own mother and then himself. Police would find reams of weblog on his computer, detailing his obsessive love for his mother. He would be Britain's first serial killer dressed entirely in baby blue. He would be forever known as that – BABY BLUE SENT DOWN TO BELMARSH! I could see the headlines now.

My Jo seemed oblivious to the mortal danger she was in, and

was actually stroking Baby Blue's cheek. Dan hadn't noticed. His own daughter was befriending a serial killer and he hadn't even noticed. I wanted to knock on the window and shout at him to take her away. And then I noticed what Dan was actually doing. His prone position had masked the fact that he was reading a newspaper. I couldn't believe it. There he was spouting on about his precious time with his daughter and what was he doing? Reading about the bloody cricket. I climbed the lower branches of the tree to get a better look at the proceedings. Yes, he was picking his nose lightly and reading the sports pages. And Jo's nappy was bulging suspiciously. The contours of it looked like poo to me. This was terrible. She'd get a rash. She'd probably get an infection. And where was her ten o'clock snack juice? I could see it poking out of the hood of the buggy, totally undrunk. She'd be dehydrated as well as stinking. And she was still holding that stupid fluorescent monkey, for Pete's sake. Dan hadn't even bothered to check her stimulation levels. Didn't he realize that she needed more than a monkey to fill her morning? She'd have the brain of a cauliflower if I let him look after her too much. Dan was getting up and stretching his legs. Good, he must be getting the juice. Either that or a new nappy for her malodorous bottom. Or maybe, just maybe, he'd have the brain to move his darling away from that weirdo murderer-baby in the sailor suit. But no. He shook out his paper, gave Jo a little pat on the head, said something to Ventriloquist Mum and headed off to the loos at the other side of the room. With his newspaper. This was a very bad sign indeed. What in God's name did he think he was doing?

Ventriloquist Mum moved in towards Jo with her weirdly staring baby and I could tell by the way her face was moving that she was doing the Ventriloquism Act on my own flesh and blood! And Jo was enjoying it, the traitor. She was actually smiling and reaching out for the ghoulish woman's face. Oh God, Jo was falling under her spell too. Maybe they'd become a serial-killing couple, her and Baby Blue? I was losing my daughter to her. Where the hell was Dan? He'd been gone a good five minutes. Five minutes! Crapping and cricket – a lethal combination. Lucky I was there keeping an eye from my hidey-tree – I was fully prepared for the moment when Ventriloquist Mum suddenly snatched my Jo and plucked her out of the room, away into her cul-de-sac of hell. When such a moment occurred, I would run into the Playhut and fell that mum right there on top of the abacus. Dan emerged from the loo looking happy and gave a friendly smile to Ventriloquist Mum. Didn't he have any sense of the danger he'd put his daughter in? Wasn't he in the slightest bit concerned? Right, that was it, I was going in. I was absolutely furious with Dan.

I was just getting down from my tree when I was approached by a man in a brightly coloured yellow jacket emblazoned with the words 'Community Warden'.

'Can I ask you what you've been doing up that tree?' he asked with dead eyes.

'I was just looking in at the Playhut.'

'Oh yes. And what were you doing that for?' he said.

'Just spying on my husband and daughter.' I smiled.

'Spying on them, you say?'

'Yes. It's my husband's first day alone with her and I want to make sure that he's …'

It suddenly dawned on me what this warden was thinking. He'd put me down as some kind of weirdo who was perving around a toddlers' playhut, for Pete's sake!

'So your daughter's in there, is she?' he asked.

'Yes she is, and for your information, I think you'd be better off questioning some of the women in there rather than accusing me of anything untoward.'

'What do you mean?' I could see that I'd got the warden's attention.

'There's a ventriloquist mother in there!'

This was clearly too big a concept for the warden.

'Come again?' he said.

'A ventriloquist. You know, like Ray Allen and Lord Charles. Remember those acts from Saturday-night entertainment shows from the 1970s? Those slightly odd men who sit puppets on their knees and do a falsetto voice to sound like the puppet?'

His face still looked pretty blank. 'Are you saying there's old blokes in there with kiddies on their knees?'

'No. There's a mother doing it to her own son.'

'Doing it to her own son?'

'Yes. Pretending to be him. Using her own voice as his ...' My voice faltered. This was ridiculous. We were getting nowhere.

'What's your name?' he said, taking out a notebook.

'Why on earth should you need to know that?'

My voice had suddenly got posher. A trick my mother pulls when dealing with people in authority.

'It is my right to ask you your name if I feel something is occurring that may be a threat to this community,' the little oaf reeled off pompously.

'Me? A threat to this community? I'm a mother, thank you very much. I've lived round here for years.'

'What's your name?'

'Britney Spears,' I said defiantly.

He actually started to put pen to paper before ripping the sheet of paper off angrily.

'Do you want me to make a citizen's arrest?' he said, taking a step towards me.

'You dare lay one finger on me and I'll ...' I made a mental note to have something prepared for future incidents like this. 'Look,' I continued. 'I'm going in there to get my daughter. Then I shall bring her out here to show you and then we shall go home. Is that good enough for you?'

The warden crossed his arms. I turned on my heel and went into the Playhut. God I was cross with Dan. This was all his fault. I scanned the Playhut but there was no sign of either Dan or Jo. A hot feeling began to swell in my chest. I had no choice – I would have to ask Ventro Mum.

'Excuse me, I'm here to collect my daughter. She was here just now with my husband. She was in her buggy wearing a multi-coloured cardi. With her father who was more interested in Freddie Flintoff.'

Ventro looked at Baby Blue, then back at me. And out it came, the little baby voice.

'What? My new little friend Jo?'

'Yes. That's right.'

I couldn't believe that I was having to humour her ridiculous act, but here I was getting information out of a baby boy.

'Do you know where they went?' I asked the baby, looking him directly in the eye.

'Well, Jo did say to her daddy dat she was very hungry and so they did go off to get their lunch.'

'That's right, little man,' said the mother in her normal voice at last. 'They went to get something to eat, didn't they?'

'Any idea where?' My voice was getting higher. I could feel tears starting to prick at my eyes. 'It's just that I might be about to be arrested.'

'Oh no!' It was Baby Blue's voice back at me now. 'Poor Jo! She doesn't want her mummy to be in prison!'

'Yes, well, thanks for being so positive.' I was arguing with a baby; this was ridiculous. 'So they've gone, you say? And when did they go?'

'Thirty seconds agoooo,' was the very plaintive reply, like an abandoned fox-cub.

I smiled briefly before running out to tackle Mr Jobsworth. He'd taken out a walkie-talkie in the meantime and was talking, very po-faced, into it. He stared at me expectantly.

'It appears that my daughter and husband left the premises thirty seconds ago.' I was starting to back away from him, almost bowing in that way that Japanese businessmen do. I turned and started to walk away. My heart was beating quite fast, but I carried on, a little faster now. He shouted at me.

'Oi! I want a word with you!'

And I started to trot. Which was the most exercise I'd done in many years, and after a hundred or so metres, when I reached the bin area, I realized how foolish I'd been to start running. There was no way on earth that I could keep this jogging up. My head was starting to feel a bit pins-and-needlesy, my armpits were dampening up and I had a stitch developing under my heart. But I had to keep going. I could hear the warden behind me. To be fair, he was the sort of man who looked like the most exercise he'd ever done was the Jane Fonda Workout. On the sofa with his trousers down when the wife was out. If I kept up a steady jogging pace I was in no danger of being lapped. To anyone observing from a distance, we must have made the most unthrilling of chases. Very slow woman running at the speed of a toddler being chased by guy in size twenty-six trousers and built-up shoes because he has weakened ankles. I was lapped by a briskly walking granny at one point.

I had to keep going though. There was no turning back. It was simply too late to stop jogging, turn round and pretend that it hadn't happened. I felt like I was about to puke my heart up, right out of my mouth, and see it juddering on the ground before me. Even my eyeballs were thumping. I could hear his voice getting louder behind me.

'Oi! Stop!'

He must be making up ground. How was that physically possible? Was he hiding a jet-pack somewhere in the folds of his jacket?

I had nearly reached the edge of the park and was starting to hallucinate with over-exertion. There was a strange gargling noise emanating from the back of my throat. I've never been a big spitter. Ever since my mum told me that's how the plague started in London, I've been careful to keep my sputum to myself. But at this point in time I was ready to hawk up enough phlegm to get the whole borough reaching for its garlic and bandages.

Just at that moment, a gaggle of primary-school kids came marching crocodile-fashion round the corner. I managed to clear the pavement and cling to the Belisha beacon before they flooded the whole area. God was on my side – the lights went red and I skipped over the road, like Billy Goat Gruff, to the freedom of the sweet green meadow beyond.

Like the Egyptians following Moses through the Red Sea, the warden was drowned in a sea of little kids, unable to extricate himself from folders and gym bags. I kept jogging down the road until I was at a safe enough distance to sneak a look behind me. There was the warden, like a piece of fluorescent meat, bobbing about helplessly in a sea of small but very aggressive sharks, all in knee-length red socks.

People looked at me with pity in their eyes as I lurched down the road. My face was streaming with sweat and my breathing was completely broken up with wracking, retching gasps. I felt like I was going through the final stages of TB. Right. Definitely time to get down to the gym. I'd turned off into the back streets and was just starting to get my breath back, hunched over a railing, when a voice called out: 'Mel. Is that you?'

I was still gasping as I raised my head and saw Judy looking at me from behind her buggy. She looked neat and bright in a Peruvian-knitted cardi and leggings.

'Hi ... Judy. Just ... had to ... run ... away ...'

'You look like you could do with a coffee. Minnie's fast asleep at this time so I always try and get out for an hour.'

I managed a thumbs-up to show I was up for it. It was good to see a friendly face after the confrontations of the morning.

We sat over cappuccinos and Judy smiled at my story. I embroidered it slightly, like saying that the community warden had pretty much produced a warrant for my arrest, but she was a willing and receptive audience, so I felt I owed it to her.

'I think you're very brave to let your husband look after Jo for a whole day. I don't think I'd dare let Gavin do that.'

'Really?' I asked. 'What about Me Time?'

'I think Me Time's going to have to wait, don't you? There'll be plenty of that once they're at school.'

I felt ashamed. Here was I, out and about drinking coffee and telling stupid stories about my futile morning, when what I should have been doing was looking after my daughter, like Judy was doing. She relaxed her foot onto Minnie's buggy and started to move it to and fro without even realizing she was doing it. She seemed like such a natural mother – so at ease in her own skin. She didn't have a hunted, manic look about her at all. Her hair was clean, and everything about her emanated a sense of well-being. I was going to have to watch her and get tips.

I suddenly missed Jo very much. I didn't even know where she was. Dan's mobile was permanently switched off. Maybe he'd gone off to join the Fathers For Justice movement. I pictured him in a

Batman suit, with Jo as Robin, straddling one of the hands of Big Ben and shouting: 'Say No To Nagging Wives. Join Us!' and me at the bottom shouting up at him: 'Dan! You haven't put her scarf on! She'll catch her death up there! The clock's about to strike three: make sure you protect her ears. Did you remember to bring her afternoon milk?'

Judy was looking at me expectantly.

'I'm sorry, Judy, I was miles away. What did you say?'

'Don't worry. I was just asking if Jo was sleeping better at night now.'

'Yes! Ever since I discovered ear-plugs!' I laughed. Judy looked taken aback.

'Ear-plugs?' she said.

'They're a godsend.'

'But you can't hear your baby with them in, surely?'

'I'll always hear her through the ear-plugs if she's really bellowing, even from our bedroom.'

'Oh! She doesn't sleep in the same room as you?'

'No.' I felt suddenly self-conscious. 'You must think we're very Victorian. You probably think we're dosing her up with brimstone and treacle.' I laughed nervously.

Judy just kept moving the buggy gently back and forth with her Birkenstocked foot.

'I mean' – I was starting to back-pedal – 'I don't put the ear-plugs in every night. God no. I'll treat myself and put them in about twice a week when Dan's on duty.' I felt my cheeks going pink. I'd had the ear-plugs in solidly for the last eight nights on the trot.

'I just can't imagine not being close to Minnie all the time, even when she's sleeping. I just love hearing her snuffle at night.'

I thought of the amount of times I'd sworn violently at Jo in the middle of the night when she'd interrupted my beauty sleep. Time to change the subject.

'So do you work, Judy?'

'I used to. I was in the music industry for years.'

I was impressed – there definitely was something boho about her. Yes, it was possible to picture her supping pints and rolling cigarettes at some indie gig.

'I was a music-rights lawyer,' she said.

'Oh,' I replied, slightly disappointed. I should have realized. The Peruvian cardi was hardly very rock and roll.

'I'd like to work again, but not at the moment with the little ones. I'd love to set up my own business. From home, you know.'

'Brilliant,' I enthused. This was sounding more encouraging. Maybe she'd do something funky with her music-industry contacts or something.

'My family are from Suffolk,' she went on. 'They've got some lovely fishermen's wear down there. I thought about designing my own range for kids.'

I was stumped. A range of children's fishermen's wear? In the middle of London?

'Wow,' I managed.

'I'll have to show you all the stuff,' she said, 'see what you think. You must come round.'

'I'd love to,' I said, seeing Jo in waders and sou'wester in my mind.

'It'd be great to get the children together,' she said, stroking Minnie's perfect porcelain cheek.

'Yes,' I said. 'Jo's a real Nobby-No-Mates. Hasn't got a single friend.'

'Really?' said Judy. 'Minnie's got quite a little group of baby-chums already. We'll have to see if we can get Jo in the gang too.'

'That'd be great,' I said, feeling a bit sad on my daughter's behalf all of a sudden. I looked at my watch. Time to find my family.

'I'd better go, Judy. It was great to see you. Let's do it again sometime.'

'Great,' she said. 'And if you need anything, anything at all, you only have to ask. I've got a whole library of baby-books at home. Let me write down my number.' She scribbled it on a napkin. 'I've read them all back-to-back anyway and with two kids I think I know what I'm doing!'

'Right,' I said, folding up the number very small and putting it into my jacket.

'I've got a big mums' network, so if you want to come out and paint the town red with us, then you're very welcome.'

'Now that sounds like a very good idea,' I said, grinning. 'Just don't get me on the tequila. I'll be arm-wrestling, lambada-ing and pole-dancing!' I said, nudging her.

She looked at me. 'Well, we've been known to go a bit wild,' she said. 'A couple of plates were broken at our last trip to the Greek restaurant, but usually we just prefer a glass of red and lots of mum-chat over a nice meal.'

What was that tiny ball of paper in my pocket? I had been screwing up Judy's phone number in my hand without realizing it. It was around six o'clock and I was pacing the living room like an expectant father. Where the hell was Dan? His mobile was still off and I'd left at least six messages on his voice mail. I was on the point of dialling Emergency Services when I heard the key go in the front door. A clatter of buggy-wheels and then Dan's voice singing an old Dexys Midnight Runners favourite. And the baby gurgling and giggling along with it.

'Come on, Eileen! Ta-loo roo-ah ey! Come on! ...' He continued to sing it while he kissed my cheek and jauntily tried to twirl me round in the hallway.

'Where the bloody hell have you been, Dan? It's after six. She must be exhausted. And why didn't you phone?'

'Battery ran out,' he said.

'And you didn't take enough snack juice. Or nappies. And what about her supper? She must be absolutely starving.'

Annoyingly, she looked totally happy and placid. I picked her up and hugged her to me.

'There are such things as shops, you know. You don't have to leave the house with four months' supplies on board.'

I decided to ignore him. 'There, there, my darling,' I said to Jo. 'You're with Mummy now. That's right, Mummy'll make everything better,' and I nuzzled into her face. She looked at me suspiciously. Then her lower jaw jutted out from her face like the drawer of a cash register. And she bellowed.

Dan could barely keep the smug look off his face.

'The estate agent phoned,' he said above Jo's caterwaul. 'Somebody's offered the asking price on the flat.'

'What?' I felt suddenly stressed. I handed the baby to Dan and the little tart immediately shut up and started gurgling. 'So soon?'

'Yup. We'd better get our skates on and find somewhere to live. Come on, little bug, it's bath-time,' and with that he lifted her nonchalantly above his head and went out of the room.

He didn't even look remotely tired. After a whole day with the baby I resembled an aged peasant who'd been working the turnip field. With the hairstyle to match. Dan had a glow to his cheek and a spring to his step. I was just following up the stairs when I stopped in my tracks.

'Dan?' I shouted up at him. 'How come you managed to get a message from the estate agent when your battery was down?'

Chapter Six

'Children's fishermen's outfits?' said my mother loudly from the kitchen. She'd come round to offer support after Dan's recent departure to Germany.

'Yes, Mum.'

'Based on real fishermen?'

'Yes, Mum.'

'This Judy woman's quite clearly out of her mind.'

I dug my nails into my hands. I was not going to have a squabble with my mum twenty minutes after her arrival.

She swept into the living room bringing a whiff of Pledge with her. She was carrying tea and some of her home-made flapjacks on a tray. I felt defensive of my new friend who'd been placed under the matriarchal microscope.

'There we go, dear. I bet that's the first time the milk's come out of a jug in this house.'

'Thanks, Mum.'

It was only a matter of seconds before she made a comment about the brown patch on the ceiling.

'Is she from round here, this Judy creature?'

'Yes, she's the first proper friend I've made since having the baby. She's part of a really good mums' network.'

Mum looked as if she'd smelled something that had gone off.

'Mums' network? What on earth do you need one of those for?

In my day we just got on with it. I went to the odd coffee morning, but honestly all this dreary sitting around in each other's houses moping and dripping. It's ridiculous. Babies get far more germs than they used to with all this enforced group activity.' And with that she bit into a flapjack.

My nails were on the point of drawing blood from my palms.

'I like the company, Mum.'

'I never made any friends through you.'

'That's not true. What about Amanda's mum?'

'Exactly.'

I began to see her point.

'And fishermen's wear? I don't see why children need all these ridiculous outfits these days. Done up like Christmas-tree fairies. In my day we put girls in sensible pinafores. I used to rustle you up some outfits from Clothkits for daywear and bibs and tuckers for best.'

I winced at the memory of my sister and I having to go to a birthday party themed around the film *Grease*. All the other girls were dressed in Olivia Neutron-Bomb-style black rocker-chick outfits with high-heeled backless shoes borrowed from their cool and sassy mums. We on the other hand were in matching red Clothkit skirts and tops, white socks and normal school shoes. My mum had provided jaunty kerchiefs for us, which she'd tied round our necks so that the knots sat to one side. This was my mum's only concession to the fact the film was set in the rock 'n' roll era.

My mother sniffed and dabbed a crumb away from the corner of her mouth. 'So, do you suppose she means to supply fishing rods to go with these outfits? The children will look like gnomes.' Mum laughed through her nose.

I let out the tiniest of sighs and counted to five very slowly in my head. 'No, Mum. I expect it's smocks and stripy trousers, that sort of thing.'

'Sounds terribly twee,' she said, putting her granddaughter onto her lap.

'Well, I think Judy's very creative,' I ploughed on. I had nothing to back that statement up with, apart from the fact that Judy sometimes wore clogs.

'Littly looks very pale,' remarked my mother. 'Has she done biggies today?'

It was hard to admit it, but Mum was right. Jo was looking somewhat wan.

'Yes, but very runny.'

My mother wrinkled her nose. 'When you had the trotties I used to let you eat coal.'

'What?' I said, almost choking on a flapjack.

'You used to eat coal like it was going out of fashion. I got so worried during those awful coal shortages. Your major source of nutrition was in danger of drying up. Bloody Labour Party.'

'But wasn't it bad for me, eating all that coal?'

'Nonsense. People are so faddy about what their children eat these days. "Oh Tabitha's allergic to dairy" and "James is intolerant to peanuts". No. Tabitha is a spoilt little hoyden and James is simply too thick.'

'What – too thick to eat peanuts?' She was teasing me with the red rag now. 'Mum,' I went on, 'in the 1970s we grew up eating faggots, junket, liver, kidneys, space dust and pork pies. Most of which was riddled with salt, sugar or mad cow disease.'

'Claptrap!'

'It's true!'

'Stuff and nonsense. "Enough is as good as a feast." That was my motto.'

And my mother put Jo down in her basket, smoothed her skirt and started humming, which is always a sure-fire sign that the conversation is well and truly closed. She continued humming a song from G&S opera *The Mikado*. She ran a finger over a nearby bookshelf and looked disapprovingly at the results. Right. The red rag was well and truly out of the bag now and being gyrated in front of my face. She'd been here for twenty-three minutes precisely and I felt my blood pressure zooming.

Ruddy Dan. I could picture him right now, on one of those open-top tourist buses being driven around Berlin. 'And on ze right, ve haf ze remarkable old cathedral viz its gothic glory for all to see.' Or maybe he was in a comfortable little bierkeller, taking five with a colleague during a busy work session. Maybe she was a female colleague? I bet she was called Brigitte and didn't have unsightly hair travelling from out of her trousers up to almost her navel. I bet Brigitte still had a sense of humour, a flat stomach and calves that didn't have a vein the size of the M6 travelling up them. Bloody Brigitte. I hated her and her corn-yellow hair, sweet-smelling breath and bagless eyes. The lack of sleep was starting to get to me – I couldn't even wear my ear-plugs now that Dan was away. The darling little orange beauties had been re-encased in their plastic box. I looked at the box longingly every night, waiting for our blissful reunion.

My mum seemed now to be going through the entire libretto of *The Mikado*. Part of me wanted to join in with a cross mid-baritone to accompany her top-end warbling. But no, that would be an admission of defeat. I was not going to raise the white flag to her quite yet. I was a mother myself now – no longer a sullen little girl in Clothkits clothes. I would rise above the pettiness of our bickering, and start an adult conversation with her again.

'So Dan's set up his own business, Mum,' I said in a confident, grown-up way, as if talking to someone at a cocktail party. She stopped mid-note.

'Well I don't know,' she sniffed. 'In our day we didn't have all this starting-up-a-business-from-home nonsense. I don't know how Dan's managing it. I had a peek in his shed. Doesn't look much like a business to me. Unless he's selling weed-killer, old plant pots and broken deckchairs.'

That was it. The red flag was flapping furiously in the wind, and this bull had had enough. I jumped up and strode into the kitchen, where I silently banged my head against the ironing board hanging on the back of the door.

'Why doesn't he just become a doctor or a lawyer, dear?' she called through to the kitchen. 'Then you could move to a lovely house with a garden. All that fresh air would be so lovely for Littly and she could have her own flowerbed. And you could afford a decent wardrobe. I saw something in the paper about people becoming doctors and lawyers when they think they're past it. I'll cut it out and send it to him. It's not too late, you know. He could be a consultant, specialize in something. He'd like that. I'll have a quiet word with him when he gets back from Germany.'

I was now lying on the kitchen floor with my legs slowly grinding at the lino, like a felled horse. My mouth was fixed into a silent scream, like the Munch painting.

'Are you all right in there, dear? What are you doing?'

I let out an elongated groan, like something you hear in an underfunded zoo.

'Sounds like you need biggies!' she called brightly. 'Oh goodness, look at the time! I'm meeting Joan at eleven in Peter Jones. I'd better go.'

The kitchen door opened. She looked at me lying face down on the floor.

'What on earth are you doing, dear?'

'Just exercising.'

'You're not suffering from any postnatal nonsense, are you? You look a bit peaky around the gills. I know you, you get very silly when you haven't had enough sleep. I remember Richard Hyde's eighteenth birthday party.'

My mum had extraordinary recall for the most embarrassing moments of my life. I wondered if I'd be the same with Jo.

'Now you know that your father and I are off to Frinton to see Auntie Beryl for a week,' she said, tucking her headscarf tightly under her chin. There was not the merest whiff of a breeze outside, but this made no difference. Blazing sun, permafrost – my mother's headscarf was a permanent feature on her head. I was feeling quite giddy with excitement at her imminent departure, and was starting to leap from foot to foot.

'Now are you sure you're going to be OK all on your own with your father and I away and your husband abandoning you in Germany?'

'Yes!' I said joyously. 'Oh yes. I've never been better.'

'What if there's an emergency?'

'Mum, I've got friends, you know.'

'Ah yes. Talking of your friends, how's Amanda coping with motherhood?' This was said with a visible tightening of the lips.

'I haven't seen her for ages, actually, but I'm sure she's fine. She's got two nannies. One for the day and one for the night.'

'Has she indeed?' My mother gave Jo a little kiss on the forehead and headed down the hallway. 'Nannies lead to one of two things,' she added, snapping her handbag shut, 'pregnancy or drugs.'

And with that, she was gone.

My mother's departure left me drained and feeling rather drunk. I was still giggling to myself when I answered the phone.

'Robin Jones here from the bank.'

'Robin!' I shouted, greeting him as if he was a long-lost relative. 'How are you? It's been ages.'

A slight pause. He was probably adjusting his special bank tie, which was grey polyester with the bank's logo emblazoned proudly on the front.

'Keeping myself busy,' he replied. 'No rest for the wicked, as they say.'

'That's good, and how is the world of finance?' I said, by way of opening the conversation up a bit.

'Well. They keep us on the hop. We've got some great new products come in, which is always exciting,' he said.

'Oh yes?' I said encouragingly.

'We're offering a new Slice Account system – you may have seen the literature last time you were in the bank – which slices up your money like a cake into a three-tier system and then sweeps all the interest between the various slices, a bit like a money trifle. The custard and cherry being the high-interest slice and the sponge being a bit like your average savers account.'

'And would that sponge make it a CURRANT account?' I said and then laughed like a drain.

There was silence at the other end of the line. 'Yes, well, I just wanted to have a bit of a catch-up about the state of play with the move. Have you found anywhere to move to yet?'

'Not yet, Robin, it's been so busy, what with me being on my own with a small baby. I don't think I told you Dan's in Germany, did I?' I could hear the slightest click of a keyboard in the background. His computer? Possibly a palm pilot. 'Anyway, it's home-alonesvillle for me at the moment, Robin. Nobody to share the dirty nappies with, just me at the coalface. Motherhood is a bit like being a miner, Robin. It's dark dark tunnels but occasionally you chance on a diamond. And like a miner, you do get very very mucky. Although not with coal, unless you happen to eat lots of it, which apparently I did when I was a baby.'

I waited for a reaction from Robin, but none came. I ploughed on.

'Luckily I don't have to wear a Davy lamp all of the time, though. That was just the midwife, thankfully!' And I threw back my head and laughed. 'Robin?'

He coughed and then said, 'Well, let me know when you ...'

'Oh yes, I will, Robin. You'll be the first person I phone. I've got about ten properties to view next week, so fingers crossed. I don't suppose you fancy coming to look at houses with me, do you, Robin? Cast your gimlet financial eye over them?'

There was a slightly uncomfortable pause.

'Only kidding!' I said loudly.

'Yes, well, I'll speak to you soon, and do keep me posted on the purchase.'

'Are you close to your mother, Robin?' I enquired gently. 'I mean, it's tricky, isn't it? There's so much love there and yet so much frustration and capacity for annoyance. I often wonder if Jo'll think the same way about me. I suppose she will. It's the nature of things. She'll look at me wearing my combat trousers and they will seem as outdated to her as my mother's headscarf appears to me. It's funny, isn't it, Robin?'

'Okey dokey,' he said, in a winding-up-the-conversation way. 'You let me know of any purchase news.'

'What? Oh yes, of course, Robin.'

'OK ...' said Robin's quiet voice at the end of the line.

'Have you ever been left alone by a partner, Robin? You know, someone you've been with for a long time, whom you're used to being around and then suddenly they're gone? Just here one day and—'

There was a click as he put down the phone, quietly and neatly, in his little booth in the bank.

Hard to admit, but my mother was right. Jo was definitely below par for some reason. She was listless, wouldn't feed properly, and her eyes looked small and red round the rims. She looked kind of waxy too. Odds on she was getting another tooth.

She needed gingering up a bit. I decided the best course of action was to take her out for a nice inspiring trip. Expose her a bit to the urban thrum of our city. She'd been cooped up with me for too long. We hadn't even made it as far as Angie's class. After that first triumph of time/baby management, I'd never quite managed to get out of the door again with such aplomb. I was seriously going to have to work on my time-management skills. But then, I thought, it takes so much time to sort out one's time-management skills, doesn't that defeat the object? Simply drawing up a timetable for the day would take me the whole day.

No, I was going to give my daughter a really good day out. We'd go on a bus and everything. Then she could see that there was a basis of truth to 'The Wheels On The Bus Go Round And Round' and mothers weren't just a bunch of demented, lying lunatics after all.

I toyed with the idea of dressing up for the trip, but decided that I simply couldn't be fagged. Scanning through my wardrobe was a similar experience to loading up clothes parcels for Poland, which we'd all done in the early 1980s. Nothing had changed. My wardrobe was full of brown and grey drooping clothes. I'd given up trying to keep up with fashion. The last time I'd ventured into a high-street clothes shop I'd been scared off by a dragoon of shop assistants wearing what looked like jackets from the Royal Air Force with footless (surely I was dreaming?), FOOTLESS fishnet tights and white stilettos. What was this? Had we all been transported back to Angles nightclub, our favourite teen venue in the 1980s, and the place where I'd snogged Adrian Mills for two hours solid?

I must be getting old. For today's trip I'd wear my usual uniform: drawstring maternity trousers (so many months after the birth, and I couldn't bring myself to let go of them quite yet) and a baggy green fleece. No makeup, hair scraped back into a bunch. I looked utterly nondescript. A cipher. A non-event. Good.

It was a matter of urgency that I find myself a new bra. Jo and I would go in search of one this very morning. It was ironic – my friends and I used to laugh a lot at our French teacher, whose boobs were so droopy they hung over the belt of her skirt. Looking in the mirror now, I realized I was fair game for local kids.

It was time to get out of this rut of appalling self-image and hold my head up high. We headed for Trafalgar Square. I felt confident that Jo would love the lions, Nelson's Column and the scores of hobbled pigeons. We alighted on this most illustrious of London squares and inadvertently managed to appear in about five other people's holiday photos. Don't you often wonder how many photo albums you feature in round the globe? Maybe I am just very self-centred, but it gives me a feeling of warmth to imagine that I feature in albums as far-flung as Kuala Lumpur and Rio. I may just be a blurred head, the end of a stride leaving the shot, but I am there, a feature imprinted into somebody else's life, and after this morning my daughter Jo had that honourable position too. The thought actually made me brim with sudden tears, and I crouched down into her buggy to share this moving moment with her. She was fast asleep. Her breathing was a little bit raspy, and her waxiness looked accentuated in the bright light of the day. The edifying delights of Nelson would have to wait.

I was at a slight loose end now. I leaned up against the plinth of a lion, toyed with the idea of going into the National Gallery but decided that was too much like hard work, and decided that I'd walk over to Covent Garden in search of the bra. I hadn't been among this rush of people and noise of traffic and bustle for months. I was absolutely shattered. I felt like one of those characters in a film who has traipsed through deserts and pitches up in an unknown town, dirty, dog-tired and dishevelled. I looked around me. Was I part of this race? Everyone looked different from me. Everyone looked neat, focused, sure-footed. I felt like an old rustic who'd come from up-country for the day.

Unfamiliar music blared out from the shops in Covent Garden and sullen shop assistants looked at me uninterestedly from their leather and cashmere palaces. Since when had everyone taken to wearing these funny little Walkmans with miniscule headphones tucked right into their ears? And at the other extreme, there seemed to be lots of young people wearing outrageously oversized earphones, like Radio 2 DJs used to wear in the 1970s. And these big ear-bowls didn't seem to be attached to anything. No wires, no tapes, nothing clipped onto the belt. So where was the music coming from? If indeed it was music? Maybe it was some kind of ear-sauna, the invention of which had totally passed me by? Or specially oversized ear-plugs? If so, I'd have to invest in some immediately.

Jo slept on while I continued my stumble through twenty-first-century London. There seemed to be many more of those people who stand in the street with clipboards, stopping people to sign up for charities and wearing netball-bibs to advertise them. Most of them looked like students, plastic identity-tags hanging round their necks and trousers with crotches down to their knees.

All of them seemed to work in pairs, so they were very hard to avoid. One lot were signing people up for a homeless organization

– I rammed myself and buggy up against a shop window and pretended to be deeply interested in a collection of walking sticks until they'd collared somebody else.

Another pair was persuading people to sign up for an environmental charity. They were leaping about, forming a pincer movement round the public like big dancing crabs. I whipped out my mobile and pretended to have an extremely emotional conversation on it – one of them looked at me suspiciously and I had to start crying loudly to get past her. I thought I was safe until I rounded a corner and almost walked slap-bang into two more of them, a boy and a girl. I scanned my surroundings quickly. High walls everywhere – no shops to dive into, my phone was stowed back under the buggy. There was no escaping this confrontation. The boy was talking earnestly to a woman in an expensive raincoat, showing her various leaflets. She was nodding earnestly – poor sucker had fallen for it. This left me to the mercy of the girl.

'Hi there,' she said from underneath some dreadlocks and a beanie hat, 'have you got a moment to spare for Kid-Leidoscope?'

'Not really, I'm very busy with my baby,' I said, motioning towards the buggy where a deeply asleep baby was giving every impression of being the least busy-inducing thing in the world.

'It won't take a second,' she said, her wide smile revealing a set of suspiciously white teeth for somebody in a beanie hat.

'Well, OK,' I conceded, 'but I'll have to make it quick. I'm very busy being a mum, you know.'

'So I see,' said the student, 'which is why you'll be very interested to hear about Kid-Leidoscope. Did you know that most kids in our country don't know how to play any more?' she said in hushed tones.

'That's awful,' I said, unconvincingly. I felt a heavy ache descend into my knees. I was gagging for a coffee and a large pastry.

'It is, isn't it? What we have to ask ourselves is: what will they be like as adults if they've never played as children?'

'I dread to think,' I said. 'They'll probably turn into those sad tossers who spend their weekends on adult go-kart tracks, or who go paintballing.'

'Well, no, actually,' said Beanie-face earnestly. 'Research shows that adults who never played as kids can end up very marginalized. They are often under-achievers, loners, and in extreme cases can end up in prison.'

This all sounded a bit far-fetched. A child who can't play? About as likely as a dog who can't pee against a lamp-post. I wanted an end to this silly encounter. And she was the only thing standing between me and an uplifted bust.

'Well, I'm sure it's a real problem, and I'd love to help out, but really, what with the baby—'

'All we ask is five pounds a month towards our knockabout play-bus scheme or our new sponsor-a-clown initiative.'

'What?'

'We send clowns into deprived areas where children have no concept of play. They can have a big impact.'

'Clowns?'

'Yes, that's right. We have a whole unit of clowns trained and ready to go.'

I looked at her, agog.

'You're asking me to donate money so that an out-of-work pissed-up mime artist can put on some sinister makeup and ridiculous flapping shoes and go and scare deprived children, as if they didn't find life scary enough already?'

Beanie's silly cheery face wasn't grinning now. She struggled to get the words out. 'The clown initiative has been shown to have very positive benefits—'

'Oh don't give me this poppycock!'

I was pleased with that. I don't think I'd ever used the word 'poppycock' in a conversation in my life. I was on a roll now.

'You saw me come round the corner pushing this buggy and you thought, Right, here's some sad old breeder whose brains have had a landslide along with her bust – I'm sure I can get her while she's down. It's immoral to get money off me like that. Especially when it's going to line some clown's pockets, which are probably hilariously oversized and covered with polka dots. You know what your charity should do if it wants to teach kids how to play? Just leave them a-bloody-lone! And then suckers like us won't have to pay you anything! Five pounds a month – I'd rather spend that trying to help deport all clowns back to France, or wherever it is they come from.'

I felt a very hot spot on one of my cheeks. I felt cleansed, though. My brain felt clear, as if I'd rolled a defluffer over it, like you do to a coat. I had taken on this ingénue, this slip of a student who had barged so ungraciously into my precious Me Time. I inhaled, smiled, looked at her and felt about six feet tall. For the first time in months, my head felt well and truly screwed on.

'Now if you'll excuse me, I have a child to bring up,' I said haughtily, 'and all being well, I shall not require the services of a clown to do that.'

A rather dignified parting shot, I felt, and I proudly wheeled my daughter out of her way. I was forced to turn back sharply when I heard a snort that sounded uncannily like laughter.

Beanie-face was pretty much doubled up against a nearby wall, holding her nose and guffawing like a mule. So was her charity-cohort, together with the woman in the expensive raincoat. All three of them were falling about like fools.

Then Beanie-face flicked her fingers towards my face and said, 'That was wicked, man.'

'You're skill,' said her slack-faced partner.

'Totally fucking hilarious,' said Raincoat Woman, whom I now noticed was holding a small video camera. She stepped forward and held out her hand, as if expecting me to shake it.

'Tasha Cameron, I'm a producer on *Tom and Tim's Saturday Stitch-up* and I'm proud to tell you that you have just featured spectacularly on our "You Fell For It!" section of the show.'

'Excuse me?' I said.

'It's a very popular part of the show where we stitch up unsuspecting members of the Great British Public.'

At which point Beanie-face had the audacity to wink at me and give me a sort of Cubs salute.

Tom and Tim's Saturday Stitch-up – I'd had the misfortune of catching this top-rating show a few times recently. The show consisted of the eponymous young presenter-chimps, Tom and Tim, basically loping around the studio patting each other on the back and laughing loudly at each other's puns. Meanwhile, various vapid members of the public were served up in front of a blood-hungry TV audience. It was pitiful really.

'Well done you,' Ms Cameron said to me with a little smile. 'You'll be on prime-time telly. Make sure you tell all your family to watch. And you've just earned yourself two hundred and fifty quid. Nice cash for your little one.' She waved distractedly towards the buggy and said unconvincingly, 'Aaaah, so cute, is it a girl or a boy?'

Whereupon Beanie-face stepped forward, pulled out an official-looking document and gave me a pen to sign it with.

'Oh God, that was bloody side-splitting. That was seriously one of the best "You Fell For Its" we've had in ages. You were so pompous. So funny,' said Beanie.

'That's just a standard release form between you and the

production company,' said Tasha. 'If you want to just sign and date it, we're all finished here.'

I looked at the piece of paper in front of me. I felt my heart and soul fall down into the bottom of my grubby gym-shoes. I felt a burning sensation in the back of my throat. I wanted to cry suddenly, to throw myself onto Tasha Cameron's raincoat and cry like a baby. I swallowed.

'You'd better send that to my agent. She deals with all my performing work.' And I sniffed, sounding scarily like my mother.

There was a suitably gratifying pause.

'You're an actress?' said Tasha.

'I do lots of different broadcasting work.'

'Local radio?' proffered Tasha.

I eyed her sourly.

'Telly.'

All three looked blank.

'What, regional stuff?' said Tasha.

'No. National.'

'Sorry, should I know you?' the bitch said and a half-smile played over her lips.

'I used to do a lunchtime show,' I said.

Tasha looked me up and down, taking in my terrible outfit. She cocked her head to one side, obviously scanning through the Antarctic wasteland that was her imagination. 'Oh my God yes!' she squealed. 'That daytime thing. I used to watch it when I was off school. You're Kim, aren't you?'

'Mel,' I said.

'That's right!' and she turned to her two colleagues. 'She used to do this lunchtime thing. It was ages ago. Oh my God, Tom and Tim will LOVE this.' She turned back to me with real excitement in her eyes. 'I reckon they'll want to have you on the show, actually. They love having a rib with minor celebs. What do you think, Kim?'

At which point I looked at all three of them in turn and then pushed the buggy through them.

'Kim! Wait!' shouted Tasha behind me. 'You haven't signed the release form!'

Like Orpheus trying to make his way out of the Underworld, I was determined not to look behind me, not even for a second.

By the time I entered a shop called Voluptuosity on Neal Street, my face had regained its normal colour. I fished my mobile phone out of the pannier at the bottom of the buggy and phoned my agent. I was put through to Ruby, her new assistant.

'Hi, babes, I'm afraid she's in a meeting,' she drawled. 'Can I get her to call you back?'

'Yes. It's urgent,' I said tersely.

At which point Jo woke up, took in the sight of many bra-mobiles dangling above her in all their silken glory, and bellowed. She screamed so loudly that I couldn't even risk looking at one bra. I gave her a bottle to try and cork the bellowing, but she pushed it away with a defiant little fist. Women looked round with pity in their eyes. Not at me. At Jo.

I pushed her, still screaming, through the bustling streets of Covent Garden and onto the bus. She was still screaming when we alighted at our stop. I pushed her, still bellowing, down our road and into the flat. Nothing could soothe her. Not milk, not muted Electric Light Orchestra, not *Teletubbies*, not a little jig around the living room. I felt awful for her, but God I was weary. I was long-ing, nay, desperate to put my feet up and settle down in front of a bit of Eddie Shoestring on UK Gold.

The phone rang. My agent. Unheard of for her to get back to me so quickly.

'Hello?' I said, Jo pressed to one shoulder and the phone to the other.

'Mel, it's me.'

The familiar, calm, totally relaxed-sounding and therefore intensely annoying voice of my husband.

'Oh it's you,' was all the wifely warmth I could muster.

'Are you OK?' he asked.

'Well, apart from a daughter who hasn't eaten for two days and who possesses the mood swings of Richard Burton, a complete disaster of a day which saw me being ritually humiliated by those two tossers Tom and Tim, and a total lack of bra-purchasing possibilities, yes, everything's going absolutely swimmingly, thank you!'

'Tom and Tim?' he said.

I paused. 'I don't believe it. You're more interested in Tom and Tim than you are in our daughter's well-being.'

Jo opened her lungs and let out a piercing yell. Dan said something inaudible at the other end of the line.

'Look, I'll have to call you back later when I've got her to sleep,' I said dourly. 'You just go back to Brigitte.'

'What?' said Dan.

'Brigitte, or whoever it is that you're working with.'

'There's nobody here called Brigitte,' said Dan. 'I'm working with a woman called Anna.'

'Oh, Anna, is it?' I said with my best sarcastic voice. 'Well, you just go off and carry on doing whatever it is you do with Anna. Does Anna know that you have a wife and sickening child at home?'

At which point, on cue, Jo let out a loud mewling noise like a cub.

'Mel, are you OK?' said Dan, genuinely concerned.

'I'm fine,' I said, eyes brimming with tears. 'Phone you later,' I said quickly and put the receiver down.

Two hours later I managed to get Jo down, with a bit of help from the great God Calpol. She was definitely hot. Brilliant. Dan goes away leaving me with ill baby.

I shuffled downstairs and put a Meal For One into the microwave. I'd got a luxurious one at the top of the price range: chicken breast in gouda sauce. With wild rice on the side. A generous helping of dry white wine in a large goblet, and I was set. Finally, here was my God-given chance to put my feet up in front of the telly. It felt a bit selfish, but it was actually quite nice to know that Dan was in Germany worrying about me. I wouldn't phone him just yet. I'd let him worry a bit more.

There was nothing on the telly, just a bit of *Tom and Tim Extra Best Bits*, and I would rather have stuck forks into myself than watch that trash. No, it was time to catch up with some old mates.

I decided to ring round the old uni pals who were my favourite group of people in the world. Just a shame I hadn't spoken to any of them in the last few months.

I tried Ewan and Sarah first. Ewan was Dan's oldest pal, and we'd had many a boozy holiday with them. I'd only seen them once since Jo was born. No reply.

'Hi, Ewan and Sarah. It's Mel. Just phoning for a catch-up. Loads of love.'

And onto the next, Mike and Chloe.

'Hi, guys! How are you both? We're missing you! Up to our ears in babydom, but we're coming through the tunnel – it'd be great to hook up. Loads of love.'

And then scanning down the phonebook. Two ex-flatmates of mine and real old muckers, Jim and Shorty. They were such a cosy couple and both mad on *Coronation Street* – surely they'd be in? I couldn't be the only one at home, could I?

'Hi, Jim and Shorty!' My voice was starting to sound slightly forced on yet another answering machine. 'Where the devil are you, you pair of gorgeous hunks? I miss you! Shorty, I've still got your jumper from that party about two years ago. Jo's gorgeous, can't wait to see you. Loads of love.'

The final call I had to make was to Pen. I hadn't spoken to her for weeks, and she was pretty much my best friend. She was always up to her ears in something cutting-edge or other, and was fiendishly hard to get hold of. The last time I'd rung her she was at a rave in Denmark, and the time before that she was in such a loud bar in Shoreditch I couldn't make out a word of what she was saying. Pen was great, though. However irregularly you spoke to her, she never gave you a hard time for not getting in touch.

I phoned her mobile – pointless ever to phone Pen at home.

Amazingly she picked it up, and even more amazingly there was no deafening thump of dub music in the background.

'Hello?' she said. I could hear a murmur of voices in the background – it sounded like she was at some cool art gallery opening night or something.

'Pen, you old dog, it's me, a voice from your past!'

'Mel?' she said.

'Yes! Now before we go any further, are you still snogging that kraut?' I laughed.

'Eva?' she said sadly. 'No, we split up two weeks ago. It was terrible. She's left England.'

Oops. God, I hadn't even realized they were serious. When they'd come to visit us in the hospital I'd assumed it was just a fling.

'Oh God, Pen, I'm sorry. I had no idea.'

'Well. You haven't been in touch for ages, have you? I thought Eva was The One. Anyway, life goes on. How are you, love?'

'Oh you know. Same old. Dan's away, which is weird. Jo's great, although she's not well at the mo, poor thing.'

'Oh little darling. Send her a kiss from me.'

Then there was a nano-pause. I felt a bit self-conscious, like I lived on the other side of the world from Pen, although in reality she was only a few miles up the road.

'Where are you, love?' I asked her.

'Oh, I'm at home.'

'Amazing!' I said. 'It sounds like you've got some people round.'

'Yeah. It's lovely actually. I was feeling a bit blue after the whole Eva thing collapsed, so I've got Mike and Chloe round for dinner, and Ewan and Sarah. And guess who showed up out of the blue – Jim and Shorty! I'd better go. I've made soufflé – can you believe it? I've got to save it from the oven before it turns into a heavy duff.'

I heard somebody shriek with laughter in the background. Shorty had probably made one of his filthy gags. Pen held the receiver away briefly from her mouth so that she could join in the laughter.

'Do you want to talk to anyone here?' said Pen.

The lump in my throat almost prevented me from speaking at all.

'No, Pen. I'd better go. Just send my love to everyone.'

'Will do. Give me a call really soon.'

'Yes, bye,' I husked, and put the phone down quickly. I looked down at my Meal For One, getting tepid on the plate in front of me.

I got into bed feeling utterly leaden. I tried Dan but his mobile was switched off. I thought about phoning Mum just to hear a familiar voice, but there was no reply. Of course. They'd be in Frinton. I checked Jo, who was sweaty and unsettled. It was only a matter of time before she'd wake up needing more medicine. The alarm clock said ten past ten. I switched the light off and curled myself to sleep in the foetus position.

I was in the middle of a curious dream about Pen and Eva. They'd morphed into Tom and Tim and were doing a bizarre, almost Brechtian version of *Tom and Tim's Saturday Stitch-up*. Both were dressed head to toe in black PVC and were marching around the studio, Pen with tears streaming down her face so that she had panda-eyes and filthy blackened cheeks. Then Eva looked at me and threw back her head and screamed. Like a chicken being skinned – high-pitched and curdling. Then she moved her face close up to mine until I could see her larynx like a cartoon, bobbing up and down inside her gaping mouth. Her screaming was relentless; on and on she screamed. The screaming sounded familiar. Strange that Eva was screaming – it sounded like a baby screaming.

I sat up in bed and looked at the alarm clock. 1:01. Pen and every other best friend of mine in the world would probably just be getting onto the drinking games without me. I shivered, put on a jumper and shuffled through into Jo's room.

As I went through the door I could almost feel the heat coming off the cot. My heart started bumping. Something was wrong here. I bent down to pick her up and for a moment thought that I might need oven gloves. She wasn't my baby any more – she'd turned into some kind of thermal appliance that explorers take to the Antarctic. She was seriously hot. I fumbled round for the thermometer and, with the help of an enormous shot of adrenalin that had suddenly been pumped into my system from God knows where, managed to wedge it and hold it under her arm to take a reading. 103 degrees. Oh God, that was hotter than boiling water, wasn't it? No, it couldn't be. Was it Fahrenheit or the other one? Oh God, she could die. She could easily die. I'd seen it all before on *Little House On the Prairie*. A feverish baby had been put to lie in its crib and then had died in the night. True, it was mainly due to the fact that they didn't have any Calpol, and also the doctor had failed to show up because he was having a marital crisis and was drowning his sorrows at the creek with a couple of itinerant miners. Oh goodness, this was ridiculous. Why was I filling my head with that when my baby was sizzling in my arms? I had to get the fever down. As quickly as possible. Where was Dan? Why the bloody hell wasn't he here? As I took her out onto the landing I almost dropped her. 'Oh my God, Jo!' I shouted. 'Spots! Spots! Oh my God, spots!'

Covering her from her crown to her feet were spots. And they didn't go away if you rubbed them. This was serious. Her voice was rasping now that she'd done so much screaming – she sounded like she'd just come out of a Metallica concert.

I stripped her down to her nappy, gave her Calpol and then couldn't think what to do. The most sensible option seemed just to walk round and round with her. In soothing familiar circles, like we'd done when she'd just been born. I sang inanities to her.

'Flintstones, meet the Flintstones, they're a page right out of history!' and 'I am the very model of a modern major-general' from G&S. A subconscious cry for my mother.

Jo didn't seem to be getting any cooler. Should I take her to A&E? Should I call an ambulance? Where the hell was Dan? Should I ring him and get him to fly home? He wouldn't get here for hours. I just had to get through the night. This night was all that mattered. I suddenly remembered in *Little House On the Prairie* when the baby had first developed the fever, the family had soaked strips of muslin in the creek and draped them all over her. Right, I needed strips of muslin, and fast. And a creek. I'd have to make do. Tea towel and a tap. Jo was attached to me so putting her down was out of the question. Oh God, I needed an extra pair of hands. I found a tea towel – a favourite of mine with a Devon cream tea on it, but it would have to be sacrificed. Now, how to tear it into strips while holding boiling baby? I wedged it round the door handle and tried to go at it with my teeth, but it was no good. I needed help. Dan's phone was still off. Mum and Dad were in Frinton, my sister lived three hours' drive away. Pen and all of my friends were drunk and I'm not sure if they were my friends any more. Irene the neighbour? Too rogue. Amanda? Too flaky. I needed somebody nearby and solid. Somebody sensible and good in a crisis. Of course, why hadn't I thought of it before?

I dashed into the hall to get my bag. I'd written down Judy's phone number on a piece of paper somewhere.

Chapter Seven

Judy arrived at about two in the morning, in culottes and clogs, looking quite sprightly considering the cruel hour of night. She assessed the baby while I hovered around going from foot to foot, uselessly.

'Get me a glass, please,' she said crisply.

'We've got tonic,' I replied quickly. 'Do you want gin or vodka?'

'No, I don't want a drink. I want to do the glass test on Jo.'

The glass test? I'd never heard of this.

'What do you do?' I asked. 'Make her look through it?'

'No. Didn't you do antenatal classes? You press it onto the baby's skin to see if she's got meningitis,' and she gave me a stern staff-nursish look.

I felt very small. And also scared. Meningitis? Thank God Judy was here. Jo might have died if I'd been on my own, and the thought of that made my heart beat so fast I thought I was going to pass out.

Meningitis was quickly ruled out, thank goodness, and Judy decided that the best thing to do was to give Jo a tepid bath. A genius idea. Why hadn't I thought of that? I followed Judy round the flat, from living room up to bathroom, doing her bidding. If she'd turned round and asked me to strip naked, cover myself in peanut butter and dance a Lithuanian folk dance, I'd have done it unquestioningly.

'No, that's still too hot,' she said, testing the bathwater with one freckled elbow. Once she was satisfied, she plunged Jo deftly into the water and then folded her gently into a towel. I was quite keen to give Jo a little cuddle, but Judy whisked her off into her bedroom.

'It's a bit stuffy in here. Open the window a bit,' she commanded.

Jo's temperature had started to go down slightly, and she looked like she was ready to sleep. I felt overwhelming love for her, and also for Judy at this point. God, I've never felt so relieved in all my life.

'I don't know how to thank you, Judy, honestly.'

'It's fine. It's what being a mum's all about. Do look up some first-aid stuff, though. I've got a good book I'll lend you.'

'Should I phone an ambulance? Those spots look pretty nasty.'

'No, take her into the GP tomorrow. The fact that she's cooler is the main thing. Just keep an eye on her through the night. I could murder a cup of herbal,' she said, heading down the stairs.

I was thinking half a pint of brandy would be more the ticket, but raced into the kitchen to turn on the kettle.

This night felt so important, so real somehow. Thank God it was Judy here rather than Pen. Pen wouldn't have known about the tepid bath – we'd probably have covered the baby in Savlon, wrapped her up really tightly and then taken her on some godawful ten-hour mission to casualty.

Judy cupped her mug in two hands, which is something I usually find annoying, but on her it looked attractively homely.

'I'll get you details about local first-aid groups,' Judy said. 'It's good to have the basic knowledge under your belt. Didn't you know about the tepid-bath routine?'

'Er … I never really read any of those baby manual books. Full of silly women wafting along the beach wearing linen. I found them a bit smug, to be honest.'

'Smug? But if you'd read them this crisis would have been averted tonight.'

She was right.

'Well, I'd better be off,' she said suddenly. 'I've got two of my own at home, let's not forget.'

'Oh God, of course. You must go.'

She picked up her car keys. 'Now, keep giving her Calpol every four hours, give her another tepid bath if the temperature goes up again, and get her to the GP in the morning.'

She reeled all of this off without averting her eyes from mine. I felt like I was standing in front of a gym mistress, being dressed down about my weak hockey tackle. Extreme gratitude won the night, however.

'Thanks, Judy, that's great advice. Oh God, you know what the worst thing about tonight was? I kept on thinking about *The Little House On the Prairie*. People were always feverish on that programme. There was one episode where Laura nearly dies from fever, and her mother's panicking and sees a sentence in the Bible which happens to be open next to her which says, "Cut it off, cut it off." She's so panicked she thinks it's a sign from God, reaches for a knife and—'

'Mel. It's three fifteen in the morning,' said Judy. She slipped her feet into her clogs, and turned down the hallway.

She smiled briefly while I stooped, waved and grovelled in the doorway.

She was climbing into her people-carrier when she looked around and said, 'Anyway, I was never allowed to watch ITV when I was a child.'

'Great,' I said and laughed foolishly as she swished off into the night.

Two tepid baths later, one at 4.30 a.m. and one at seven, and I collapsed onto a heap of towels outside Jo's door. The phone rang at nine and I hobbled into our bedroom to answer it. I'd slept with one shoulder up by my earhole. My head felt like rats had taken possession of it and were slowly gnawing at my eyeholes and brains.

'Yes?' I mumbled.

'It's Dan, how's Jo?'

I felt stung. What about me? Miss Madam had been bathed and canoodled all night. I was the one who needed TLC round here. I looked like something out of *Fright Night*, for Pete's sake.

'Dan, where the bloody hell have you been? I've left you about ten messages.'

'Yes, I got them this morning. I'm really sorry. I couldn't find my phone charger.'

'What about the good old-fashioned landline, Dan? What about a friendly little goodnight call?'

'I thought about phoning you but it was late at night, Mel. You're usually asleep after nine.'

'Asleep? Asleep? Jo had to have a meningitis test done, Dan.'

There was a pause.

'Oh my God. Has she got it?'

'No, Dan,' I said. 'Luckily we did the glass test.'

'What?'

'Didn't you listen during antenatal classes, Dan?'

There was a grumpy silence.

'You said "we". Who's we?'

I was beginning to enjoy this conversation. I was half on the point of pretending that I'd worked tirelessly through the night alongside a hunky male nurse called Geoff. That would annoy Dan.

But frankly I didn't have the energy. I barely had the energy to stand upright. I just said, 'Oh, me and a friend.'

'Who?' said Dan.

'Judy.'

'Judy?'

'My very nice new local mother-friend, Dan. She's amazing. Dependable, so nice, *so* knowledgeable. Just brilliant. Someone who's really there when you need her. A real friend in need, Dan.'

'Look, all right, you've made your point. I feel bad enough about being away from the two of you as it is. You don't have to make me feel worse.'

'Have a lovely easy day, Dan. And if you do get a minute between watching your films, snoozing and doing whatever it is that you do with that Brigitte-person or whatever her name is, just spare a thought for me. I'll be the one with the Ken Dodd hair, eyes like a ghoul's and some sort of chronic pox spreading over my entire body which I've contracted from my daughter.'

'How is she?' he asked.

'SHE'S BETTER!' I shouted and put the phone down on him.

I hardly left the house for the next three days. Once to go to Dr Sweeting's surgery, where she diagnosed Jo with a nasty post-viral rash. She also checked on the computer and asked if I'd heard from the hospital about my haemorrhoid referral. I told Dr Sweeting that I hadn't, and she said she'd chase it up. I suddenly felt about seventy years old. This is how life was going to pan out – my body was going into total disintegration already. You have children, you bring them up, they leave home, and then all you have to think about is your crumbling health. I could see it already with my own parents.

'Hi, Mum,' I'd say to her on the phone. 'How's Dad?'

'He's fine, darling. He's very excited, actually.'

'Oh yes?' I'd say optimistically, thinking that my dad had joined a book group, or taken up squash.

'Yes,' Mum would continue, 'he's just trotted off to the chemist. They've got him something new for his corns! And I've just finished my prescription for the heartburn, so he's collecting a new one for me too. It's all go here.'

And my heart would sink. I'd try to change the subject.

'Any news from the family?'

'Ooh, now. Yes, your Auntie Barbara's lumbago's come back, which is a shock to her, and Kenneth just can't kick that nasty infection, so he's back on the antibiotics. And little Sammy's still wearing the built-up boots – can you believe it? The hospital says he might be in them for another nine months.'

I hate to admit it, but Dr Sweeting's haemorrhoid plan was music to my ears. Since giving birth I'd developed enough arse-grapes to produce a fruity little Bordeaux from my own personal vine. At times the sensation was almost as painful as labour. It was great for the thigh muscles, however. I spent so much time hovering over chairs, too scared to sit down on them.

The other times I left the house during the baby's recovery were for vital supplies, like large quantities of chocolate and Bacardi Breezers. Every time I put my nose outside of the door I would inevitably bump into Irene, the neighbour. She asked her usual.

'So how's the little lad doing?'

'He's better, thanks, Irene.'

'What's his name again?'

'Joseph,' I'd say, 'after his father.'

'Oh, that's lovely. But he looks awful peaky, doesn't he?'

'Yes, Irene. He's got syphilis, leprosy and beri-beri.'

'Oh, has he now? Poor little lad. He looks constipated and all, doesn't he?'

I'd made it up with Dan, thank goodness, via a series of texts. It was so much quicker that way. And, unbelievably, my agent had been in touch.

'Darling, it's wonderful news about Tom and Tim. They said you were hilarious in the stitch-up. It's really exciting. You know they want you to actually go on the show, live?'

'Yes, to take the piss out of me.'

I could hear her sucking deeply on a fag.

'But what a comeback. Woof! You've had your baby, and now boom! Here you are back on prime-time telly with Tom and Tim. It's GREAT for your profile.'

'I don't care. I hate my profile anyway. I've got five chins. Like my maternal grandmother. And the last thing I need is that pair of dick-weeds Tom and Tim patronizing me.'

'But Tom and Tim are so cute and just so bloody hilarious, darling. Their show pulls in a massive audience, you know.'

'Yes, of half-witted baboons,' I said, pompously.

'Babe, try and have a bit of a sense of humour about it.'

'Look' – I was starting to pace around the kitchen now – 'if you'd just had the few days that I've had ... babes ... you'd find it pretty hard to have a sense of anything, least of all humour. I don't need laughs, I need work.'

There was a light noise at the end of the line – she was fiddling with a biro, maybe.

'Darling, gone are the days when performers were judged by how good they were or how much they worked, sweetie,' and then she exhaled the fag. Christ, she had the lung capacity of Kiri Te Kanawa. 'These days it's profile profile profile, honey. It's column inches, it's ... you know ...' and she took another big draw on her cigarette.

'Listen, I'd rather have my piles plucked by a blind Sicilian goatherd than appear on *Tim and Tom's Live Saturday Night Arse-Crawl* or whatever it's called,' I said.

'Oh babe, go get some oats and a nosebag.'

'I'm sorry?'

'I think your high horse needs feeding.'

Two days later and Jo's spots were starting to fade. She was now smiling as cheekily as ever, thank goodness. Her appetite was back with a vengeance. It was miraculous that babies could bounce back like this. Wish the same could be said for the parents. As babies continue to bounce, getting ever stronger and braver, their parents seem to deflate ever so slightly. Like very very slow punctures, just a little bit of their vital air is expelled every passing day. I was wondering what sort of pump could be invented to reinflate parents, when the doorbell rang.

It was Judy. She looked fresh and scrubbed in olive-green polo-neck and Capri-cut jeans. I looked like a patient from *One Flew Over the Cuckoo's Nest*. It was eleven in the morning, but I still hadn't quite managed to crowbar the grey flannelette dressing gown from my cheesy-smelling body.

'Thanks so much for the flowers, Mel,' she said.

'It's nothing, Judy. You saved my baby's life,' I replied, and had to look at the floor to blink away the tears welling up in my eyes.

'I've brought you these,' she said, handing me a carrier bag full of magazines. 'There are some back issues of *Parenting*, *Junior* and *First Aid Monthly*. I think you'll find them useful. I also dug up some good patterns for baby clothes, if you like sewing – I noticed Jo's drawers in her nursery weren't exactly overstuffed with clothes. Oh, and there are some lovely healthy recipes in there too. Maybe Jo got ill because she's not eating properly?'

'Er ... I think her diet's fine actually.'

'I find it really helps to make meal times fun, Mel. Don't just give them mush. I often try to create a little tableau when I make supper. Why, just the other day I made a building site – I made the mashed potato into a pile of cement, and used little chunks of cooked vegetables and batons of chicken to make little builders and their tools. Honestly, it really works.'

I was starting to feel dazed.

'Right. A building site. Good idea, Judy.'

'Oh and we're doing a mums' night out next week. Let our hair down a bit. Have a meal somewhere where you won't see anybody under two foot and dressed in a babygro. Do you fancy coming?'

I was still trying to process the building-site concept, and had only just taken on board Judy's suggestion that Jo might neither be dressed nor fed properly, but had to brush this all aside, however. I owed Judy the life of my baby, so I wasn't going to let a couple of comments get in the way of a new friendship. Was she a friend? I had a sudden pang for Pen. She would scoff at the idea of a 'meal out' as a night on the tiles. A couple of Es and an Access-All-Areas backstage pass at a White Stripes gig were more Pen's way of letting her hair down.

'Yes, I'd love to, Judy,' I said. It was nice to be wanted.

'Great. I'll let Alison know; she's in charge of this one. She'll probably phone you and tell you to bring something.'

'Oh yes?'

'We normally have a silly theme, make it a bit light-hearted, you know.'

'A theme?'

'Yes, last time we all had to wear a silly hat during dessert. It was a hoot.'

The smile on my face was forming into a rictus but I managed to force a little laugh from somewhere.

Once Judy had gone, I slackened off my cheeks, which was a relief after all that smiling, and put the magazines down on the floor next to Jo, who was propped up with cushions. She grabbed an issue of *First Aid Monthly* and started to pulp it round her mouth with copious amounts of spittle.

'Good girl, Jo!'

The idea of reading up about new methods of bandaging really didn't appeal to me at present. Thankfully, the phone rang.

'Hello, you.'

Steve, the boy estate agent. I could hear the smug smile in his voice.

'Steve,' I replied, adopting the tone my mother uses with tradesmen.

'I think I've just found your dream house.'

'Oh good. I hope it features a rubber room so that I can lie undisturbed and draw crayon pictures on the walls with my feet.'

Steve laughed a little too loudly. 'No, but it does have a lovely street-facing kitchen, so you can watch the world and his wife go by all day.'

I was on the point of explaining heatedly to this upstart adolescent that I had plans, big plans, for my life, and did not intend to spend it watching other people's out of my kitchen window all day – but I didn't have the energy.

'I'll book in a viewing, shall I?' he asked chirpily.

'Suppose so,' I replied. Now who was the teenager round here?

Quite suddenly, the sun came out. It showed up the thick layer of dust that had accumulated on the shelves. It made me feel weary. My mother would have been up there and at it in a pair of Marigolds, humming 'Just A Spoonful Of Sugar Helps The

Medicine Go Down'. But I simply couldn't compute the idea of housework as well as looking after a baby. Surely it would be a strain on my ovaries?

Time for some fresh air. Good for both of us.

I kept my head down as I walked past the public gardens. I didn't fancy bumping into that fascist again. Jo and I jumped on the bus no problem, and she grinned all the way into town. For some reason I thought it'd be fun to head into Piccadilly Circus. I hadn't actually ever bought Jo a toy and I thought the two of us would go to Hamleys toy store as a treat.

Regent Street was buzzing. Everyone was smiling. I felt like we were in a musical, and wouldn't have batted an eyelid if a couple strolling along in matching Burberry coats suddenly leapfrogged into a complicated dance routine in the street, using water hydrants, lamp-posts and traffic cones as key props and crucially revealing tight black dancers' body-stockings underneath their coats.

Jo loved the shop window. It was filled from top to bottom with a fully functioning mechanical farm. A cow came trundling out of its little shed while a milkmaid whizzed in to meet it, sitting on a stool, and actually pressed her head down near to the cow's udder. A farmer chuffed by on a tractor and had a real bit of smoke coming out of his pipe. There was even a large cowpat that a dog appeared to be rolling around in. It was wondrous. Jo was completely rapt, her eyes shining. She was too engrossed to make any noise at all, and her little fists were clenched, moving up and down in a slow, blissful rhythm. This felt pretty great. I winked at a passer-by who touched the brim of his peaked cap. Sheer musical.

The other window was magnificent. It was fully taken over by the Ken and Barbie Medieval Fairy Wonderland Castle. There was a lifelike banquet with plastic haunch of venison and minute

Perspex goblets. Ken and Barbie, resplendent in matching velvet outfits, had his 'n' hers pet dragons on the end of ribbons. I imagined myself in their pristine world where nothing gets spilled, thrown, chewed, spewed or mushed. I longed to be at the court of Ken and Barbie, with a little hourglass figure, long velvet dress and permanent smile on my face. My reverie was broken by a familiar pungent smell curling round my nostrils. I looked down at Jo in her buggy. Her eyeballs were straining, and she was completely red in the face. Finding somewhere to change her nappy round here would normally have sent me into a spiral of stress, but not today. Ken had given me Zen, and Barbie just smiled through the glass as if to say, 'That shit is your shit, not my shit!'

If Ken and Barbie ever have a baby, I bet even the poo will be pink and covered in a bow.

I turned round the corner into a back street and chanced upon a smallish, discreetly posh hotel. The sort of place an MP could take one of his aides for a quick mattress-test.

I dived in and a very nice bob-haired receptionist directed me to a ladies' loo. It amazed me how helpful people could be sometimes. She'd feature in my London musical – she'd probably do a tap dance right there on the desk.

Opposite the loo there was a smart-sounding function going on behind the closed double doors of the Bloomberg Suite. I slipped into the ladies', which was large and brightly lit with a rather ostentatious chandelier in the middle. The whole area was carpeted, which was nice for Jo to lie down on.

'Abboo! Abbadooo!' I said to her, and she gurgled back at me with delight.

A woman with too much fake tan gave us a patronizing smile as she stepped round us in high heels, leaving a blanket of heavy perfume in her wake. I wiped the poo carnage away in a few deft sweeps. I was feeling pretty damn good about this whole mother-hood thing. All that was needed was a nice clean nappy, and bingo, the job was a good 'un. I reached into the changing bag to fish one out, but could only feel cream, rattle, nappy bags and juice bottle. Ah. I must have put it into the pocket on the back of the buggy or underneath in the basket. Nothing there. Surely there was one in my handbag? No, just the usual detritus: a crumpled tissue, some pile cream, several bus tickets and an old custard cream. Musk-woman emerged from the loo, rubbing her nostrils frantically.

'I don't suppose you've got a spare nappy on you, have you?' I noticed that she was carrying the tiniest of clutch bags in her French-polished talons. It was a silly size of bag. It would have struggled to contain the toiletries of an elf, let alone a large bulky crap-catcher. She cackled with laughter, and fiddled with several of the large diamante brooches pinned to her jacket.

'Sorry, love, nappies ain't my thing,' she said with a smirk, and wrangled her massive jewelled belt over her skinny hips.

Loo paper was not going to solve the problem. There was no way of attaching it to Jo's body. No, I was literally attempting to paddle up the creek of aforementioned doo-doo with nothing absorbent to strap to my child's bottom. I could feel the sweat creeping into my armpits, and my neck and hairline were starting to moisten up with stress too.

By the washbasin some hand towels were rather poncily laid out. I circumvented Musk-woman, who was now pumping out some more of the ghastly stuff and shaking her hair around in front of the mirror like an epileptic pony.

'Excuse me,' I said, and whisked a hand towel away from under her nose.

It now fell upon me to tie a nappy in the old-fashioned way

and I had very little idea of what to do. I knew that it involved a triangle and some sort of fastening at the front. Jo wasn't helping matters by squirming round and arching her back.

'Stop it!' I snapped. The abbadoos and coochy stuff were forgotten now. The tricky part was tying the whole thing together. Of course, my mother would have had a selection of those big safety-pins. I had nothing pin-like to hand, but suddenly had a brilliant idea.

'Excuse me,' I said politely to Musk-woman, 'would you possibly mind lending me one of your brooches? It's to tie up this makeshift nappy that I've made for my baby here.'

She turned to me with her hands on her hips.

'I can post it straight back to you if you give me your address,' I added reassuringly.

She folded her arms and looked me up and down. 'Do you know where I got these pieces from?' she said.

'Camden Market?' I ventured cheerily.

'They're exclusive. J-Lo designed them. So no, you can't.'

She stared at me coldly. Jo was starting to get bored lying on the floor. 'Ssssh' was all that I could offer her. I had more pressing matters to deal with.

'It would really help me out if you could give me your brooch,' I said calmly. 'My child needs it to hold her nappy in place.'

'So?' was her reply. 'I need it to hold my basque in place.'

'And which is the greater need here, do you think?'

My voice had risen several tones and my heart was bumpy, but I crashed on: 'I'm actually amazed you want the services of a brooch. I wouldn't have had you down as someone who wants their clothes to stay up.'

She sucked her teeth and looked at me with shark's eyes.

'Bit rich, isn't it,' she snarled, 'for someone to criticize my

141

clothes when they look like they're dressed to go out and do some gardening for the council.'

And she tottered out, leaving a trail of her filthy musk behind her.

I looked in the mirror. She did have a point. Green fleece, drawstring trousers with a greenish hue. With a pair of wellies on the bottom I'd have the full municipal plantsman look down to a tee.

'You silly bitch!' I shouted half-heartedly once she'd gone through the door. It's really not in my nature to swear at other women.

Jo started to scream. I picked her up and tried to soothe her in a rather frantic, sweaty way. This of course had the opposite effect, and she squalled and thrashed around in my arms.

The London of musicals had completely dissipated and I was left surrounded by its tatters. Gone were its lavishly painted sets and brightly dinging bells, and in its place was the reality of a city of nasty people on the make, and people who snarl at you on buses if you try to meet their eye.

Why was the world so un-child-friendly? If we'd been on the *Titanic* with that clacky-heeled Musk-woman she'd have been sure to knock us off the life raft.

I sat Jo on the hand towel in her buggy and was rummaging round in the bag, when I heard the door open again and a familiar voice boom out: 'I mean it's not physically possible to get your figure back that quickly. I reckon she's been sticking her fingers down her throat again, don't you?'

I looked up and saw Amanda applying lipstick in the mirror. Job done, she pouted at herself coquettishly.

'Amanda,' I said.

She turned round and looked down at me still on my haunches. It took a moment for her to compute who this ruddy-faced, makeup-free woman was.

'Mel?' She always addressed me with a question mark, as if eternally hoping I might morph into a slightly different, better-dressed person. She suddenly remembered that we'd known each other all our lives and gave me a non-committal hug.

'So you decided to come after all?'

'What do you mean?' I said, still crouching and trying to jiggle Jo up and down at the same time.

'Tania Bryant's do. The party for her little girl.'

My face was blank.

'Remember I told you about it ages ago? Oh it's fabby in there, Mel.' She looked at my outfit. 'Oh. Are you getting changed?' she added hopefully.

'No. I was actually changing Jo and stupidly realized I came out without any nappies ... '

'Ah. She's cute, isn't she?' she said, without looking at her.

'You haven't got a spare nappy on you, have you, Amanda?'

She looked confused.

'I don't carry them. But Lyn does. She's through there in the party. You've met her, haven't you? She's my nanny. I'll take you in, we can get a nappy for Flora—'

'It's Jo.'

'And I'll introduce you to Tania. Or do you know her already? She's so lovely. I've been training her since her last baby. She's got incredible upper-arm definition.'

'Bitching outfit too,' said Amanda's friend who was putting on mascara. 'I love her fuck-me boots.'

'Oh, Mel, this is my friend Hayley. She's doing PR for somebody very famous who we're not allowed to talk about,' said Amanda excitedly.

At which point I was presumably supposed to ask the identity of this mystery person. I was simply not going to give either of them the satisfaction. They looked at me expectantly, but I just smiled blankly.

'It's Enrique Iglesias!' Amanda shouted.

I had a vague recollection of a bloke in a woolly hat with a large mole on his chin, but hadn't the faintest idea what he was famous for.

'God, he is gorgeous,' said Amanda, rolling her eyes. 'Is he going to marry her, Hayley?'

'Maybe they already are,' replied Hayley enigmatically.

This almost pushed Amanda over the edge. 'Noooooooooo! How the hell did they do that without the paparazzi getting a sniff of it?'

'Why do you think he employed me?' said Hayley smugly, and then made for the door. 'Come on, the photographer's nearly ready.'

'It's so exciting – a photographer from *Up Close* is here to take exclusive photos. Come on!'

And she chivvied me and buggy through the door.

'How's Balthazar?' I asked her in the corridor. I hadn't seen her baby in months. But she never replied. She was too busy preparing herself to enter through the double doors of the Bloomberg Suite.

The room was large with windows running all the way down one side. The view was dismal – the back end of another set of buildings. Despite its size the room was claustrophobic. The windows looked unopenable. Hotel policy presumably – management afraid of people jumping out of the building. And rightly so – I'd have been tempted to jump out of Tania Bryant's do if the window had been open.

The atmosphere was languid. There were lots of stick-thin, über-trendy women sitting around in ludicrous designer clothes looking bored. Some of them had overdone it on the fake tan and looked like satsumas, while others had gone tweezer-mad so that their eyes looked like boiled balls with no eyebrow to give them relief. I felt like I'd just stepped out of the *Beagle* rover on Mars. The atmosphere was certainly cold and dry enough to be Martian. It was the sort of party you could only fit in at if you had extremely narrow feet. In such surroundings my own feet felt extra-clompy and steak-like. Which reminded me, I was absolutely starving. Jo was momentarily silenced as she processed her new surroundings. She looked watchful.

Waiters were making their way round the room with trays of canapés that were waved aside, untouched. As soon as a whiff of a tray came past my nose, I grabbed unceremoniously at about five little salmony things on puff pastry. I shovelled them into my mouth, one on top of the other.

'Hhhmph,' I growled. 'Thss bedder.'

Amanda looked at me sorrowfully. 'When you've finished, I'll take you over to meet Tania. Oh and that's her daughter over there.' She motioned over to the far end of the room.

Ah yes. The birthday girl. I looked round for a little girl whose Big Day it was, the one who traditionally runs around direction-lessly, ripping the paper off presents and filling her face with jelly.

All I could see was a smallish huddle of babies and toddlers, surrounded by a group of women sitting down on the floor. These women looked less trendy than the mums, and they weren't offered drinks, I noted. Obviously nannies and au pairs. A few of the kids wore rather desultory paper hats and there was a lavish pile of as yet unopened presents in the corner. A photographer had set up a little booth and one by one a mum would be handed her child by a helper and they'd pose together in front of a banner saying 'HAPPY 3rd BIRTHDAY AMETHYST'. One of the mums, who looked thin enough to drop right through a drain, stubbed out her fag, held her baby and then plastered on an enormous grin while kissing her child's cheek.

My heart sank as I saw Musk-woman emerge from behind the photographer's stand. She started to talk earnestly with him while sucking on a cigarette. Scanning the room, she caught sight of me and glowered. I noticed that Amanda looked longingly in their direction – she was clearly dying to be asked to step forward and have her photo taken.

'Who the hell is that piece of work over there?' I said, referring to Musk-woman.

'She looks fab, doesn't she? I love that ironic Page Three look she's got going.'

'Who the hell is she?'

'Sharon Homes. Tania Bryant's PR. Very powerful, knows all of the paps and the journos.'

'Right,' I said, feeling immediately depressed. 'And what about party games for the kids? Is there going to be an entertainer or something?'

'Oh my God, look over there,' said Amanda, sotto voce, grabbing my arm.

'What?' I said vaguely. 'The jug of lilies?'

'No no no. Three o'clock from the jug. It's Cornwall.'

I was confused. Was there some sort of West Country display featured on the table? A selection of scones with clotted cream?

'It's Cornwall! Cornwall!' she whispered.

'What, the whole county?' I whispered back.

'No, the model. Cornwall Smith. The one with her legs draped over the umbrella-holder thing. Oh my God, I don't believe it. I must tell Hayley!'

She ungripped herself from me.

I needed to get out of here fast. If Dante had created an extra little anteroom in his version of Hell, this would be it. The Ninth Ring of Hell – Celebrity Child's Birthday Party, as featured in *Up Close* magazine. Talking of Rings of Hell, my daughter's bottom needed immediate attention. It was only a matter of time before the hand towel became acquainted with my daughter's insides, and it was a meeting I was very keen to avoid.

'Amanda, the nappy. Would you mind?' I said, but she was already flapping across the room towards Hayley.

Firm action was required immediately. I'd find Balthazar and his fabby nanny myself, get a nappy with all possible haste and make a dash for the door.

Amanda's son was easy enough to spot. He was the only baby decked out entirely as a mini-rapper. He had a baseball cap on back to front, an oversized T-shirt emblazoned with 'BABYZ IN DA HOOD', and a set of baggy camouflage trousers with ludicrously large, spongy trainers on the ends. He was the baby least likely to become a rapper in adult life. He was pudgy, with small blue eyes and a look of Count Bismarck about him. I gurned in his general direction, but there was no way he was going to reciprocate. Fair enough: I was putting on a pretty miserable display.

Poor Jo was starting to show signs of wilting. She was writhing round in her buggy so much that the hand towel had completely lost purchase of its crucial target.

I barged into the nannies' coven unceremoniously.

'Hi there – which one of you is the fabby Lyn?'

A pale and slightly spotty woman in her early thirties put up her hand.

'Hi, Lyn. I'm a friend of Amanda's. Could I possibly borrow a nappy from you?'

With its dry bulk safely in my hands, I felt like Aladdin must have done when he found the lamp. My world could revert to its normal state as soon as I'd taped this wondrous object round my daughter's waist.

'Thanks,' I said, and turned towards the door. I breathed deeply. Freedom was merely metres away.

I strode to the door, keeping it in my sights.

Suddenly Amanda popped up in our path from nowhere, like some awful puppet from a Punch and Judy show.

'Mel, you've got to come and meet Tania. She's actually recognized you from the telly, and if she sees us together ...'

'Amanda, I am not having my photograph taken with you and our children.'

'Oh no, I didn't ... I mean, I'd just love you to meet her. Please, Mel.'

Something about her desperation moved me. I still couldn't shake this absurd loyalty to her.

'All right, I'll say hello, but I'm not having my photo taken in that bloody booth.'

'Fabby!' and Amanda's eyes shone with genuine happiness as she ushered me forward into the throng of scary stick-women.

Tania had a delicate flute of champagne dangling in one hand, and her racehorse legs were crossed, a pair of monumentally high sharpened stiletto heels on the end of each foot. She was chatting to a friend.

'Tania!' Amanda butted in enthusiastically. Tania and friend looked lazily at the pair of us.

'Hi, Amanda,' said Tania. 'Oh God, you're not going to get me on the floor doing squat-thrusts are you?' and turned to her friend and laughed. 'Amanda's my gym-bitch.'

'No.' Amanda grinned delightedly, pleased to be a member of Tania's court. 'Tania,' she said, 'you must know Mel,' and the silly cow nudged me forward so that I slightly lost my footing.

'No, I don't think so,' said Tania, looking me up and down. Bloody Amanda: this woman obviously had no clue who I was or why I was crashing her daughter's birthday party. She continued to look at me out of glacial green eyes.

'Are you here looking after one of my daughter's friends?' she asked me.

'No. I'm … I'm …' I had no idea who or what I was any more.

'It's Mel. She's on the telly.' Tania sized me up again, as if I was a vegetable on a market stall.

'No, I don't think I know you. Are you someone?'

Finally, to cap it all, old Musky arrived. Jo took one look at her and started whimpering. I picked her up protectively as one of the witches noticed her dear little bare bottom with disgust.

'Hi, Sharon,' said Amanda, breathless at all the attention we were now receiving. 'Fabby party.'

Sharon smiled poisonously at her and then turned to me. 'Hello, Alan Titchmarsh,' she said, scanning my outfit again.

'We're just going actually,' I said to everyone in general.

'Don't go,' said Sharon. 'It's Mel, isn't it? Won't you stay and have your photo taken?' she continued, smiling. 'I'm sure the readers of *Up Close* would love to see what's happened to you after all these years.'

I was speechless. My mouth grappled for some words, as the circle of women looked at me, their plucked eyebrows arched expectantly.

There was a brief pause before Jo replied for me, in an eruption of brown/green noxious ooze which spouted forth like a large cow's protest at being loaded into the back of a trailer. I looked down as the brown/green merged with my outfit. It was quite a good colour match. The hand towel remained fluffy-white in the buggy. Amanda's jaw was down by her bustier. Tania flared her nostrils like a horse. Sharon was evidently going to throw up. All eyes in this semi-circle of grotesques were fixed on me. Jo gave what sounded like a little giggle. I grinned.

'Shit happens!' I said, and turned on my heel.

Chapter Eight

I've never been so pleased to be contained within the four walls of our smallish flat as I was that evening. Jo was safely in her cot with enough wadding to stymie an explosion of Krakatoan proportions. I had an enormous bowl of wine on the go. The green outfit was soaking in a bucket by the sink, and a large cream slice awaited my attention on the little nest of tables by the telly. My husband had deserted me, my friends no longer cared about me. I was a televisual has-been. I was packing a few too many kilos. Work was non-existent, and we hadn't sorted out our house move. But this was all as nothing. These were the tiniest bacteria on the Petri dish of life compared to the absolutely over-whelming feeling of pride that was surging through me, pride in my daughter who had pulled off the most brilliant social coup of the century.

I saw Steve the estate agent's dream house the next day through a mist of wine and cream-slice hangover. Annoyingly, he was right. It was by far the best house we'd looked at and seemed pretty perfect for us. When I said I wanted to put in an offer straight away, Steve began to strut around on the pavement like a cock. He put on his sunglasses and phoned through to HQ on a miniscule silver phone.

'He shoots, he scores,' he said into it, followed by a loud volley of laughs.

I busied myself with my own, rather larger phone. 'I'm putting in an offer, Dan,' I announced.

'You're sure?'

'Definitely. You're going to love it. It's exactly what we wanted. Spacious but cosy, wooden floors. Not too fussily done out. Lots of room for us to put our own stamp on it. And a really sweet little garden. It's a house, Dan!'

'And it's got a shed?'

'Dan, it's got a luxury Swedish-style workspace-shed with power points, carpet and everything.'

'Wow.'

'The street is very quiet compared to here.'

'Is it still within Greater London?'

I laughed.

'Of course it is. It's about twenty minutes away from here.'

'And you're sure I'll like it?'

'Definitely. Shall I put in the offer?'

'Yeah, go on.'

It had started to strike me that I hadn't really stood up straight since giving birth. Motherhood seemed to require you to maintain a permanently hunched position. I was always rummaging around at floor level. I remembered wistfully that there was once a time when I walked the streets with my neck held proudly above my shoulders.

I felt like I was strapped into an invisible yoke all of the time, and that I was ploughing through life with not much to show for it. It was great being a mother, but it wasn't the type of job that gave you a sabbatical. I suddenly remembered at college we'd been given a rather preposterously titled 'reading week'. All us Modern

Languages students bundled off and stayed in some college in the countryside to edify ourselves with the literature of Jean-Paul Sartre for the week. In reality, things had turned out rather differently. Our friend Shorty discovered a field of magic mushrooms just behind the students' hall, and we spent the whole week off our heads, then getting the munchies and swaying up to the local garage for Hobnobs and Liquorice Allsorts.

I longed for a reading week. Or how about a sleeping week? Just seven days to step off the treadmill and catch up with myself a bit. It would give me the crucial time to do all those things like get a proper haircut, shave my armpits, read a newspaper. People say that you feel out of touch when you've had a baby. I had real difficulty remembering not only what the date was, but what the month, or even more worryingly, the year was. Time was when I could reel off the names of the shadow cabinet. Now I had to search around the jellied remains of my brain for the names of my own family.

My mum didn't offer much solace on the subject.

'You may not have a fully functioning brain, but at least you've got a washing machine, darling,' she told me on the phone. 'The only piece of technology we possessed when we had you girls was a small transistor radio. Imagine me, up to my ears in soap flakes, scrubbing your father's underwear on a board. Not like all of you have-it-all types with your instant this and your quick-fit that. You'll have a machine to change Littly's nappy next. God knows you've got them for everything else.'

I wasn't expecting a medal or anything, but some kind of certificate might be nice. It would do wonders for morale.

Pen was booked for babysitting duties so that I could attend the mums' night out. Apart from looking forward to seeing an old friendly face, I was keen to touch base and check that I was at least remembered by our old mates, even though I wasn't seeing them at the moment.

I phoned Alison to check the details for our night on the town. She was a breathy woman who had overly ruddy cheeks, as if she had permanently walked in from a hearty hill-walk. She dressed her entire family in cagoules all year round, saying that you never knew what the weather was going to be like from one day to the next. She'd booked a table at a local Italian restaurant, and was positively fizzing with excitement.

'We're going to do something a little bit wacky.'

My heart sank instantly.

'I'm going to bring a board that we can assemble easily next to our table, and I'll bring drawing-pins too.'

Far from wacky, it sounded boringly like Pin The Tail On The Donkey. Maybe an adult version of it? Pin The Penis On Tom Or Tim perhaps? In which case I'd try damn hard to aim for the head.

'What I'm asking everyone to do is to bring a photo of themselves as a child and pin it up on the board,' Alison said, giggling, 'and we all have to take guesses as to who's who. It's a bit of a laugh. I did it once at work.'

Which must have been at least a decade ago. Alison surely hadn't had time to create her four cagouled children overnight.

'That sounds like fun,' I said flatly.

'It's a bit of a giggle. I'll ring round to remind!' she said, as one of her brood yelled 'PAPER ME!' loudly in the background.

I'd been trying to block out a feeling of dread about the mums' night out. I'd seen Judy a couple of times in the last fortnight, once when she'd taken me through some basic first aid in a café using a rubber doll as a baby, and the next time when she'd brought some of her fabric samples for her children's fishermen's outfit designs to show me.

I'd managed to take Jo to several weeks' worth of Angie's Actions. I couldn't work Angie out. Underneath the sing-song voice and pea-green sweatshirt/slacks combo, there lurked a brooding soul. She really seemed to dislike me. I could tell from the very tiniest things. When we were singing 'Ten Little Speckled Frogs' she would always make sure that every other mother in the room got a squeaking frog to join in with the chorus. But when it came to me, there would be no frog left in the basket. When gathering in the instruments at the end of a 'free-music session', there was something aggressive in the way she took the rainmaker out of my hand. Throughout the class she would throw little barbed looks in my direction. Her lip curled over a bit whenever she spoke to me. It was nothing anyone else would have noticed, but it was there, in the air. For the sake of Jo, I tried to do everything right. I tried to stay in tune, made a brave fist of all of her actions, except during 'I'm A Little Teapot' where I did inadvertently mess up the pouring action by using the wrong hip. But apart from that I was an exemplary mum. I talked to Judy about it after an Action class.

'I think Angie's got a problem with me.'

'Hang on a sec. Good girl, Minnie! You're holding that juice beaker very very well!'

Judy looked at me for confirmation of the fact that her daughter was some kind of child prodigy for holding a plastic cup.

'Isn't my daughter great?' said Judy.

'Yes,' I replied, wondering if Minnie would be put up for the Nobel Beaker-holding Prize.

'Sorry, what were you saying?' asked Judy.

'Angie. She doesn't like me. She offered everyone else a Penguin biscuit last week, and when it came to me, she offered me an unwrapped Nice one.'

'That means she likes you if she offered you a nice biscuit,' said Judy, in a long-suffering way.

'No, a Nice biscuit.'

'Exactly.'

'A Nice one. As in the brand-name "Nice". It wasn't actually nice. It was un-chocolatey and rather bleak and reminded me of my mother's coffee mornings.'

'Well, to be frank, I think you're overreacting, Mel.'

'Please don't be frank. Be Judy!' I said, laughing.

Pen and I had always done this puerile little gag with each other, and it still made us laugh.

Judy gave me an empty look. She clearly thought I was a bit of a prat. 'Oopsie daisy!' she said, suddenly swooping down into Jo's buggy. 'Do watch out for those smaller toys, Mel. Jo could have choked on that.'

'Oh yes,' I said lamely. 'I'd noticed that.'

I was too slow. Judy was down there and prising a mini plastic football boot from Jo's slobbering jaws. I was beginning to resent Judy's self-appointed role of guardian angel over my child. OK, she'd saved Jo's life, but she didn't have to rub it in all the time.

Things had taken a strange turn for the worse the following week. I decided to take positive action and confront the Angie situation head-on. If she wouldn't make friends with me, I'd make friends with her. It was very much the same tactic I'd applied in the school playground when Samantha Bright bullied me for many months. After torturous breakfasts and school-runs full of howling and tears, my mother had given me a stern talking-to outside the school gate.

'You have to go in there and turn the other cheek.'

'I've already turned it. I don't have any more cheeks,' I wailed.

'The only way to deal with the enemy is to befriend them. Like Neville Chamberlain.'

The name sounded familiar; I think he was in Year Six.

'Now just go in there, darling,' Mum continued, 'and kill her with kindness.'

Whereupon I'd gone right over to Samantha Bright, smiled at her and given her a sweet. She'd booted me hard in the shins.

I wasn't worried about Angie kicking me in the shins, but I wouldn't have put it past her to spit in my face or pull my hair. I girded my rather tired loins and, after the session, I decided to extend the olive branch of friendship by offering to help her stack the crash mats.

'Let me give you a hand with these,' I said.

'They go in the corner. Lengthways along the bench. And don't tread on the soft-play materials.'

I sensed that an ice-breaker was called for.

'So!' I said brightly. 'That was a great class today, Angie. Jo's really loving it. We do all of your songs and actions at home now, even when I'm cooking. 'Cook cook cook the pastry! Doesn't it taste really tasty!' I warbled.

She looked at me sourly.

'It's bloody hard work doing these sessions, you know,' she said.

'I'm sure it is,' I said encouragingly, 'all those actions. And rhymes. Must be exhausting.'

'You can't just waltz into a job like this, you know. It's taken me years to build this business up.'

I nodded empathetically.

'I see some people try and do what I do in this area. Tina's Tumbling Tots. Jackie's Jumpabout, Janine's Jive Gym-boree. Rank amateurs the lot of them. They fail. They always fail.'

My nodding was getting too vigorous. I slowed it down.

'I've trained, you see. Three years at drama school, six in rep, followed by a decade in Theatre in Education.'

'Wow,' I said positively.

'So you work on the telly,' she said, as she shunted a box of balls roughly into its allotted space.

'Yes,' I said modestly. 'Haven't done much for a while, though.'

'Well paid, is it?' she asked pointedly.

'That really depends on what the job is. It can be if you're presenting something that's popular.'

She sniffed. Her eyes narrowed.

'You don't get paid much for appearing on *Crimewatch* though,' I added light-heartedly. 'Crime really doesn't pay, does it?'

There was a silence.

'Ah, dearie me,' I added for no reason.

'Don't suppose you've ever done live performing like this?' she said.

I was momentarily confused as to what she was referring to. Then it dawned on me that she was referring to her role as leader of the class.

'Did you train?' she asked me then.

'No,' I confessed.

'I was Juliet in our final-year production at drama school. One agent said that it was a better performance than Judi Dench's at the National. And, to be frank, I agree with her to this day.'

'Don't be frank. Be Angie,' I half whispered. Thankfully she didn't hear, but continued to put beanbags away into a box, and was gripping one of them so tightly I thought it would explode.

'Well, it's been great talking,' I said, hoping for a little chink in the conversation to allow me to escape. But it was not to be. Angie was on a roll.

'You see in those days, we learned a craft. We grafted. We sweated. We slept with everyone and anyone in a position of influence we could lay our hands on. There was commitment, you see. And love. Real love, in all of its stark-bollock nakedness.'

I was starting to back towards the door, but Angie just kept on going.

'I could have done telly. Oh yes, I could have done bloody telly, but you know what? I was too good for telly. Telly couldn't contain me. I needed the room and freedom that only theatrical space could offer me' – and here she waved her hands expansively around the church hall of St Martin's to illustrate her point. 'Television's just full of talentless cipher-people, propelled into all this fame and money. I could have made pots of money. I just didn't want to.'

I was starting to back dangerously up against the hot-water urn. I had nowhere to go now. I could hear the water inside approaching boiling point. I didn't really fancy the idea of the Burns Unit.

'Angie, the urn ...' I faltered.

'So did you make a lot of money in telly?' she asked me, close enough now for me to notice that her canine teeth were extremely yellow.

'Sometimes,' I said. 'I just need to move away from this boiling water ...'

'I'll bet you did. I'll bet you were VAT-registered and everything. Well, you can keep all that. You've never had this, have you?'

'I can feel the steam, Angie ...'

'All this that I've got. It's my thing. I'm in charge. Bet you've never had that on telly. If you're on the telly, you're a yes-man. I'm not a yes-man. All this is mine.'

At which point I would have been on the receiving end of a very intense neck sauna if Angie hadn't suddenly strode into the main body of the hall, allowing me to jump away from the now-rumbling urn.

She had the space now to really project her voice.

'Romeo, Romeo, wherefore art thou, Romeo?' she belted out, followed almost immediately by: 'I have ten little fingers and they all belong to me!'

And she held up her fingers, as the action dictated, and thrust them all towards me. Was she going to strike me, just as Samantha Bright had done?

I didn't wait to find out, but scurried away to the Free World outside. I left Angie inside, working her way through a speech from something heavy. Possibly *The Seagull*. Even though I'd paid up front for a full term of Angie's Actions, I decided Jo and I would be playing truant from now on.

On the day of the mums' night out, I received a phone message from Robin at the bank. It was funny – he'd stopped ringing the house of late, and had started calling my mobile phone, which I was much less likely to answer. He confirmed that everything was fine with the mortgage on the property; our lawyer had also said that we could get things moving. Just as well Dan was on his way home in a few days.

I was quite keen to lose a few pounds before his return. I didn't want him to think that I'd just let myself sag during his absence. I had four days to lose the weight. Which diet could do that?

Pen was good with this sort of dilemma.

'Speed and Jack Daniel's,' she said matter-of-factly.

'Pen! I can't look after Jo under the influence.'

'Better to be drunk than inflict phallocentric rubbish on her like, what's this? Fireman Sam?'

'OK, OK.' I laughed.

Pen was rolling around on the floor with Jo, who was shouting with laughter. I don't think I'd ever heard Jo laugh like that. She often giggled and gurgled as any nine-month-old does, but this laughter was heartfelt and natural and it made me swell with happiness.

'Now, come on,' said Pen, 'go and get changed, for God's sake. Your cab's coming in two minutes,' and she rolled Jo onto her back and started tickling her.

'I am changed,' I announced.

'What?' The tickling stopped abruptly.

'Yes. I'm going out like this.'

'That flowery shirt and cardi?'

'Yes.'

'And those weird trainers?'

'They're not weird. They're cheap, Pen.'

'Oh dear,' she replied.

Pen spent all of her money on clothes. Tonight she was sporting tweed plus-fours, high-heeled ankle boots, a ruffled shirt with waistcoat over the top and a new tattoo on her wrist. Her hair was two-tone, a wedge of jet-black underneath a bottle-blonde outer pelt. It made her look like a badger. She'd finished the look off with mulberry-coloured lip-gloss and a sequinned scarf. And this was what she wore to go babysitting in.

'So what do you wear to actually go out in, Pen?' I had enquired, giving her the once-over.

'I'll wear this. I'm going out later,' she said glibly.

'But I might not be back until ten thirty, or even eleven,' I said.

Pen had simply stared at me with a mixture of pity and disbelief. I'd forgotten that not everyone in London is in their winceyette pyjamas by eleven.

I looked down. Pen was right. What was the adjective to describe my outfit? Mumsy. That's what it was. I looked mumsy.

'Pen. You're right. I'm going to get changed into something a bit more …'

'Of this decade?' she suggested.

'Ha bloody ha,' I said, ascending the stairs.

'They've made all sorts of advances in fabrics, you know,' she shouted after me. 'Denim is very "in" now, as is corduroy if you're feeling daring.'

I came down several minutes later with the lemon off-the-shoulder number I'd bought. Pen gave it the go-ahead and pronounced me fit to go out.

'Now, Pen. Just a couple of things. Jo's in a great bedtime routine. Using a night-time voice, i.e. gentle and lilting, put her into her cot, and then creep away from her, still maintaining eye contact while singing something soothing, yet rousing. I usually opt for Status Quo's 'Whatever You Want' – you know the sort of thing. Creep creep back to the door, like I'm doing here. Give her a reassuring smile, and then leave the nursery. Leave the nursery and on no circumstances go back in. OK? It's really important. Check that her blackout blinds are in place, and—'

'Mel?' said Pen. She motioned down to Jo in her arms. 'Well done,' she continued. 'You've actually managed to bore your own daughter to sleep.'

And I looked down on her little face, as serene as an almond. My heart twisted with love. A car horn beeped outside. The cab had arrived.

'Don't drink all the bloody Bacardi Breezers,' I told Pen sharply, 'and no long-distance phone calls.'

'Just go and have fun with all your new friends,' said Pen,

and then added: 'Don't take the E with a Mickey Mouse on. They're shit.'

Pasquale's restaurant was only a ten-minute journey by cab, and I was soon being welcomed into its convivial bosom by a man who insisted on ushering me to the table with his hand on the small of my back.

'Here we are, signorina,' he growled.

There were ten or so mums already at the table, looking strangely fluffed and powdered compared to the usual rather worn figures I was used to seeing at Angie's Actions or in the local parks. There were a lot of soft fabrics round the table. Angora, mohair, flannel. Sitting down was like immersing myself into a fleece-covered barrage balloon. Alison was positively giddy with the fun of it all, and sat proudly next to a child's blackboard on which was mounted a large piece of cork. All of the baby photos had been neatly pinned onto it and Alison had fashioned a notice above them saying 'WHO AM I?' in big sparkly letters.

I called out a general 'hi there' to everyone, and sat down at the one available chair between Alison and a woman in round glasses who introduced herself as Bridget, mother of Sam and Laura. I was expecting Judy, as the person I knew best there, to stand up and make room for me at her end of the table, but she merely smiled and waved at me. She was surrounded by a gaggle of laughing mothers, most of whom lived in the same street as her.

'Glass of wine, Mel? Go on, you only live once,' said Alison.

'Make that a bottle,' I said to get into the spirit of it.

'Well, we've only ordered three bottles, so I think one glass per person at this stage—'

'Just joking,' I said quickly. 'Wow, the photos look great.'

'Don't they?' Alison looked proudly at her handiwork. 'Between courses we'll start the quiz. I've brought a whole load of felt-tips and a big scribbler pad from Edward's craft cupboard, so we can all write down our answers in secret.'

'Aren't felt-tip stains a nightmare to get out of clothes?' said one mum opposite me with brown frizzy hair. 'It drives me spare when they say, "Mummy, can we do colouring?" Amber got red pen all over her First Holy Communion dress. I was livid.'

'White wine vinegar's what you need,' piped in Judy from the other end of the table. 'Dilute some with water in a bucket and leave the clothes to soak. It really works.'

'Thanks, Judy,' said Frizzy Lady, blushing with pleasure, and then turned back to me and said confidentially: 'Judy's so amazing. She's full of clever tips.'

'Yes' – I had to agree – 'she was brilliant when my daughter was ill the other week.'

'Oh yes, we know,' said Frizzy, looking at me pitifully. 'Judy told us. 103 she went up to, didn't she? And nobody had even done the glass test until Judy arrived. You were very lucky.'

I felt a hot spot on one cheek. So Judy had been recounting the lurid details of my poor mothering skills to the entire group, had she?

'I'm sorry,' I said to Frizzy, 'you already seem to know so much about me, and I don't even know your name.'

'Jane,' she replied, and waved girlishly from across the table.

Thankfully the felt-tip-stain discussion was swiftly curtailed as the food was swept onto the table by a flock of waiters. The mums giggled and tinkled with girlish laughter as one after the other they were called 'darling' or 'beautiful signorina' by the mob of men. I found it tiresome, and when my steaming cannelloni were set in front of me by an ageing Lothario with the words,

'Eat up, beautiful baby,' I had half a mind to flick one right into his face.

It seemed so pointless and annoying that the waiters were putting on this pathetic, patronizing act of trying to woo a bunch of mothers. What on earth could they be hoping for? That one of us would go home with them, strip off the alluring all-weather protection Pac-a-mac down to a pair of tantalizing reinforced slim-silhouette support-pants, nursing bra complete with sodden breast pads, and then wrap a matching set of wobbling thighs and upper arms round them and say, 'Giovanni, I feel so good about myself right now. And I've got so much time on my hands what with my three children under five, so I'm sure I could fit in a steamy affair with you on a Wednesday afternoon between Kerry's swimming club and Max's tae kwon do. How about it, big boy?'

And here was this bunch of tittering women going along with it. I drained my glass of red wine grumpily.

'Ooh, my lasagne's delish,' said Jane.

'So's my tagliatelle,' added one of Judy's cronies at the end of the table.

'Has anyone tried that scrummy lasagne recipe in the Annie Carmichael book?'

'Oh, it's wonderful,' said Judy. 'I always put a couple of little spaceman figures and a rocket on top, and pretend they've just landed on Lasagne Moon.'

There were a few appreciative noises. Was there no end to Judy's creative skills? I wondered if she cooked a dish for her husband and then put a little figure of a crumpled man mowing the lawn on top of it.

'The Annie Carmichael book is a total life-saver,' said Alison. 'It's so brilliant to be able to whisk up a really healthy smoothie for them, isn't it?'

'Yes, and I love her pocket pitta ideas. So useful if you're on the move.'

I'd never heard of Annie Carmichael, but anyone who creates something called a pocket pitta needs to be kidnapped and never released into the world again.

'How's your cooking for Jo going?' asked Judy in my direction.

I bristled imperceptibly, feeling once again that Judy was putting my care of Jo under the microscope. I was also slightly flummoxed. 'Oh, you know, fine, I guess. I do like using the ice-cube trays for freezing in advance. Although don't do what I did and put a block of spinach and sweet potato into your vodka and tonic thinking it's ice.'

Nine pairs of tired eyes looked at me in disbelief, and a chorus of 'Nooo!' ensued. A couple of them giggled helplessly.

I felt a little glow of warmth creep through my body as my little anecdote, untrue of course, seemed to have hit the spot.

'Oh, I'm not surprised she did that!' said Judy, keen to speak loudly over the laughter. 'Mel's flat's very wacky, isn't it, Mel?'

I wasn't sure if this was a compliment or a criticism. I decided it was the former.

'I'm not sure. Maybe it is a bit.'

'You go in there,' Judy told everyone, 'and you feel like you're a student again. It's all cluttery and fun.' Her smile in my direction was broad, but I felt uncomfortable meeting her eye so I dropped mine to the table and poured myself another glass of wine.

'Oh, I forgot to tell you all,' said Bridget. 'Jenny can't make it tonight – her babysitter fell through.'

'Fell through what?' I quipped.

A slight silence fell on the table. I felt the ground I'd made pull away from underneath me.

'So!' said Alison loudly. 'Once everyone's finished their firsts, we can kick off with the quiz!'

I sighed and looked over to the board. There were ten photos, all cut up neatly and sitting there in rows. Maybe it was the red wine creeping into my bones, but I felt maudlin. What had happened to those ten open-faced babies with everything, the whole greatness of life's adventure, in front of them, to be grabbed, wrestled to the ground and feasted on? It was difficult to imagine, but maybe round this very table were women who'd explored the wilds of Borneo, got their Ph.D. in Post-Feminist Peruvian literature, hang-glided, tripped their nuts off dancing to The Orb, shagged David Blunkett. In which case why were we all sitting here talking about felt-tip stains and ice-cube trays, for Pete's sake? Had life become so small? And I wasn't any better or bigger. Like every mum round the table I was sitting with my mobile phone in front of me, like a paranoid MI5 agent. If only ... I'd far rather answer the phone and receive coded orders from a craggy boss somewhere in Whitehall than the inevitable twitterings of a babysitter:

'Tilly put her left foot out of her duvet and it feels rather chilly.'

'Quick! Put it back inside and phone me back as soon as it's warmed up again.'

'Bradley just came downstairs.'

'Did he say anything about me? Is he OK? Does he need the loo? Phone me back if he does it again.'

'Kelly had a bad dream.'

'Did she say what it was about?'

'She mentioned big horses.'

'Oh God, it's her fear-of-abandonment one. Right, if she has it again, phone me straight away.'

I looked from mum to mum and caught snatches of conversation – the problems of getting toddlers out of night-nappies, how difficult it is when molars are coming through, is she holding her head up yet, how much pocket-money should you give to a five-year-old? I wanted to shout: What about climate change? The threat of terrorism to our city? The Olympics? Surely there was more to life than the dilemma of what to wash your child's trainers in?

I watched the earnest faces nodding at each other, advising each other, bonding with each other over their children's ups and downs. I tried to strike up a conversation with Jane about going away on holiday, but it ended up, inevitably, on the subject of which holidays are more child-friendly than others. Gradually everyone else cottoned on to what we were talking about, and a whole open discussion ensued about the problem of finding a child-friendly holiday.

'Well, we rented a cottage in Devon and the brochure said there was highchair and cot provided, but it was an absolute lie,' said a blonde mum with a T-shirt emblazoned with a large photo of her two children on it.

'It's awful, isn't it?' said Judy. 'We never leave anything to chance any more. I always pack everything into the car – I'd take the kitchen sink if there was room.'

I needed some air.

'Just going to the loo,' I mumbled and slipped into the ladies'.

It was nice to sit on the loo with my head in my hands. God, what had happened to my life? Who was this weird woman in drawstring trousers and grey wings of hair I saw every time I looked into the mirror? Where was the girl with the cheeky riposte to everything, the head for vodka and the rather dashing line in footwear? I looked down at my trousers crumpled up round my ankles and shuddered at the sight of my trainers. Pen was right, they were weird. They were white and spongy and looked like they belonged to a sixty-year-old American tourist. I needed to get out of here. I simply couldn't face the idea of sitting round with deflating tiramisus, trying to guess who belonged to which baby photo. I thought this evening was supposed to be about being an adult? And here we were, turning ourselves back into babies, so that we could simply carry on the conversation about our own babies, whom we'd come here to avoid talking about in the first place.

I dialled home. Pen picked up and I could barely hear her shouting 'Hello?' above a racket of loud music. Sounded like Led Zeppelin.

'Pen?' I shouted as loudly as I could: 'PEN! PEN! TURN DOWN THAT BLOODY MUSIC, IT'S ME!'

She continued saying 'Hello?' a few times and then put the phone down on me. Great. I dialled again.

'HELLO?' she shouted.

'PEN!' I shouted at the top of my lungs.

'OH! HI, MEL! I'VE GOT THE STEREO ON! HANG ON!' and she went to turn it down.

'That's better,' she said. 'Don't tell me. Someone's brought out the speed, you're going to a club and you're not going to be back till four.'

'The only thing anyone's going to break out here is a pair of knitting needles.'

'That bad?'

'Look, I need you to do something for me. Give it about ten minutes and then phone my mobile, OK? I'll pretend something's up with Jo and then I'll be able to cut and run. Ten minutes, OK?'

'Yeah, cool,' said Pen. What a diamond.

I came out of the cubicle and started as I practically bumped into Judy who was washing her hands. My upper lip began to prickle with sweat.

'Oh, hi, Judy. I didn't hear you come in.'

'Everything all right at home?' she asked innocently.

'Yes. Yes, absolutely fine.' I was damned if I was going to show more chinks in my mothering armour to Judy again.

'You're not going to suddenly whisk away because there's some drama at home?'

'No. God no. No no no no no.'

'Talking to your babysitter?' she asked.

'Yes. All's fine.'

'That's good,' she said. 'I just got a text from hubby too. Are you having a good time?'

'Yes,' I said airily, 'it's lovely.'

'We're a fun bunch, aren't we?'

I didn't reply.

'I'm glad I invited you, Mel,' she said and patted me on the arm. 'Well, we'd better get back in. Alison's starting the quiz.'

And we went back to the table.

'Now, ladies, you've each got a pen and a piece of paper. Just have a look at the photos up on the board and match the number of the photo with the name of the person you think it is. Then fold up your piece of paper and pass it on up the table to me! And no peeking, ladies!'

A few giggles and then the mums were heads down and studiously writing their answers.

My phone rang. The ringtone was a White Stripes song I'd downloaded to give me an air of cutting-edge, possibly even danger. 'Hello?' I said.

'It's Pen. Blah de blah de blah. You'd better come home, Jo needs you. Is that OK?'

Why had she phoned just at the moment when the table had fallen totally silent? All eyes looked up expectantly at me. I wasn't sure, but I felt that Judy was looking at me extra beadily.

'Oh, hi there! That's great!' I said, smiling.

'Mel, it's Pen. Something about Jo. Something bad. God we need you here. You'd better leave immediately.'

'Sleeping soundly, you say? Thanks so much for letting me know. See you later!'

And I hung up.

'She's sleeping soundly,' I explained to the table.

'That's very efficient of your babysitter,' said Judy. 'Ours only phones me to tell me to get back home double-quick. You're not being summoned home, are you?'

'No no no no no no no,' I said. 'She just likes to keep me abreast.'

I'd just taken the lid off the felt-tip pen when the phone went again.

'Hello?'

'Mel, what the hell are you doing?' Pen was speaking very loudly. 'I'm phoning you to get you out of that godawful knitting circle. Just get your buns back now for Pete's sake while you can.'

'Oh, she's sucking her thumb. That's so sweet. I'm so glad that it's all going so well.' I mouthed to the group: 'It's the babysitter again,' and then wrapped up the conversation with a: 'Yes, I shouldn't be too late. Help yourself to the shepherd's pie I made,' and hung up again.

Jane looked concerned.

'Everything all right?' she said. I couldn't help looking down at her answers to the quiz written neatly on her paper like a fourteen-year-old's exam.

'She's not trying to get you back there for a crisis?' said Judy with her eyebrows raised.

'Oh God no, no no no no no.' The phone rang again.

'Will you all excuse me for a second?' and I picked up the phone and walked away from the table.

'Pen, stop phoning me!' I hissed.

'I thought I was supposed to.'

'The plan's changed. I'll be back in an hour.'

'What was all that crap about a shepherd's pie? I'm starving. There's nothing in the fridge except some eye-shadow and a rotting marrow.'

'Got to go.' I snapped the phone shut and went back to my chair.

'Righto, folks!' said Alison. 'Time's up,' and she picked up a little egg-timer she'd obviously purloined from Edward's craft cupboard. 'Pieces of paper to me, everybody,' she said, rubbing her hands together gleefully.

I looked at Alison, ruddy-faced and smiling goofily, and slowly shook my head. Was she genuinely excited by the outcome of this ridiculous quiz? Had her self-esteem fallen so low that she was actually proud to have been given charge of it? Had motherhood rendered her so brain-wobbled that fashioning this board with drawing-pins was her main achievement of the last month? And did I have any right to assume that I was any better than these mums here? No. I'd achieved less than Alison in the last month. Nobody had given me the charge of a quiz, and I certainly hadn't made anything useful from the contents of a craft cupboard. I was exactly the same as every woman-jack of them, and that was the most painful thing about it.

The only way of dulling the pain was a large Limoncello liqueur. Which the oldest waiter provided with a lascivious wink and a: 'Here you are, beautiful baby.'

'Look at my photo on the board, mate,' I said, pointing to the one with froggy eyes and bulbous head. 'A beautiful baby I certainly was not.'

'Mel, I can't BELIEVE you just did that,' said Alison. 'I'm

afraid you can't take part in the quiz now you've given away your identity. That's a real shame.'

Several hours later and I was stretched out on the sofa with Pen sitting at my head, acting as therapist.

'And another thing,' I said, 'all of you lot met up the other night for a jolly cosy dinner and I wasn't even invited. That hurt.'

'You never return anybody's calls, Mel. Jim and Shorty and all the guys were complaining about it the other night. I've given up asking you out to do things.'

'I have a child, Pen.'

'So? Does motherhood prevent you from picking up the phone?'

I was slightly stumped.

'It's very difficult being a mother, Pen. You can't just pick up the phone every time it suits you. You're tied into things. Rinsing, loading, dandling … jiggling.'

'Jiggling?'

'Yes, Pen. I know it doesn't sound like much to you with your fancy-pants life and your trendy job, but I spend most of my life jiggling now. I jiggle her from dawn till dusk,' I said, and added woundedly: 'It's actually bloody tiring.'

I wasn't sure but I think I heard Pen stifle a slight giggle.

'Anyway, I can't go out. I've got nothing to wear.'

'That's certainly true,' said Pen, putting on her jacket. 'Look, I'd love to stay and wallow in more of your self-pity, but I've got a life.'

'You cow,' I said, throwing a cushion at her.

'Oh by the way, my rate is £3.50 an hour.'

'I bet it is,' I said. 'And is that for the full service?'

'Ha ha ha,' and she kissed me on the lips. Pen always does that. She knows I get a bit unnerved by it and she likes that.

'Thanks for babysitting, Pen.'

And she was off into the night.

I lay on the sofa for another hour or so, mulling over the evening's events. Thank goodness Dan was coming home at the weekend. All this self-analysis was getting embarrassing. I couldn't wait to show him the new house.

Chapter Nine

Jo had the bare-faced audacity to utter her first proper word as soon as her father showed his face back in the homestead.

'Dada. Dada.'

The cow. All these weeks I'd spent with her, and just one look at his face prompted this most significant of achievements. And his was a rosier, chubbier face too after a few weeks in Germany – he had a rather yeomanly look about him. I tried to avoid mentioning his weight gain, but I did enjoy gripping him by the love-handles whenever our paths crossed in the flat. Which was pretty much all the time considering its size and our amount of stuff.

To add to our inventory of goods we now had a baby-walker in the shape of a car, a multi-shelved baby-changing station on wheels, a paddling pool filled with balls, and my latest purchase – a daybed I'd ordered from a Sunday supplement. It looked so wonderful in the photo, all white-painted brass and rose-patterned cushions, that as soon as I clapped eyes on it I ordered it.

The problem was that our old brown sofa now made me feel sick. It was too intimately linked with that tunnel period of post-birth madness. I figured that the daybed would add a fresh spriggi-ness to the room, and also to me. It had been in the room for two weeks now.

'Just as well we're moving,' said Dan, sitting rather forcefully on the daybed so that it groaned. He tried to stretch out fully on it, but found that his legs were too long.

'Brilliant,' he said. 'I can't even lie on it.'

'Well, it's mine,' I said ungraciously. 'It's my reward for being a single parent all these weeks.'

Dan was unimpressed.

'You can barely open the door with this ludicrous *Ruhebett* in it.'

Annoyingly, Dan had started to drop a lot of German words into his everyday chat.

'Well, I'm sorry, *Damen und Herren*, but the *schlafen-sie-gut* is staying,' I said, snuggling into its rosy gorgeousness.

It was a relief to have Dan back. Mainly because it gave me the chance to become reunited with my ear-plugs once again. No longer was I the lone wolf on duty at night. I was passing the baby-buck, nay, positively flinging it in Dan's general direction.

The very night he got back, I scampered upstairs to bed, leapt into my cool cotton jim-jams and pressed the little orange lovelies into my ears. Nine twenty precisely. If all went to plan, I could be looking at a nine-hour kip here. I hugged myself with excitement and shut my eyes.

Several minutes later I gasped in shock as I felt something scratchy rubbing on my neck. It felt intrusive and smelled weird. I opened my eyes to find Dan kissing my neck and mumbling something or other.

'What?' I said gruffly.

Still nothing. He was moving his lips but I couldn't hear a thing.

'Hang on a minute,' I said grumpily, levering out the orange beauties from their beloved hidey-holes and glancing at the clock. Nine twenty-three. He'd better have a bloody good excuse for this, I thought to myself.

'What do you want?' I snapped.

'I just want to be intimate with you. You're my wife.'

'But I'd just put my ear-plugs in.'

'Mel, it's twenty past nine.'

'Soon to be nine thirty if we carry on chatting the way we are.'

'If I was still in Germany, I'd just about be starting to think about dinner now. Not putting on my bloody nightcap and moustache net.'

'Well, listen. You're back in Britain now, which must be such a disappointment to you. And I've been up since five forty-five this morning. Hang on, are you saying that I've got a 'tache?'

'No. You're gorgeous and ... lovely ... and do you actually remember the last time we had a bit of nookie?'

Oh dear. I had been praying this wasn't going to rear its head. I'd got rigidly into a routine of being on my own, and I'm not sure I wanted to get intimate with Dan at all.

'It's been eons,' he said mournfully.

'It's only been a couple of months, Dan.'

'Exactly. I just think it's sad that we can't be close like that any more. It worries me that we'll start to drift apart.'

'We're closer than we've ever been, we've got Jo,' I said, half trying to convince myself.

'Well,' said Dan, stroking my hair, 'I think we should make a bit more of an effort to get back on the *Steckenpferdchen*.'

'What's that?' I asked grumpily.

'It means hobby horse. Although in Westphalia you can also use it to mean a painted fairground horse.'

I couldn't help suppressing the tiniest of yawns. Nine twenty-seven, the clock said. If Dan stopped talking I'd still have a chance of hitting the nine-hour kip target.

He sighed.

'I'm sorry,' he said and kissed the tip of my nose. 'I don't want to be a twat.'

'I'm sorry too,' I said, kissing his forehead. 'We'll get it together soon, I promise. We'll be like a pair of crazy love-baboons.'

Dan didn't say anything but looked wistful. I sneaked a look at the clock before marrying plugs to holes again. Nine twenty-nine. Result!

The hospital appointment for my piles assessment had come through at last, thank goodness. Dan offered to come with me, but it was quite embarrassing enough to have to go at all, let alone with him in tow.

My name was called out and I was ushered into a brightly lit, nondescript consulting room. An Italian doctor in a white coat and smart suede brogues shook my hand warmly. He had the Mediterranean five-o'clock-shadowed handsomeness to a tee, and annoyingly I found myself blushing for no reason. It's such a shame that it's always the good-looking ones who have to see you at your worst. I remembered a gorgeous Danish anaesthetist who'd come in to oversee my epidural when I was in labour. All he ever saw of me was a pair of pallid buttocks sticking out of one of those paper gowns that open all the way up the back.

'OK. So we're going to take a look at these haemorrhoids, are we?'

He had nice eyes, and lovely hands. Chef's hands. Hands that could slice a courgette really finely.

'Yes. They've been a real pain in the arse,' I said and laughed. He smiled.

'Are you drinking lots of water? Exercising?'

'I've just had a baby,' I said quickly.

'OK. You take the trousers and pants off, behind the screen, and we take a look. OK?'

God, even the way he said 'pants' was sexy.

'OK, up on the bed,' he commanded. 'On all fours is best.'

If only he'd said that to me in other circumstances. After a candle-lit dinner, perhaps. I was going to have to create an out-of-body experience that would take me far far away from this little booth. Failing that I could always go down the good old middle-class route of polite and inane questioning to circumvent life's messier elements.

'So you're from Italy?' I asked. 'Which part?'

'Milan,' he replied, prodding something round the general area. I sincerely hoped it wasn't his finger.

'I don't know Milan,' I said in a high-pitched voice. 'I went to Orvieto once. Where the vineyards are. Lovely grapes,' I said and then laughed. Oh God, I would never be able to look him in the eye. He'd already looked into all of mine.

There was a knock at the door.

'Come in,' he said.

I couldn't see from behind the screen, but it sounded like about six people had just entered the room.

'You OK for everyone to take a look?' the good doctor enquired.

'I beg your pardon?' I squeaked.

'They are medical students. You ticked the box here on your form giving consent for them to come and have a look.'

The pressure was on now to get our flat sale completed and move into the new house. It was all looking promising. Surveys had been done, the money was ready to be transferred; we were simply waiting to exchange the contracts.

I rang Robin at the bank. He didn't answer his phone, but a bored-sounding PA took the call.

'Can I speak to Robin, please? It's Mel.'

She cupped the phone with her hand and I heard her reedy voice and a male voice chatting in low tones. She was soon back.

'Can I take a message? He's actually in a meeting.'

Ah. That old 'in a meeting' excuse.

'What sort of meeting?' I demanded.

'A meeting meeting,' she said, chippily.

'But with whom? For what reason? How long? With what outcome?'

'Hang on a minute,' and she went back to the phone-cupping and rumbled away with the male voice. It occurred to me that the male voice belonged to none other than Robin himself. There was a certain familiar high twang in it.

'He's just told me he's in a meeting, that's all,' she came back, sullenly.

'He's just told you? You mean he's standing right there next to you? What sort of meeting is this? Please tell him to phone me straightaway. It's urgent. OK?'

'When he's out of his meeting.'

This really riled me.

'Oh stop pretending he's in a meeting. Just lean over to him now and ask him to call me. Will you do that for me?'

'I can't just interrupt him when he's in a meeting.'

'Look, the only person he's in a meeting with is you. Now please pass on that message.'

'I will. He's out of his meeting now.'

'Well, can I speak to him?'

'Sorry. He's just gone into another meeting.'

I couldn't believe that we were going to be moving into a house. A proper house! In a matter of weeks we'd have a back garden and little driveway in the front. I would miss our flat. A lot had happened in it. There were still marks on the hall floor where Pen had danced in tap shoes. We'd had some good parties here, sometimes fifty people squashed into this flat. Dan would always fill the bathtub with ice and stash the drink in it. I'd make vodka jelly and then put tons of fairy lights and candles round the place, which would annoy Dan so he'd go round turning all the main lights on. The front door was scuffed where Dan had slammed it violently after a row. And upstairs a window was still cracked where I'd flailed at it drunkenly while Dan tried to sober me up in the shower. Stuff had happened in this flat.

There is a pub in north London that still bears the bullet holes of where Ruth Ellis, last woman to be hanged in Britain, was shot at. We didn't have marks quite as dramatic as that, but looking round all the rooms I felt that we too had left some sort of archive. I would miss our neighbourhood with its old locals, tramps, itinerants and trendies. There was a buzz here, a sense that we were part of the city. But it was time to move on. We needed more space, a bit of peace and quiet.

'I've sorted out the removal people,' sad Dan, edging his way round the daybed. I was sitting on it playing a Polish tickling game with Jo that my dad had always done with me. I'd been doing it since ten that morning. It was now nearly lunchtime.

'God, I hope I get some work soon,' I said, 'and we're going to have to think about some childcare. It's impossible for me to do anything in the house when Jo's in it.'

'I think we should get a lodger in the new house to help with the mortgage,' said Dan.

'Fine by me. I'll put an ad in the newsagent's,' I said. 'We might as well get the ball rolling.'

The following week was Judy's daughter Minnie's first birthday. Minnie was to have ten of her closest friends round for a teatime get-together. I hadn't seen Judy or any of the others en masse since the mums' night out, so I thought this would be a good opportunity to reconvene. I was rather ashamed looking back at that evening – I felt I'd judged them all too harshly. Anyway, it was more important for Jo to make friends than it was for me. Even if I thought the mums were all ghastly, it was vital for Jo to have a social life.

I dressed her up in a jolly orange dress with matching orange sneakers and orange tights and a little orange toggle in her hair. Dan said she looked like an EasyJet employee, but I didn't care. She was crawling brilliantly now, which was a source of both wonderment and hives-inducing stress. The flat was her realm. She always made a beeline for the hall. Despite the money we'd shelled out on developmental toys, all that interested her was systematically licking the row of shoes by the front door. No amount of saying 'no' in that kind but firm manner that one's supposed to adopt, like a dog-handler, would work.

We rang Judy's doorbell and waited. Judy's road was about ten minutes' walk from us and in a much more upmarket neighbourhood. At the end of our main drag with its Everything-For-A-Pound shops and pubs where you could order anything from pints and peanuts to guns and hand-grenades, you walked on a bit further and suddenly it was like stepping into a painting. You were in the world of Maida Vale. Even its name sounded leafy and restful. Long boulevards with redbrick mansion blocks, lots of smart elderly people walking equally smart dogs. A garden centre, not garish and advertising a hundred bulbs for a fiver, but selling exquisite wrought-iron benches and little fountains with water spurting out of cherubs' mouths. Suddenly there were no tramps. The booze shop was brightly lit and peopled with non-alcoholics.

Judy had a large maisonette flat in one of these blocks, and it was immediately clear which flat was hosting the party due to the amount of bikes with child-seats attached parked outside. There was one rather smug contraption which had a trailer attached to it, with room for two toddlers and a lot of yellow flags.

I checked my hair in the brass work on Judy's front door, and then buzzed. I put on a friendly but relaxed smile. I was determined to really be myself this afternoon and not let anything get to me. I was going to try to see the party through Jo's eyes. After all, it was for her sake that I was here.

Judy answered the door in a mob-cap, long skirt and hobnailed boots, with a woollen shawl tied round her shoulders. She looked me up and down.

'Oh,' she said, disappointed.

'Oh!' I said, surprised.

'Where's your costume?' she asked me.

'Costume?' I said.

'Didn't you get my message? About the Victorian theme?'

'No, Judy, I didn't,' I said, determined not to get annoyed.

'God, I hope I did leave you a message, actually,' she said after a brief pause. 'Minnie's got so many friends, I might well have forgotten you.'

My poor Jo. Her first rejection.

There was a sticky moment at the door when I thought we weren't going to be allowed into the party. Thank God. We could get home to the daybed and the Polish tickling game.

'Don't worry, we'll find you both some bits of costume. Come on in,' she said.

In we went, and I greeted the collection of Victorian mums with a suitable amount of oohs and aahs and 'Wow, what an amazing costume you've got on!'

'So why the Victorian theme?' I asked Judy, as she handed me a mob-cap and shawl. They looked blatantly ridiculous on top of my drawstring trousers, trainers and cheap roll-neck jumper, but I thought it'd be churlish not to show willing.

'Well,' said Judy, handing round a plate of black blobs, 'a group of us went on a trip to the Museum of Childhood the other day.'

Great. Nobody had thought of inviting me. The blobs came my way. I looked at the plate slightly nonplussed.

'Handmade liquorice tablets,' said Judy.

'Great,' I said, popping the smallest one I could find into my mouth.

'It was a wonderful outing,' said Alison enthusiastically from under a bonnet. 'The babies all had a go at lying in a real Victorian cradle.'

The liquorice was creating a black froth inside my mouth, and some of it was working its way into a filling.

'And then we washed some of the babes in a big Victorian pot,' said Bridget, pronouncing the word 'pot' the French way, so that it sounded like Po the Teletubby.

'It was very special,' said Jane. 'So amazing to see how mothers looked after their infants in those days.'

'They had so little, and yet so much,' said Judy, sitting down to join the rest of us on the floor. Why is it that groups of mums always sit on the floor? I long for the day when I'll be offered a chair again.

'You're so right, Judy,' said Alison. 'Here we are buying our little ones endless toys and plastic gee-gaws' – now that was a word I thought only my mother used – 'and there they were in Victorian times, happy to play for hours with only a stick and a ball.'

All of the mothers nodded sagely. I wanted to shout out 'I love plastic gee-gaws! Our flat's full of them!' but couldn't because my teeth were stuck together with liquorice.

'Which is why,' said Judy, getting up again, 'I asked Gavin to fashion some of these for our babies to play with!' and she fetched a big basket from one side of the room and began handing it around.

'Oh, Judy!' sighed Alison. 'You are truly amazing.'

The basket was full of whittled sticks and little wooden balls, one for everyone to take away with them.

'What a brilliant idea!' said a mum with a large mole on her chin, sitting at the back of the group.

'Gavin got his Sunday-school group to make them last week. He had plenty of balls already.'

I stifled a snigger. Surely he didn't have any balls at all if he went to Sunday school and whittled sticks, for Pete's sake.

'So nobody caught TB then?' I asked with my mouth completely lopsided, still wrestling with the liquorice tablet.

The mums looked slightly puzzled. Luckily two of the babies started crying, which was the vital decoy for me to declamp the liquorice from my mouth and park it into a nearby fig tree.

'Right, folks!' said Judy brightly. 'I'll call in the older children from the garden – they've been having a wonderful time with hoops and sticks – and we'll have tea, shall we?'

The mums heaved themselves up with the grace of a group of water buffaloes.

Judy had laid out one big kiddy-proportioned table in her large kitchen, with lots of mini chairs set round it.

'I borrowed the table and chairs from Tumblers Nursery,' said Judy. 'Here we go. There's traybake, shortbread, mini jam dicks and toffee apples.'

'Wow!' said Alison. 'A proper Victorian tea!'

'I just don't know how you manage to do all of this,' said Bridget, totally awestruck.

I caught myself grinning like an idiot, and then remembered my plan – to be myself this afternoon. I unclenched my smiling muscles.

'Well, if you were all round at mine for Jo's birthday,' I said, rubbing my hands together, 'it'd be Wotsits and some shite shop-bought cake with Smarties on top. Now, did you say there was a dick on offer? It's been a long time since I got my teeth round one of those.'

Judy blinked several times and then announced 'Time for some music!' and approached the record player. 'Look what I found!' she said, holding up a dog-eared record sleeve to show everybody.

'I don't believe it!' cooed a short mum with the hairiest face I'd ever seen. Not the downy pale stuff, but thick black wiry ones. It was mesmerizing. 'You managed to find some Victorian nursery rhymes!'

Again, awed whispers circulated round the room of Wonder-Judy's myriad of superhuman achievements. Was there anything the woman couldn't do? She could probably make a soufflé, trim the rosebushes, make an origami sailing boat and give her husband head all at the same time.

The record grated into life with that old foot-tapper 'Georgie Porgie Pudding and Pie'. I'd have happily listened to the National Orchestra of Albania playing the back catalogue of The Dooleys rather than this mournful collection of nursery dirges. No wonder the infant mortality rate was so high in those days – kids were probably throwing themselves out of nursery windows when these songs were sung to them.

'Diddle diddle dumpling, my son John! Went to bed with his trousers on!' warbled the Victorian mums like a bunch of deaf nuns. They'd gone into default toddler-group mode, which meant that they started speaking in high-pitched voices to their children and repeating every line in the nursery rhyme with its appropriate Angie action.

Something about nursery rhymes automatically makes me think of horror films – those angelic little girls in nighties singing 'Ring a Ring o' Roses' very softly. Meanwhile, Satan has gripped their souls and starts to make them perform acts of unspeakable wickedness, such as fire-starting, ripping the heads off their dolls and then chopping their mother's feet off and burying them. The front doorbell rang. I hoped it was the Grim Reaper come to get me.

An apparition on a par with the Grim Reaper walked into the kitchen. A figure with copper hair under a thunderously large Eliza Doolittle hat with what looked like a piece of roadkill strapped to the top. A funereal black Victorian governess's dress cinched in at the waist and a watch pinned to her ample right bosom. Black hobnail boots on the bottom and a whiff of bloomers showing under the skirt. The whole look was completed up top with some scarlet lipstick applied liberally over her large wrinkled mouth.

'Angie!' shouted Judy. 'How lovely to see you and what a fantastic costume,' and the women embraced, which sent a shudder through me.

Angie surveyed her women and children. We were so lowly at our one-foot-high table that it suddenly felt like we were in a Victorian poorhouse, with this scary black-dressed woman as our cruel warder. I clung to Jo. I could not meet Angie's eye, but busied myself rearranging the little mob-cap, which Jo kept pulling off her head.

Angie plumped herself down in a Lilliputian chair and was

waited on hand and foot by her adoring protégés. She was brought tea and bread and dripping. The older kids didn't touch any of the strange birthday fare at all, and the babies seemed perfectly content eating their own hands or one of Gavin's balls.

I'd never really seen Judy with her five-year-old before now because he was at school whenever Judy and I met up. He was a pale lad who seemed rather withdrawn. Judy was obviously keen for him to eat some of the birthday tea.

'Come on, darling. Try just a little bit.'

But the little lad just sat with his head hung down over his plate, unbudgeable.

'Try a piece of the shortbread, darling. Mummy made it specially.'

He simply shook his head.

'It's Minnie's birthday, Oliver,' said Judy sharply, 'and you'd better do as Mummy says otherwise it's straight into the Naughty Nook.'

A quietness fell on the group – always the way when parental discipline is being meted out. Nobody wants to miss the chance of seeing somebody else in action and judge their technique.

'Come on, Oliver' – there was a steely edge to her voice now – 'eat up the birthday tea.'

'I want to watch telly,' said Oliver, who was growing in my estimation by the second.

'Telly?' Judy laughed at the group. 'We don't watch telly, Oliver, except on a Thursday between three twenty and three forty-five.'

'I don't want to wear these stupid clothes.' The poor boy was in pedal-pushers and a peaked cap. 'I want to watch *Transformers*.'

'Right, everybody. I'm afraid Oliver hasn't listened to Mummy even though Mummy gave him two chances, and Mummy's going to put Oliver into the Naughty Nook.'

And with that she whisked him out of his place and out into the hall. He began to wail in earnest and Judy's voice was heard above the racket: 'Mummy's very very disappointed with Oliver. Very very disappointed. And you will stay in the Naughty Nook until I say.'

'NO,' he screeched back at her.

'Yes,' she shouted, 'and you will NOT be getting a star on your Good Behaviour Sticker Chart this evening.'

'NO NO NO NO NO!' he screeched.

Several of the mums exchanged the tiniest of facial expressions with one another. Angie slurped at her teacup as if nothing was happening. Oliver just carried on bellowing until Judy finally yelled back, red in the face: 'STOP SHOUTING!'

There was a momentary silence before Oliver started wailing again. The hall door slammed and Judy was back with us, re-arranging her shawl and putting her mob-cap, slightly askew, back into place. Her eyes were still glittering with anger, but she smiled fixedly at everyone.

'Right. The birthday cake.'

On one of her spectacularly clean surfaces sat a mountainous, rich fruitcake complete with marzipan and white royal icing. At a guess, I would have said that a baby would be more likely to eat the contents of a llamas' enclosure in a zoo than that. It made rather a pathetic picture among a group of one-year-olds. It didn't stop me from helping myself to a gargantuan slice, however. There was a bit of a silence over the group, which was broken by Angie: 'Naughty naughty. He's been caughty.'

The five-year-old group at the other end of the table were a subdued lot too. They were probably wondering if they were going to be next for a dose of Naughty Nook. It seemed absurd to punish the boy for misbehaving at a birthday party. That was the reason they were invented. I tried to cast my mind back to one where I had behaved with absolute decorum and couldn't think of a single one. My behaviour at my eighteenth where I ended up vomiting over somebody's windscreen must surely have earned me a lifetime of Naughty Nook. The poor chap was still crying out there in the hall. Judy pretended not to hear and was showing Minnie how to blow out her candle.

We all sang 'Happy Birthday' to her, which I thought would be the ideal opportunity to bring Oliver back into the fold and give him a big hug, but no. As we sang, he wailed.

Jo was having a very merry time of it all. She wasn't the slightest bit interested in any of the other babies. I'd given up trying to position her right in front of them. All she wanted to do was find some shoes, and finally she chanced upon a few pairs in the corner of the kitchen.

'Oh no! No no no! She mustn't chew those, that's disgusting,' shouted Judy.

In a move that must have defied the natural laws of gravity, I got out of the mini chair pretty sharpish and flew over to Jo.

'What's she doing?' I asked, out of breath and imagining something terrible like a poisonous mushroom or a Stanley knife.

She was munching on the strap of a little sandal, perfectly happy.

'Oh that's OK, she loves chewing on shoes, don't you, noggin? She's like a puppy.'

'Well, I don't think it's a good idea, Mel. All sorts of terrible germs lurk around shoes, you know,' said Judy.

'You've smelled my feet then?' I said.

Judy shook her head and turned to the sink. Her shoulders were high up round her ears.

'Parties are stressful, aren't they?' I ventured, now that we had a chance to talk on our own. All the mums and kids had gone off to do some of Angie's Actions in the living room.

'I've just got too much on my plate at the moment,' she confided. 'I really want to try and get my clothes collection off the ground. I've never done this before, but I'm thinking of looking for a childminder for Minnie for a few hours a week.'

'It's absolutely the right thing to do,' I said firmly, glad to be in the driving seat for once. 'Just because we're mums shouldn't mean that we have no life. I want to find a childminder too, you know. I need to do some work. We're about to move, for God's sake. We need the money.'

'Well, if you hear of any good ones let me know,' said Judy. 'All the ones round here are booked up.'

'OK. I'll do that,' I said. It was ridiculous, but I felt a warm glow spread all over me. Here I was. Finally, part of a network. 'I'll let you know,' I promised.

'Now, can you pass me that cloth? No, not that one, that's Minnie's face flannel. The blue one. That's my glass-cleaning cloth. Thank you.'

I was starting to feel excited. Suddenly the world was opening up with possibility.

'I'll start to put out the feelers. There are some good websites.'

I felt proactive, positive and together. Judy smiled at me. Gone were the days when I didn't know what a glass test was, for goodness' sake. I was going to go out there and find myself a childminder. Jo and I said goodbye to everyone half an hour later and put our coats on in the hall where Oliver was still occupying the Naughty Nook, very quiet now.

'I'll be in touch if I hear of anything,' I said to Judy.

'Great. Now, Mister Man,' she said gruffly to Oliver, 'are you ready to be released from the Naughty Nook?'

'Yes,' he said flatly.

'Good. Now back to the table and let's see you tackle some Dundee cake.'

The next month was a flurry of house-moving chores. Documents were signed, removal men booked, and I was sure that my finger-prints were beginning to disappear because of all the newspaper I was handling in the packing process. I became a sort of wrapping automaton and began to look at objects simply in terms of how much newspaper they would use, and from which angle I would tackle them. The teapot presented the most tricky wrapping chal-lenge – should one take the spout as your main point of packing or the body of the pot? As is clear from this sad wrapping obses-sion, there hadn't been a single call from my agent during the whole month.

'He's a pale little thing, isn't he, dear?' said Irene, whom we met on our way to the shop to buy more wrapping paper.

'He's incredibly well, Irene,' I said defensively.

'Ah, a city's no place to bring up a baby. He looks just like his dad.'

'Yes, doesn't he?'

'You'll be wanting a girl next?'

'Yes, Irene, I'd love to have a daughter.'

'Well, good luck with the move. You'll come back this way much, will you?'

'Oh yes, Irene. We're not moving too far. Only twenty minutes away.'

'Ah well. I've brought you these anyhow. They're for the baby,' and she handed me a rather bulky plastic bag filled with something soft. 'They belonged to my husband, but he doesn't need them now, God rest his soul.'

'That's very kind of you, Irene,' I said, slightly puzzled as to what this mystery object could be. 'Shall I open it now?' I asked.

'Ah go on, you might as well.'

I opened the bag and pulled out a pack of incontinence pants. Large size. Male.

'They're unused,' she said.

'That's good,' I replied, totally stumped. 'Thank you, Irene. That's really ... thoughtful of you. Thank you so much.'

'Ah well, it all helps, doesn't it?'

She took such a deep drag on her fag I thought her whole face was going to be sucked into the enormous pits of her cheeks.

'He wears a lot of pink for a boy, doesn't he?'

It was strange to say goodbye to Jerome the cafe owner. It was even a bit sad to say goodbye to the resident drugs dealer who always sat on the little wall in front of our house. I'd never actually spoken to him. He was about seventeen, a good-looking boy with a very cool range of clothes, always immaculately laundered, and the most intricate array of patterns shaved into his head and eyebrows. In that paranoid London way, I was a bit scared to make eye-contact with him or engage him in too intimate a conversation. It might lead to trouble – he might think I was patronizing him and pull a huge club or stick on me. Or worse, he might be thinking that I wanted to buy drugs from him. We were two days away from moving, however, and I was feeling a nostalgic affection for the place already, even though we hadn't left yet. I was determined to look on everyone as a friend.

'Morning,' I opened up with. A nice ice-breaker, nothing too confrontational.

'Morning,' he said. Very pleasantly and articulately. I was surprised.

'We're moving in two days,' I announced, 'so you won't be seeing us round here as much.'

'Oh goodness. Well, I hope the move works out really well for you. Going far?'

'Into the St Stephens area.'

'Very nice. Probably a better catchment for schools up that way. Some nice architectural bits and bobs too. There's a lovely early example of a Great Western Railway-inspired coach house. On the corner of Bathurst Avenue.'

'So. How's business?' I ventured, emboldened by our civilized chat.

'Oh you know. Softly softly catchy monkey.'

'Is street trade quite buoyant at the moment?'

'Yes, it is.'

'Ah well, good luck with it all. And see you around.'

'You can be sure of it. Goodbye, and good luck with the move.'

The day of the move was clear and sunny, the sort of weather that showed our flat off at its best. The old red front door looked majestic and imposing with the light bouncing off it, and the mutations in brick-colour made the front of the flat look like an autumnal patchwork of red, orange and brown. I felt like we were about to say goodbye to an old and dear friend. Would the next people love it in the same way that we had? Would they work out the technique of opening the front door when it rained and the wood swelled up? Would they remember to feed the robins who'd suddenly appeared two Christmases ago? Would they understand the language of the house as we did, the gurgles of the boiler at night, the hissing of the immersion heater, the strange clunking of the gas and electric cupboard door on a windy day? I could hardly see the dustbin, my eyes were so full of tears. I placed a pretty fero-cious nappy in there, the last thing I would ever throw into it. It was fitting somehow. Jo had been born into this flat and she was leaving it a final goodbye present.

Wandering round the new house, with all of our belongings still in boxes, was strangely liberating. For the first time in months our lives were clutter-free. The only objects out were two plastic cups and a bottle of Cava. The first person I rang as soon as the landline was operational was Robin. I hadn't spoken to him for ages. I'd tried to speak to him on numerous occasions, but he always seemed to be out of the office. He was away on an IT course. I felt sure that he'd have wanted to know how our move had gone, what we thought of the new area and its inhabitants, whether we were settling in.

My mum had taken Jo for the day to give us a chance to unpack the essential boxes. She was obsessed with the one and only break-age: a bottle of soy sauce all over an armchair that had belonged to one of her aunts.

'You see, I told you you should have bubble-wrapped your condiments,' she kept saying. 'When your father and I moved into our first house I wrapped each item of his underwear in tissue paper before it went into the box. Imagine that.'

She was still twittering as I despatched them off in the general direction of anywhere. She'd already called the house 'drear' and 'suburban'. It did look a bit shabby without the previous occu-pants' life filling it. Outlines of their pictures on the wall remained like ghosts, in frames of dust. I found a puppet with big shoes in one of the built-in cupboards, and somebody had very helpfully left an enormous floater in the upstairs loo. It felt deathly quiet. You could actually hear birds singing in the trees. Only if you strained your ears could you just about make out the rumble of a big road some distance away.

It made our old flat and our old life seem like another country. Now we were in the land of pampas grasses planted in diddy front gardens, Neighbourhood Watch stickers in windows and neat little cars parked up in driveways. There was a distinct lack of dog poo about the place. Dogs around here obviously had the good manners to hold it in until they got to the park. The houses were Edwardian with white wooden porches. The first inhabitant we saw on Brook Grove (Grove! Even the name sounded villagey) was an old woman pushing a zimmer frame into her house a few doors up from ours. Dan gave her a cheery wave but she scuttled in quickly without turning.

'I wonder if there are lots of kids round here?' I said.

My answer came in the form of an elongated silence. It didn't look like a child-heavy street. There were too many gnomes and little stone wheelbarrows in front gardens for that. Not a single people-carrier was parked in the road either. Instead, neat boxy cars were parked one after the other, with no telltale internal evidence of crisp, biscuit and banana-skin detritus.

An old man with an even older dog emerged from the house opposite. Both had grey mangy coats.

'Morning,' I ventured.

Neither dog nor man responded.

'Come on,' said Dan, putting his arm round me, 'let's go and unpack.'

As we went over the threshold (I'd dissuaded Dan from carrying me over it for fear of rupturing his spleen), we heard a cheery voice behind us.

'Coo-ee!' it said, like something out of a sitcom. We turned round to see a couple in their fifties, in matching his 'n' hers grey windcheaters with purple piping, carrying a plate of something covered in silver foil.

'Welcome to Brook Grove,' they said in unison. They were a couple who'd clearly been together so long they'd started to look like one another. Both had a good head of grey, bouncy hair cut into soft helmets, and I was gratified to look down and see that both were sporting the essential item for the over-fifties. The grey spongy shoe.

'I thought you might need something solid inside you,' said the wife, 'so I've brought you some of my apricot sponge.'

'Not for the faint-hearted!' said the husband jovially, rubbing his stomach and screwing up his face in pretend pain.

'That's so kind of you,' I said, taking the astonishingly weighty plate from her. 'I'm Mel and this is my husband, Dan.'

'Frank,' said the man, holding out a hand and revealing a wrist forested in black hair. 'And this is Mrs Frank,' he added, giving us a wink.

'Cheryl. Pleased to meet you,' she said, offering us both a handshake as soft as a bruised fruit.

'So, how are you settling in then?' said Frank.

'We literally arrived two hours ago,' said Dan. 'The guys are getting the last of the things inside.'

'Well, it's nice to have some young blood in the street.'

'We were the young 'uns before you came along!' said Cheryl, and they both broke into peals of laughter. 'You're going to make us feel old.'

'Are there any families in the road?' I enquired.

'No,' said Cheryl firmly.

'Just old biddies and ancient gits,' said Frank, and did a remarkable impression of a very old man doddering with a walking stick.

'Most people in this road just die and then the houses get broken up into flats full of itinerant foreigners. Do watch out for number 36' – Cheryl had lowered her voice to a whisper – 'house full of New Zealanders. God knows how many they've got packed in there, but there have been some break-ins in the area recently, and I don't think it's a coincidence,' and she tapped the side of her nose confidentially.

'Well, we'll let you young 'uns get on with it,' said Frank. 'Any time you fancy coming out for a pint and a game of darts' – and he winked at Dan – 'I'm your man.'

'Great,' said Dan.

'Well, we'll see you soon no doubt,' I added. 'Our daughter's with my mother at the moment, but she'll be back soon.'

'You have a daughter?' Cheryl looked suddenly wistful. Maybe they'd never been able to have kids. Childless couples often wear quite expensive matching waterproof gear, I've found.

'Yes, she'll be a year old quite soon.'

'Ah. Isn't that lovely. You'll have to bring her round for a game of dominoes.'

Definitely childless.

'Fantastic,' I said, and Dan and I plunged into our house.

'Well, I don't think we'll be having any late-night whisky and guitar sessions with our neighbours, do you?'

'Oh God. I feel like we've moved into one of those retirement complexes. Do you think this is it? Is our life over?'

'We'll just have to have loads of mates over all the time,' said Dan confidently.

'Yes,' I replied, 'all of our mates that we see so regularly.'

'Come on. We've got to start having dinners, parties, rambling lunches that go on all day, sleepovers.'

We'd gone upstairs. All that had been placed in our bedroom was our large double bed. It stared at us from the middle of the darkened empty room.

Dan came up behind me and started kissing the back of my neck.

'How about we christen our new bedroom?' he mumbled. 'Your mum won't be here for a couple of hours.'

'How about we have a nice cup of tea and some of Cheryl's apricot sponge?' I said, disentangling myself from his embrace, and then humming loudly all the way downstairs.

Chapter Ten

A couple of weeks later and the house was starting to smell like it belonged to us. That heady combination of dirty nappies, mushed spinach, Dan's ancient aftershave and my greasy hair – it smelled like home. We'd started to make our mark on the house by painting Jo's little bedroom. At Pen's request we'd done it out in the official feminist colours: purple and green.

'Are you sure these paints aren't too dark?' I asked Dan, as I finished up a skirting board.

He stood back to admire our ten days' handiwork. We'd fallen into that fatal freelance trap of spinning out a domestic chore well beyond its natural lifespan.

'I'm afraid they do look like the official colours of the Wimbledon tennis championships,' admitted Dan. 'Basically what we've done here is recreate Steffi Graf's changing room.'

He was right.

'Yes, but we agreed that we wouldn't paint her room the colour of old ladies' cardigans.' Why must it be the fate of baby girls to suffer the octogenarian hues of candytuft, sickly lemon and lavender? 'Oh, Dan, I forgot to tell you. A girl rang about renting the spare room. She sounded really nice, Eastern Europe by the sounds of it. I've told her to come and check the room out this afternoon.'

'Great. I'll check my diary to see if I can be around,' he said.

'You're always around,' I mumbled to myself. 'No need to check your diary.'

'What?' said Dan sharply.

'Czech ... and ... wiry. That's right. She sounded Czech and wiry.'

'Oh,' said Dan, looking puzzled. 'Right, I'd better go and get on with work then,' and headed towards the patio door.

I knew Dan was feeling sensitive about his newly acquired freelance status, but I felt as his wife I had a right to know what exactly he was doing in the shed.

'Oh you know. I've got lots of calls to make. Things to set up. That sort of thing.'

'OK,' I replied. 'Well, I'd better go and get on with some work too then.'

There was a pause. Dan rubbed his hands together briskly.

'So, what "work" are you doing at the moment?' he asked.

'Oh you know. I've got to speak to my agent. Do some admin. Get things going, you know.'

'Great,' he said. 'Fancy a bit of lunch when Jo wakes up?'

'Cool. See you in the kitchen for some pasta and pesto.'

And he actually whistled the song 'Heigh ho, heigh ho, it's off to work we go' as he made the five strides between house and shed.

It had two windows and was an altogether swisher model than the little tumbledown hidey-hole in the backyard of our old flat. Thanks to the power points, Dan had been able to set up a computer and blow heater inside. I had to hand it to him – at least he turned on his computer every day. My work was in complete flat-line. Since the Tom and Tim debacle I hadn't heard a squeak from my agent. Except for the mandatory basket of muffins that arrived special delivery via her office – their usual offering when clients moved house or had a birthday. When you secured an enormous contract for her, however, then you got the special super-deluxe muffin basket that also contained champagne, egg sandwiches and chocolate truffles. I'd obviously never seen one of those myself. The muffins arrived throttled in acres of cellophane and green gingham, with a huge green ribbon and little card. My agent hadn't signed it, but had simply initialled it and scrawled a few air kisses. I sat lugubriously on the stairs and ate the muffins one by one. There were eight of them.

Five minutes later, Jo woke up. I've never seen Dan run faster into the kitchen for lunch, and it was only 11 a.m.

At a quarter past three, the doorbell rang.

'Dan! I think the girl's here about the room,' I called.

I didn't have to raise my voice. Dan hadn't actually made it back to his shed after lunch but had spent the intervening two and a half hours sorting Sellotapes, masking tapes and insulating tapes into separate sections of a kitchen drawer.

I smoothed my trousers, put on a welcoming smile and opened the front door to find not one girl, but two. Both were skinny-hipped and rangy. The Cheeky Girls sprang to mind. One had long tresses of bottle-blonde hair arranged in sort of knotted flaps, while the other sported a neat cap of vivid brown hair the colour of a chocolate brownie. Both had enough makeup on to ice a large Christmas cake. It gave their faces an unfortunate beige colour, and highlighted each pit, pore and spot smattered across their wide Slavic foreheads. Both had vivid blue eyes, clogged up with mascara. They looked very neat and laundered with buttons, zips and stitching done slightly on the cheap. One wore a long furry waistcoat and a raspberry silken shirt. She'd tucked a pair of ovary-crushing jeans into a pair of zip-up pointed boots. Now, I'd noticed that rather a lot of people on the streets of Britain had taken to tucking jeans into boots. What the hell had happened to the country? The last time I'd seen someone tuck jeans into boots was when Lesley Judd went on safari for Blue Peter circa 1977. And my Uncle Chris, who was a pig-farmer in Devon. He said it was imperative if you wanted to save your turn-ups from being filled with cow shit.

The other girl wore a skirt no longer than a belt. A 'pie crust', my mother would call it. It sat atop two legs the length of motor-ways, mottled with leopard-print tights running all the way down into patent ankle boots.

Add to the sartorial mix lashings of lip-gloss, about a hundred glittering hair-clips, shiny clutch bags, mini mobile phones on strings, a bizarre array of gonks hanging off keyrings, dangling earrings and nails the colour of Dolly Mixtures, and their look was complete. I felt as if a Christmas cracker had been pulled on the doorstep, and this was the treat inside it.

'Hello, do come in,' I said. I was amazed how grown-up my voice sounded. Mind you, I was probably old enough to be their mother.

'Thank you, thank you,' they chorused, and stepped into the bare-boarded hallway. A sickly blanket of perfume followed them into the house. I could make out two different smells clash-ing for airspace.

'Ah. Very nice, very nice house,' they said encouragingly. Both held their backs tremendously erect as they walked, which I found impressive.

'I'm afraid it's not very nice yet,' I apologized.

'Hello there,' said Dan, coming forward to shake hands. He suddenly looked old and daddish in their presence too. When had he acquired those new vertical wrinkles running upwards from his eyebrows?

'We only moved in recently,' I explained, 'so the room we're renting out is very simple.'

'Simple, yes,' said the blonde girl in a whispery, slightly Marilyn Monroe voice.

'Simple very good,' said the brown-haired girl, in an altogether deeper voice. 'We have plenty many stuff and things.'

'Cup of tea?' said Dan.

'Maybe yes,' the brown-haired girl said. 'You have lemon?'

'Sure,' said Dan, rubbing his hands together.

'There's nothing as English as a cup of tea,' I said brightly. They nodded.

'Except cricket,' said Dan. Both girls looked at him expectantly. 'Cricket? It's a traditional English game,' Dan explained, adopting a batsman's stance. 'You see, you hit the ball like this. Boff. Leather on willow it's sometimes called, and the aim is to …'

'Yes, cricket. And tea.' I laughed lightly. 'They go together actually.'

A pause. They weren't big conversationalists.

'Goodness! We haven't introduced ourselves. I'm Mel. And this is my husband, Dan.'

'I am Sonata,' said the blonde girl, 'and this my sister, Ruta.'

'Ruta? That's an unusual name,' said Dan. 'As is Sonata. Well, I suppose you'll live by Moonlight then!' and he laughed.

The girls registered no reaction.

'So,' I said, mentally scouring the room for the life-raft, 'where are you both from?'

'Our country is Latvia,' Ruta replied.

'Ah, Latvia,' said Dan, as if he knew it intimately. 'Very nice to meet you. And a great host for Eurovision you were too, several years ago. That host was extraordinary, wasn't he? Was his hair real?'

The girls looked at Dan in a puzzled way. I was going to have to get him a *Guide to the Latvian Sense of Humour* for Christmas this year.

'So, which one of you is looking for a room?' I asked breezily.

'We both,' said Ruta, matter-of-factly.

We were in the kitchen now, and the girls sat perched, not quite knowing how to fold their giraffe-like bodies round the chairs.

'Oh dear. I'm afraid we've only got one room available,' I explained, enunciating each word clearly like a primary-school teacher.

'This is no problem,' said Ruta, clearly the spokeswoman for the duo. 'We like share the room please.'

'Well, I don't know,' I said, looking at Dan for back-up.

'We were really only looking for one person,' he said.

A squawk came through from the living room. We'd left Jo on a rug playing with a shoe.

'You have baby?' said Sonata, her eyes lighting up.

'Yes. A daughter.'

'I can see her?' she asked, getting up onto her tottering tower of boots.

'Of course, she's through there.'

And Sonata clattered into the living room, where we heard much Baltic cooing and squidging. Sonata brought Jo to the table where she was bounced and tickled broadly.

'She really likes you,' I said, delighted.

'Very beauuuutiful baby! Very beauuuutiful!' and Ruta joined in the general adoration of my daughter by chucking her cheeks. As I watched the girls handling her so naturally and confidently, a plan was starting to formulate in my mind. I looked over at Dan. Was he thinking the same thing? In my mind's eye, I was seeing Dan and me out at the cinema, just like the old days, holding hands and eating nachos. Then I saw us out with friends, laughing together round some friendly gastro-pub table. Then the two of us having a cosy tête-à-tête dinner in a little Greek taverna. What I was seeing was a world of evenings out, opening before me like some glorious glittering canyon. Otherwise known as Latvian babysitting on tap.

'Would you like to see the room anyway, girls?' I asked enthusiastically. Dan shot me a confused look. 'Maybe we can come to some sort of arrangement?' I said, smiling.

And so it was that the two Latvian sisters moved into our new house three days later. A friend of theirs called Rimas pitched up with a clapped-out white van and the three of them took a good couple of hours unloading boxes, grip-bags, bin-bags, suitcases, wheelie-cases, Tupperware storage boxes and an unending stream of carrier bags. To the sounds of The Sugababes blaring out of a tinny ghetto-blaster, they worked on their room all through the day and evening, until at ten o'clock it was ready for our perusal.

We entered into a sort of fairy grotto, with twinkling lights attached to every wall and perfumed candles on all available surfaces. They'd rigged up a pink mosquito net above their bed, which was barely visible underneath a mound of cuddly toys. It looked rather like a children's ward in a hospital. There were enough toys – bears with hearts, a pig in a skirt, dog on silken lead – on that bed to open up a fairground stall. They'd covered the chest of drawers with a purple velvet throw, and had rigged up a nest of tables out of crates, all covered in a range of ornaments from a red London bus to a porcelain weeping clown and a vase filled with plastic flowers. They'd set up a clothes rail, which groaned in one corner of the room. It looked like a rack of outfits belonging to a pair of showgirls. Feathery collars poked out from behind sequinned scarves and leather jackets. With row upon row of shoes and boots stacked up underneath like a fancy-dress shop.

Both girls were beaming with delight at their handiwork, and I couldn't help my eyes from filling with tears. It could have been the emotion or the stink of the vanilla-scented candle to be honest.

I was slightly concerned about the proximity of mosquito net to candle. Something I'd have to tell them when we ran through the house rules with them.

'Please,' said Sonata politely, 'is possible we put things in bathroom?'

'Oh yes, of course,' I said.

They followed me into our smallish bathroom, wheeling an air-hostess suitcase behind them, and unpacked a shopful of toiletries into piles round the room. Unguents, oils, splashes, gels, waxes, scrubs, powders, hairdryers, tongs, crimpers, straighteners, and the pièce de résistance, an enormous heated box of old-fashioned hair-rollers. Dan obviously don't know what they were and glanced over with panic in his eyes. Our toothbrushes and Jo's set of yellow rubber ducks suddenly looked very tiny next to this invasion.

Back in their boudoir we all drank a vodka toast, but had to keep our voices down for fear of waking the baby. The doorbell rang at about ten fifteen. I was bounding down the stairs wondering who could possibly be calling round so late, and opened the door to find the neat little form of Cheryl standing on the doorstep.

'Didn't want to disturb,' she said, 'but I did see the lights on so I thought I'd chance it.'

'It's lovely to see you, Cheryl. Fancy joining us for a nip of vodka?'

'Ooh no, thank you very much, ta. We're watching a smashing whodunnit on the telly and I popped over in an ad break. Got my slippers on, look. I just wondered if I could get that plate back? The one that had my apricot sponge on?'

'Oh yes, of course, Cheryl, come on in and I'll get it.'

'It's all right, ta, I'll wait on the doorstep. I didn't want to disturb.'

I ran through to the kitchen to get her plate and handed it over to her. She took a step closer to me and whispered, 'We saw a white van parked here today, and a lot of foreign chattering going on.'

'Yes, Cheryl, they're our new Latvian lodgers.'

'Latvian?' said Cheryl, looking horrified. 'Where are they from then?'

'Latvia, Cheryl.'

'Oh dear. I've not heard of there.'

'It's one of the Baltic republics, Cheryl.'

'Baltic? Ooh, I don't like all that spicy Balti food. Frank had that once and got a terrible Delhi belly. Well, I'd best be off. It'll be starting in a mo.'

She was just going through the little gate when she stopped and looked back at me.

'Your pampas grass looks healthy,' she said.

'Oh. Thanks,' I said. 'I didn't know we had one, to be honest.'

'Ours has withered a bit this last year,' said Cheryl, striking the long soft fronds of our pampas. 'You'll have to give me some tips.'

'Righto,' I said, which was the first time I'd ever used that particular word in my life. Our new life in the 'burbs was clearly seeping into my system already. Cheryl winked at me and scuttled off back into the night. Dan and I were going to have to work out a way of creating some distance between ourselves and the inhabitants of number 53.

As soon as I shut the door, the phone rang. It was Pen.

'So how are you, Margot Leadbetter?' she said, guffawing with laughter. 'Been to any WI cake sales yet? And how are the residents' association meetings coming along? Has poor old Mrs Winnet found a solution to the leaves clogging up her driveway?'

I laughed grimly through my nostrils. 'I can't believe we're only twenty minutes from the old flat. It's like another world here,' I said.

'That's London for you, honey. Sorry I haven't been round yet. I'm setting up a big webcast for The Ringworms in New York at the moment. It's going to be massive.'

I hadn't an iota of a clue what she was talking about, but I said 'wow' supportively anyway. 'Well,' I said, 'come as soon as you've finished casting your web, or whatever. Come for the day and we can spy on the neighbours. We're all at it, hiding behind our pampas grasses.'

'Pampas grasses?' asked Pen.

'Yes,' I said.

'How funny,' she said and laughed.

'Why are you laughing?'

'Didn't you see that thing in the papers?'

'Pen, I have a baby. The last paper I read was about two years ago. I still think that Tony Blair's got brown hair.'

'It's just weird that you mentioned pampas grass because it was in all the weekend papers.'

'What?'

'Well, there was a massive survey about sexual mores in Britain today, you know the sort of thing. Well, apparently, if you grow a pampas grass in your front garden it means you're a swinger, and you're advertising it. It's like a code. It started in the 1970s.'

'That's ridiculous.'

'Apparently not. Look out of the window now. Who's got pampas grass in their front garden?'

I craned my neck to look through the little hall window at what could be seen under the streetlights, and relayed my findings to Pen.

'Right. I can see two gardens with pampas at the far end of the road. And up here – well, I'll be blown!'

'There's a good chance of that, with a pampas grass in your front garden,' said Pen dryly.

'Our neighbours Frank and Cheryl have got one in the corner by their gate. It is kind of withered. Cheryl said it was.'

'Well, there you are then. Swingers. Without a doubt.'

'She came round specifically asking me to give her some tips for her pampas, Pen.'

'She saw your pampas and took it as a sign.'

'Oh God.'

'What?' said Pen.

'She stroked my pampas.'

'Uh-oh.'

Sonata and Ruta left the house the next afternoon in full war paint, off to their jobs – Ruta as a waitress and Sonata as a hotel receptionist. I'd explained to them that they were welcome to cook in our kitchen sometimes in the evening, and to be very careful about burning candles in their room. I also stressed the importance of being very very quiet when they came in at night, so as not to wake up the baby. I then showed them a technique I'd worked out for opening and shutting the front door so quietly that it only made the faintest of clicks.

Dan seemed to get on with them well. Ruta spoke excellent German, so if conversation in English got tricky, the two of them could sort it out that way.

'*Tschüs!*' she said to Dan.

'*Tschüs!*' he responded, shutting the front door behind her.

They seemed to take my house rules in good grace and I felt heart-warmed. It was good to know that our new house was being used to its full capacity, and that we'd have some regular cash coming in from the lodgers. Jo was going through a really good patch too, with teeth and bottom areas behaving normally, which was a miracle. Such were my feelings of all-round positivity that I decided I was ready for the Big One. They were in my drawer where I'd left them over a year ago. It was time for my trotters to enter the world of denim once more. Yes, I was going to try on a pair of pre-pregnancy jeans.

I opened the drawer and took them out. It felt weird to hold them in my hand. They felt chilly, as if they'd been transported from far away. I found it hard to believe that my body had once been indelibly linked with them. It was time to re-establish contact. I heard the soundtrack of *Close Encounters* in my head as I circled around them, like a scientist looking at a piece of asteroid that has just landed out of the sky. With a good deal of spleen squeezing and shifting of resources, I managed to crowbar the jeans on over thighs and rump, bar the top two buttons. The look in its essential form was not attractive. But with a longish jumper going down to mid-thigh, it was all pretty acceptable. Almost a year after Jo's birth and I was saying goodbye to those drawstring maternity trousers at last. This was a big moment.

Spurred on by these new feelings of self-worth, I walked downstairs rather stiff-legged to see if Dan would notice anything different about me.

'Notice anything different about me?' I asked him.

He scanned me up and down. 'Hair a bit greyer?' he asked cheerily.

'Cheers, Dan. You really know how to make me feel good.'

'But I love those streaks,' he back-pedalled. 'They make you look distinguished.'

'Go lower,' I hinted.

'You're not grey down there too, are you?'

'No, Dan.'

'No bra on?' he said suggestively.

'Dan, I'm wearing enough corsetry to power Helena Bonham-Carter's career for the next decade.'

'Sorry, they look a bit ... unhoused ... that's all.'

This was rapidly turning into a self-hinder workshop. He was stuck, and shrugged his shoulders.

'Jeans, Dan. I'm wearing normal jeans,' I said and turned on my heel.

'They look great,' he shouted lamely after me.

I was not going to let go of this upbeat mood. I winched myself down into the chair by the phone. I was going to make it my mission this very morning to find a childminder for Judy and myself. I was going to show her what a together, motivated mother I'd become, thanks to these jeans.

Since Minnie's birthday party I'd been completely out of touch with the mums' group – I was so busy moving house it was quite a relief not be worrying about whether I was cutting it on the mothers' circuit. Judy had sent a nice house-moving card drawn by her son in one of his rare moments of release from the Naughty Nook. It was a very sweet picture of a wobbly house with some cotton wool smoke coming out of the chimney. The hand of Judy was clearly visible in the frighteningly neat duck-pond made from blue glitter.

I'd done some research into childminders in the area with no real result. Some were already fully booked and couldn't take on any more kids, and others didn't sound very inspiring. There was one I still hadn't phoned who'd been very highly recommended by somebody at Playhut. She was new to the area but had years of childminding experience, and apparently lived in a nice house with a garden. Her name was Marcia, and I decided to give her a ring. She sounded very nice on the phone, very calm and sensible. The fact that she didn't speak in a high-pitched squeak was an immediate plus. It seemed to be the norm among nursery workers. I made an appointment to go and see her the very next day.

All in all it had been a very positive Tuesday, and Dan and I put Jo to bed feeling that parenthood was great.

'Actually, Dan, can *you* put Jo into her cot?' I asked.

'Sure, Mel. You OK? You sound kind of breathless.'

'I'm fine. I don't think I can lower her … in these jeans.'

He took Jo from me, leaving my hands free to grapple with the buttons on the jeans, leaving them gaping appallingly but blissfully comfortable.

Later that night, Dan and I were both reading in bed. Dan was immersed in a cricketing book about spin bowlers, and I was ploughing through a biography of David Essex. I'd been reading this book for the last two years and I was damned if I was going to leave it half finished. Not exactly *War and Peace*, I know, but everyone said I would never read a book till Jo was sixteen, and I was determined to prove them wrong.

'Oh, I bumped into Frank this evening,' said Dan.

'Oh yes,' I said, Frank's pampas springing immediately to mind, 'and what did he have to say?'

'He wondered if we wanted to go round for a drink some time soon.'

I let my book drop, so that David's face nestled into my bosoms. 'What, just the four of us?'

'I think so.'

'Nobody else invited?'

'I don't think so.'

'I thought as much.'

'What?'

'Dan,' I said, looking at him seriously, 'Frank and Cheryl are swingers. They're only interested in us as potential sexual partners.'

Dan practically spat out his Horlicks.

'Where the hell did you get that from?'

'Pen,' I said, as if that was all the authority needed.

'Pen? Now why doesn't that surprise me?'

'It's been in the news recently. Apparently if you have a pampas grass growing in your garden, it's a kind of coded message that you're a swinger. And if you make contact with another pampas-owner, then that's basically asking them if they're up for a bit of … swingerage. That's why they've invited us, Dan. They've taken our pampas as a sign.'

'That's ridiculous,' he said, laughing, 'and I suppose they think we've moved into this particular house because there's a pampas in the garden?'

'Probably,' I said, deadly earnest.

'That's ludicrous,' said Dan. 'I can understand moving to a house because the schools are good in the area, or the original features are pretty, but because of a pampas grass? Come on, Mel, wakey-wakey.'

This was the phrase in Dan's lexicon that annoyed me the most.

'Look. We've moved to a very pampassy area. I've noticed a lot of them around. Maybe this is a very sexually permissive part of town and we just don't know it yet.'

'Oh yeah,' said Dan, 'old man and his dog and lady with zimmer frame. Everyone's at it round here. It's like Studio 54. Lock up your daughters.'

'Well, I think Frank and Cheryl are sinister,' I said, starting to lose my rag.

'I think they're rather sweet.'

'They're fascists, Dan,' I said loudly.

'OK, I'll admit that they're on the rightish side of the political spectrum, but I think we should show willing and at least have a drink with them.'

'Which is probably what Neville Chamberlain agreed to do with Hitler in 1938, and look how that turned out,' I snapped, rolling over so that my back was turned to my husband. I switched my bedside light off defiantly. Actually, it was quite useful to end the evening off with a bicker – it was the perfect way to quash any sexual advances.

In the darkness, several moments later, I could hear Dan rustling around and sighing. I pretended to be asleep.

I was in the middle of a very exciting dream where I was the head of an all-girl dance troupe not unlike Pan's People. I think my name was Scarlett, which I was pleased about. We were all dancing around a lamp-post to motivational music in tight, camel-hoof-hugging jeans. But although they were denim, they felt non-existent, they were so comfortable and stretchy. And as our dancing became more frenetic and gyratory, the jeans started to stretch away from our bodies in big strands of denim-coloured chewing-gum. As I pulled long strings of semi-liquid jeans away from my body and attached some to the lamp-post, some to a wall, I felt liberated and alluring. But something was wrong. The jeans were starting to show gaping holes. I was starting to fall out of step with Carol, Tiger, Bee-Bee and the rest of the girls. I was exhausted, clod-hopping around like an old shire horse in a yard. My feet were hitting the ground louder and louder, clip-clop, clatter clatter, clip-clop, clatter clatter. The noise was endless. The magic jeans were starting to fall away from my body completely. Clip-clop, clatter clatter. The noise was getting nearer and nearer, until I woke up with a start and took my ear-plugs out.

I was relieved to see that my familiar tartan pyjamas were in place and that I wasn't wearing liquid denim. But I could still hear a clip-clop clatter clatter in the corridor. I heard the bedroom door open across the landing and the sound of a light being switched on, and remembered that we had lodgers, and that one of them was home from work. Damn. Why hadn't she taken her shoes off in the hall? Why did they wear those stupid stilettos anyway? You couldn't do silver service in those, surely.

I heard her moving about her room, and my whole body was braced as I waited for Jo to wake up. I strained my ears to hear. Nothing. Dan was snoring a bit, but Jo was silent. My jaws were clenched in anticipation. I heard the light switch being turned off again, the creak of a bed, and then quiet. Thank goodness. Still nothing from Jo's room. I inserted my ear-plugs once again and fell into an insubstantial sleep. Dan's snoring went up a notch and I had to jab him hard in the side. I rolled over, tried to push the ear-plugs further down into my canals. They didn't seem to be working so well any more. I had just drifted into sleep again when I heard the front door shut with a bang. That was it. I was out of the bed and pacing round. I pulled the ear-plugs out, threw them across our bedroom and stood in the darkness with my hands on my hips. This was worse than having a newborn baby in the house. At least there's some point to waking up in the night if you have a helpless mouth to feed, unpleasant though it is. But this, this was utterly pointless. What did these ridiculous people want me to do – make them a hot drink, tuck them up and sing them a bloody lullaby?

To cap it all I heard them whispering and giggling as I pressed my ear up to their door. And then there was a yelp from Jo's room. I waited in the corridor, frozen with stress. Please please please don't wake up. There was a snuffle and then nothing. I crept back into my bed and lay there awake for the next hour worrying about my ear-plugs and drafting a letter of complaint to the manufacturer in my mind. This did the trick and I drifted off once again.

The next morning Jo was up at her usual 6.30 a.m. I dragged

myself downstairs with her, and as we passed the lodgers' door, I felt like banging on it to wake them up. My eyeballs felt sandy and my teeth felt like somebody had stuck fake-fur on them in the night. Dan came down at eight looking like a cosy badger emerging from his den.

He yawned at the kettle and scratched his hair for an unfeasibly long time.

'Sleep well?' I asked pointedly.

'Mmmmm,' he said, and smacked his lips.

'Glad someone did,' I snapped.

'Was Jo up?'

'Didn't you hear the Riverdance routine going down the corridor at God knows what time this morning?'

'I slept so soundly,' said Dan and yawned once again.

I would need to have extremely stiff words with the Latvians. I had a speech prepared in my head, and waited for them to come downstairs. Midday passed, then one o'clock, still no sign of them. At ten to three I heard them pottering round in the bathroom, but had to leave the house to go and see Marcia the childminder. I walked quickly past Frank and Cheryl's house. I didn't want them to spot me and collar me with any more pampas chat.

Marcia lived a ten-minute walk away in a friendly house filled with toys and games. She was in her forties, with two grown-up children who were both away at college. She had dark bobbed hair that was starting to show threads of grey, but she was dressed effortlessly in combats and a sweatshirt. She was looking after two children, a brother and sister, who seemed very happy with her, running round playing and squealing. Vicky, the sister, introduced herself and her little brother Nathan, who was one. Jo liked it there straight away and was soon giggling and playing on the floor, barely noticing that I was there at all. Marcia looked on calmly, and intervened occasionally when required. We stayed with her for an hour while Jo played and I drank peppermint tea. Marcia was so mellow, it was a relief to be in her company after the over-intense smothering mothering I'd encountered in the mums' group.

'I like cooking,' said Marcia, 'and I try to get the kids onto normal adult food with proper flavours. I found with my kids that it was the best way to get them eating properly.'

How sensible. No mash-potato building sites then; what a relief.

'I don't go overboard with playing either,' she said. 'If they need me to help then obviously I will, but I don't like to get in their faces and over-organize their games. It's much better for them to learn to play by themselves.'

The woman was fast turning into a guru. I'd be lighting candles at her feet soon. She asked loads and loads of questions about Jo, and was really natural with her. I explained to Marcia that I was looking for someone to look after Jo on a slightly ad-hoc basis, when I needed time for work, or an audition, if that likelihood were ever to arise again this century. I walked home on spring-loaded shoes, my grumps with the Latvians all but forgotten. I phoned Judy on the way to tell her the good news.

'I think I've found a childminder, Judy, and she's very happy to take on two more. She's wonderful.'

'Great,' said Judy. I detected a note of slight annoyance in her voice, possibly because she hadn't been involved in its instigation. I was secretly pleased and couldn't disguise the smugness in my own voice.

'Hang on a sec, Judy. Let me give you her number,' I said.

'OK. Then I can go and visit this wonderful Marcia for myself.'

I came back home to find Dan and Ruta in the kitchen. It was four thirty and Ruta was still in a pair of satiny pyjamas, drinking something out of my mug.

'*Ich bin noch im Pyjama und es ist schon Nachmittag.*'

'*Mensch, das wäre mein Traum, den ganzen Tag im Pyjama rumschlurfen,*' replied Dan.

'Hi there, Ruta,' I said with forced jollity. 'Sleep well?'

'Bed is very very very nice,' she said, lifting one be-bunioned foot up and crossing the other leg with it. She then started to pick persistently at one of her toes, pulling at a little bit of skin round the nail. I had to turn away.

'*Ich trinke gerade meine zehnte Tasse Tee. Ich bin ein echter Engländer!*' said Dan, sounding like something out of a war film. It was obviously hilarious because Ruta creased up into giggles.

'Care to share the joke, you two?' I snapped.

'We were laughing about the English. Ruta speaks brilliant German, you know.'

'German is better than my English,' she said and then said something very long and complicated to Dan in German.

'Well, as the only non-German speaker in the room, I'm going to stick to English, if that's OK? Ruta, I'm afraid you and Sonata will have to be a hell of a lot quieter when you come in after work. You were clattering up those stairs and I heard everything.'

'Excuse me?' said Ruta.

Dan translated into German, and a look of horror came over Ruta's face.

'Sorry. Sorry, very sorry. Tonight will be very very silent.'

'Good,' I said.

'The girls are going to babysit for us tomorrow night,' said Dan. 'They've both got the night off.'

'Fantastic,' I said sheepishly, suddenly feeling terrible for my grumpy outburst.

Judy phoned later that day. She'd been to visit Marcia. Typical Judy. She must have been straight round the moment we'd got off the phone.

'Yes. She seems really competent,' said Judy a tad begrudgingly, 'but I'm not sure if her toys for pre-toddlers are quite developmental enough. I'd like to see a few more shape-sorters and hand/eye-coordination games in there, but it's something I'll talk to her about. I'm going to leave Minnie with her two mornings a week so I can work on the Christmas Fair collection.'

It had been a long time since the subject of the Christmas Fair had reared its head. She was making it sound like a Stella McCartney catwalk show, for Pete's sake.

'Great,' I said, trying to steer the conversation away. 'Well, I'm going to leave Jo at Marcia's for a trial run while I go and see my agent next week.'

'Are you still up for helping on my stall?' asked Judy.

'At the Christmas Fair?' I said.

'Yes,' she said.

I was on the verge of saying no, I didn't want to, and that I thought her collection of fishermen's clothes should be thrown into the Atlantic to join the depleted cod population. But memories of that night when she saved Jo's life came flooding back again, and I said, 'Of course. I'd love to.'

'Great. I'll fill you in on exactly what needs to be done nearer the time.'

I went to bed early, determined to make up for the previous night's disturbances. The plugs were wedged down the ears, all was looking good. I went to bed with a mantra going round my head: I will not be disturbed. I will not be disturbed.

And then at some dark ungodly hour I sat bolt upright in the bed again. The clock said 2 a.m. I had heard the faintest merest whiff of a click from the front door, and could now hear the most silent of feet padding almost noiselessly up the corridor and into the bedroom over the landing. Everything was carried out nearly noiselessly. It was just me. Oh damn, this was turning into a Princess-and-the-Pea nightmare. I lay in bed rigid and awake for the next three hours. I had a twenty-minute doze before Jo woke up, ready to start her day.

The lodgers had been with us for two weeks now, and Dan and Ruta were having yet another very jolly conversation in German at the kitchen table. This was a regular occurrence these days. As the two of them rabbited on about God knows what, I clattered around and cooked Jo's lunch as loudly as possible. Ruta was still in her pyjamas, but I detected a hint of makeup about her. I wondered if she'd applied it in Dan's honour. She'd clearly said something hilarious because Dan practically doubled up with laughter. I hadn't seen Dan laugh like that in ages. Certainly not since the birth of the baby.

He wiped his eyes, caught me staring at him impassively and then looked sheepish.

'Ruta used to work in Cologne. She knows a lot of the same places I do. We were just talking about a bar. It's a well-known pick-up joint.'

'Really?' I said sourly. 'Well, maybe you'd like to pick yourselves up out of the kitchen. I've got work to do in here.'

Ruta shuffled out of the room quickly, and Dan came over to me and tried to put his arm round me.

'No, Dan,' I said, prodding him in the chest with a whisk, 'just keep away from me and the baby.'

'Mel. What the hell's going on? You were really rude to poor Ruta just then.'

'Oh Ruta this, Ruta that.'

'What is the matter?'

'I've had two weeks of sleepless nights, Dan.'

'Well, there's no need to go off on one at poor Ruta.' That was the second time he'd referred to her as 'poor Ruta'. 'I'm off to the shed. See you later. Don't forget we've got drinks round at Frank and Cheryl's tonight.'

'Oh, please don't make me go.'

'It's only a drink.'

'You won't be saying that when we wake up in their house tomorrow morning tied to their bed and dressed up as nurses and doctors. Frank's probably a dab hand at drink-spiking. I'm going to watch him like a hawk.'

Dan gave me a worried look and shook his head as he left the room. I saw a reflection in the kitchen cupboard. It was a woman I didn't recognize. She had strange hollowed-out eyes and was brandishing some sort of weapon. Then I realized it was me.

I'd have to get a firm grip on myself.

Chapter Eleven

Which is exactly what Frank did to me that evening. He gripped my hand so tightly I thought it was going to come away at the wrist.

''Ello, 'ello, 'ello!' he said with the classic policeman's knee-bending action.

Dan laughed politely but I couldn't find it in me to do so. My mood was still icy, and it had worsened when I'd discovered Dan and Ruta having a cigarette together outside in the garden just before we were leaving to go round to Frank and Cheryl's. Dan had all but given up smoking when Jo was born, and I was livid to catch him chuffing away with this new cohort of his. I gave Ruta a filthy look, which I then had to change into a weird sort of friendly grimace as I left her and Sonata babysitting Jo.

Frank ushered us with big leathery hands into number 53, which was positively alive with varying patterns of thick, shag-pile carpet. Framed photos filled the hall – Frank and a group of male friends with golf caddies, Cheryl visiting Windsor Castle, Frank and Cheryl together holding oversized tankards at a beer festival. I scrutinized several of them intensely for any telltale signs of the Pampas Code. Were there any other couples featured in the pictures? Were any of them wearing kaftans? Was there any sign of post-coitus glaze in Frank and Cheryl's eyes? Frank caught me analyzing a heavy brass-framed picture.

'Me and my Sealed Knot buddies,' he said proudly.

'They're always in each other's pockets,' said Cheryl, who glided noiselessly down the stairs in a cerise velveteen tracksuit with matching soft house mules.

'Ah right,' I said uncertainly. I'd heard of these Sealed Knot societies but hadn't the faintest idea what they did. Something creepy and Masonic, no doubt.

'Now who's for sherry and who's for something stronger?' announced Frank, showing us into their pristine front room, which was arranged entirely round an enormous television set. Frank and Cheryl had matching leather armchairs of an unfortunate colour – I was reminded of cats' diarrhoea – the kind that swing back at the touch of a lever, forcing your whole body to extend. Almost as if the chair is inviting someone to leap on top of you.

'Admiring my chair, dear?' said Cheryl, suddenly very close by my side. 'Have a go if you like: it's very comfy being on your back.'

A vision of Cheryl's cerise velveteen figure launching herself on top of me, prone and helpless in the chair, suddenly came to mind.

'Er … no thanks, Cheryl,' I stammered. 'I'll sit on the sofa here, thanks.'

I didn't want to commit myself entirely to its leatherette confines, so I sat myself down rather primly on its edge. It squeaked rather suggestively as my bottom made contact, prompting Cheryl to say 'Whoopsie pardon!' and then put her hand on my knee.

Everyone sat down, and I had the time to glance around the room. My eye landed on a large bowl in the centre of the smoked-glass coffee table. In it was a set of keys. This was all the evidence I needed.

'There's an ashtray there. Do you smoke, Dan?' asked Frank.

'I'm fine, thanks, Frank,' said Dan.

'Dan only smokes with attractive women in the garden,' I said cuttingly.

'In which case my garden or yours, Dan?' said Frank, winking. 'I'll have to take it up again, won't I?' and he and Cheryl roared with laughter.

'Sherry, Mel?' said Frank, collecting himself.

'No way,' I said quickly.

Dan shot me a look.

'I mean, no thanks. No alcohol. Something soft. Please.'

Frank moved over to a drinks trolley and, with his back to me, started to open up a can of something. What was he doing exactly? Did that large signet ring of his have a secret flap with powder hidden beneath it? Was he right this moment tipping in a sleeping draught into my drink?

'I'll pour it out, Frank,' I said quickly.

Cheryl looked at me, bemused.

'I'd like to. I get to do it so rarely these days,' I said, searching for some kind of explanation, 'what with being a mother.'

'OK, love,' said Frank, handing me the can of bitter lemon and the glass. All eyes were now on me. I started to pour the drink.

'Ah. That's great. Just like the old days. I love pouring,' I said and coughed.

Dan looked at me, and I tried to manoeuvre his eyes down to the bowl with the keys inside. He looked at me and mouthed 'What?'

I was awe-struck at how dense men could be sometimes.

I mouthed back the word 'keys' to him, but was interrupted by Cheryl, who gave us both a rather suspicious look.

'How's the drink, Mel?' said Frank, twisting his ring round.

'Great. Just the right amount of bitterness and lemon-ness.'

'Not spiked with anything,' Frank said mischievously.

'Except Rohypnol,' I said over-loudly and then laughed like a hyena for way too long.

There was a silence during which Cheryl folded her little house mules one on top of the other.

'Are you all right, Mel? I haven't known you long, but you look a bit peaky to me,' she said, gently laying a hand on mine on the sofa.

'No, Cheryl, I'm fine,' I answered, pulling my hand out from underneath hers. 'Fine, yes. Yes, absolutely fine.'

'And here you go, young man,' said Frank, handing Dan the most enormous crystal glass of whisky I'd ever seen, the sort you see in James Bond films.

'Spiked with pure Scottish peat, that one!' laughed Frank.

'Bring it on,' said Dan.

'That'll put lead in your pencil,' said Frank, winking at Dan.

I shot Dan a warning look. If Dan were to pass out on whisky, leaving me pinned in the reclining leather chair for Cheryl and/or Frank to straddle, we'd be toast.

'So,' said Dan, glugging back some whisky, 'how long have you two lived here, then?'

'Forever and a day,' laughed Frank, and Cheryl joined in too.

'The people who used to live in our house,' I enquired breezily, 'did you get it on with them … I mean, get on with them?'

I felt my cheeks flush at my mistake, and Dan stared into his whisky tumbler.

'Wendy and John were very good neighbours. We were quite intimate with them, weren't we, Frank?'

'Yes, we were.'

'They gave us that bowl, actually,' said Cheryl.

All four pairs of eyes in the room were forced to focus on the bowl in the centre of the room, with its bunch of keys nestling inside.

'Nice bowl,' I said, not daring to look at anyone, and trying to work out where the nearest available exit was in the room. The window. I'd leap through the window if any unexpected moves were made in our direction.

'We tend to leave our keys in it, I couldn't tell you why,' said Frank.

Yeah right, I thought to myself. I think we all know exactly why, you pervy creep.

'So what do you drive?' said Frank to Dan.

OK, I could see where he was going with this line of chat. He was cunningly steering the conversation round to the subject of car keys, before making his scheduled pounce. I was wise to his game.

'Our car is actually quite rare,' I said.

'Really?' said Frank, turning to me.

'It is a Volvo. And it looks like a normal one, but actually it's not,' I said. 'It's keyless.'

There was a silence. Dan was analyzing a selection of fireside accessories very carefully.

'Keyless?' repeated Frank.

'Yes. It was a technique that Volvo started to develop in the 1980s but they didn't pursue into the 1990s. Keyless cars. They turn on with a switch-thing.'

'Extraordinary,' said Frank. 'You'll have to show me that in the light of day, young man. Still, I suppose it's useful. Means you don't have to go round carrying a big bunch of keys.'

'No, we certainly don't have any keys to put in your bowl,' I said hurriedly.

'I'm always losing my keys,' said Cheryl, warming to the whole subject. 'Always leaving them at people's houses ...'

'Right, well, it's been lovely, but I think Dan and I should be getting home,' I said, starting to prize bottom away from sofa. 'The babysitters are on trial and I think we should go back and—'

'You can't go. Dan's barely sipped his malt,' said Frank, alarmed.

'It's all right, Mel,' said Dan. 'Jo'll be fine.'

I sat down again with an ignominious squeak, and sipped at my bitter lemon. I was sure there was something fishy about the taste of it, and looked at a brass wagon-wheel on the far wall to check that I wasn't seeing double.

I breathed deeply. I was obviously overtired and had blown this whole situation way out of proportion. Of course Frank and Cheryl weren't swingers. They were a childless, suburban, well-meaning couple who would provide us with years of helpful neighbourliness, lending us shears, giving us eggs when we ran out, dispensing the odd tip about compost and tutting cheerfully when our youthful music got a bit too loud of a Saturday night.

'So, Dan and Mel,' said Frank, as if he were the landlord of a country pub, standing with legs astride in front of a roaring fire. 'Do you swing?'

The bitter-lemon glass fell from my hands. Dan's bottom jaw fell down to his chest, and Frank and Cheryl continued to smile like Cheshire cats. 'Come on, Dan,' I said with a voice that had gone falsetto. 'We're leaving.'

'OK,' mumbled Dan.

'What?' said Frank jovially. 'What's the matter with you two? You're as jumpy as a pair of bunnies tonight, aren't you? I'll have to get you out on the golf course, won't I, to try and calm the pair of you down.'

And Frank reached behind him and took a golf club out of a brass umbrella stand. I thought for a terrible moment that he was about to cosh Dan over the head with it and then make his move.

'That's why I asked you,' he said, swinging the golf club with largesse above his head, 'do you swing?'

Two hours later I was in our front garden, frantically pulling at the pampas grass with my bare hands. Dan was at my side, holding a spade.

'This is totally unnecessary, Mel,' he whispered. 'We made utter twats of ourselves at Frank and Cheryl's. The man's a golfer, not a sex addict.'

'I'm still not taking any chances,' I whispered back, and grabbed the spade from him. 'This disgusting sex-pampas is coming out, roots and all.'

An upper curtain twitched at number 53. Dan and I looked up and caught Cheryl moving away from her bedroom window.

'You need some sleep,' said Dan, shaking his head slowly and watching me scrabble at the roots of the pampas like a woman possessed. 'And you need a good seeing to,' he added.

'What?' I said, standing up to face him.

'You're completely obsessed with sex,' said Dan, 'and you're totally on edge. I think you need a good rogering.'

I had half a mind to slap him right across the chops.

'How dare you?' I shouted. 'You have no idea what it feels like to give birth, do you? No bloody idea whatsoever. Imagine, Dan, a flume in a swimming pool, the sort that kids slide down. Imagine that flume with a large juggernaut squeezing down it, Dan. That's what it feels like. And frankly I don't want anything near my flume again for a long time.'

'It's been months,' said Dan quietly, 'and it's not exactly a large juggernaut that's on offer here. More of a small Renault 4 really.'

'It's all sex with you, isn't it, Dan? Sex sex sex. Sex this, sex that. We have a child, Dan. We can't just lounge around in bed all the time.'

'It won't take very long,' said Dan forlornly.

'Yes, it'd be great to smother each other with food and spend six hours licking it off, but you know what? I haven't got six hours, and I'm smothered with food half the time anyway – the stuff that gets thrown at me by my daughter!'

And with that I turned on my heel and stalked into the house, leaving Dan and the remains of a very limp pampas grass behind me.

It was late November and I felt it right down into my boots. I felt like a mirror held up to the bleak autumnal weather. My hair was its piles of leaves, scattered every which way. My skin was its pallid cold skies, damp and lifeless, and my body was its exhausted earth, full of dead summer flowers and lifeless bulbs. I had permanent rings under my eyes, like an old terrier.

The Latvians had got the front-door-opening technique down to a tee and now gained entry into the house in the wee hours with a click no louder than a box of Tic-Tacs being opened and shut. This made no difference to my sleeping, sadly. I heard the tiniest whisper, the merest pad of stockinged foot on floor, the smallest squeak of a hinge. They paid their rent on time, they were lovely with Jo, but Ruta and Dan's obvious growing closeness annoyed the hell out of me. She'd bought him a couple of German books, and I was gutted to see that he'd given her a German film on video in return. He never bought me presents like that for no reason. The two of them continued to smoke fags in the garden, and I was getting to the point where I was contemplating asking the girls to leave, even though they brought much-needed cash into the house. I was very short with Ruta whenever we spoke, and I got pleasure out of treating her sister with much more obvious friendliness and largesse. I started to notice that I hummed loudly round Ruta, just like my mother did when she was brooding.

She paid an unexpected call at the end of the month.

'Oh dear, you do look tired,' was her opening comment as she came into the hall.

'Mum, I don't believe it!' was mine.

'What, dear?' she said, taking off a rather trendy-looking new suede jacket with a belt round the middle.

'You're wearing trousers tucked into high-heeled boots.'

They weren't quite Latvian in their scale and height, but there was quite a lot of elevation there, and my mum had teamed them with some rather natty grey tweed trousers and a roll-neck.

'Yes. Nancy and I went on a rather naughty shopping trip – don't mention it to your father. We went to one of those dreadful places: they call it a "designer outlet". Have you ever been to one?'

'No,' I said flatly.

'Well, Nancy got me trying on a whole array of things – some of it simply awful, but some really super stuff too. I bought three pairs of shoes, can you imagine, dear? I spent two thousand pounds – don't tell your father. Oh, and I got a sweet pink furry jerkin, really cosy.'

I was speechless. And then my mother did something I've never seen her do before, a sort of boogie right there in the hall. It quite took my breath away. It only lasted seconds but it was terrifying. She twisted the balls of her feet round and pumped her arms in a chicken-wings manoeuvre. Maybe she'd had a tattoo done too?

'I rather love November,' she said excitedly. 'It's so full of possibility, isn't it? The death of one year and, hey presto, we're into another.'

I was starting to wonder whether my mother was on drugs.

'Now where's my beautiful granddaughter? I've bought her a mini poncho and cowgirl boots which I'm simply dying to put on her!'

'She's having a sleep,' I told her, offering her a chair, which she refused with a wave of her hand.

'Your father and I are thinking we may just go away for a few months and see a bit of the world. I know, it's amazing – your father who baulks at a trip to the supermarket on the ring road.'

'Wow,' I said, sloping over to the kettle in my Garfield slippers.

'One of your father's pensions has come through, and you know what? We're thinking we might just enjoy ourselves a bit. We're in the autumn of our lives, and it's time to relish the fruits!'

This was turning into a thoroughly depressing morning.

'Is that the green fleece you used to wear during the sixth form?' my mother asked me.

'Yes, Mum, it is.'

'Oh, darling.'

'I don't need your pity, Mum.'

'No, you need somebody to coordinate your wardrobe. Shall I send Nancy?' she said, rummaging around in her new Burberry handbag.

I fished around the shelf for some teabags. I was too depressed to even contemplate that somebody Mum had met through her church flower-arranging rota could hold the key to my sartorial rebirth.

Mum was checking her eyes in a little powder compact. 'Nancy's going to take your father out too, can you believe it? Try and get him out of that dreadful old game-keeper's jacket.' She finally sat down and looked around her. 'Well, it all looks very lived in, I must say,' she said, surveying the kitchen. She had the demeanour of a Surrey tourist arriving at the mud hut of a distant tribesman – smiling, polite, but a bit snooty.

The floor was covered in baby toys and the remains of Jo's breakfast; every available surface was strewn with ingredients of our three previous meals. A pile of flour with some half-finished fish-cakes. A saucepan of beans with cans scattered round the cooker, a whole area by the sink cluttered with shoe-cleaning equipment, where Dan had suddenly decided to polish every single item of footwear in the house. And half an attempt at sweeping, with broom and big pile of dirt in the centre of the floor next to an expectant dustpan, waiting for somebody to magically finish it. Everything was half cocked, half eaten, half digested. Here was my mum, suddenly deciding to live life to the full, and here was me, living this sort of half-life. I sat down too and rubbed at my eyeballs, wishing that this low-level itchy tiredness would just disappear. My mum scanned me up and down.

'Don't worry, darling. It's only like this for another twenty years.'

'Thanks, Mum,' I said wanly.

Still, there was a lot to be thankful for – my mother's evangelical belief in the power of Nancy seemed to have diverted her attention away from nagging me. In normal circumstances she'd have had the Marigolds on by now, bossing and tutting around the place. She seemed perfectly happy today, admiring her booted foot, which was up on a chair.

'And how are you settling in with your boarders?'

Mum refused to refer to them as 'lodgers'. She thought the phrase very non-U and insalubrious.

'Mmmm,' I said non-committally.

'What's *mmm* when it's at home?' Mum replied.

'Oh nothing. One of them seems to have developed rather a close friendship with my husband, that's all.'

A pause.

'Well, are you surprised?'

'Mum! I was looking for some support here.'

'If you will go around dressed like a drab day out then you've only yourself to blame. I'm going to ask Nancy to call you tomorrow.'

At that moment the kitchen door opened, and in it stood Ruta and Sonata, looking in rather shyly. Both were in pistachio-coloured satin pyjamas. Their faces were un-made-up and spotty, and their bare feet revealed nails of the chipped-scarlet variety. Sonata was carrying a package of something bloody in a white butcher's bag. My mother looked them up and down very sharply, turned to me and said, 'Which one, dear? They both look rather shop-soiled to me ...'

'This is my mum,' I practically shouted, to prevent her from saying anything else. Sadly it was not to be.

'Hello. I expect you're off out to work, aren't you, girls?' Then she added haughtily, 'And what is it that you do?'

'We work in the night,' said Ruta.

'Oh dear,' said Mum, and then looking at me said, 'Yes. You'd better watch your back.'

'They work in a hotel and restaurant, Mum,' I said firmly.

'Yes, they all say that,' was her tart reply.

There was a cringe-making silence.

'Please,' said Ruta, 'my sister has brought food.'

'Is OK to cook?' said Sonata in her soft voice.

My mother looked at me with one eyebrow arched. She clearly thoroughly disapproved of our ménage.

'Of course. Go ahead,' I said.

'Give them an inch,' said my mother.

They started to clatter around the kitchen, searching for the right implements and tools, pulling out things they clearly weren't going to need such as a bread-maker and little soufflé ramekins. They seemed to take up an awful lot of space for such skinny people. My mum and I ended up slowly edging our chairs back till we were both practically touching the walls.

'Childminding lady working out all right?' shouted Mum across the room.

'Brilliant,' I shouted back. 'Jo adores her. She's a godsend. I actually made it to a meeting and an audition last week.'

'Is she qualified, dear? Is she a Norland nanny or something proper like that?'

Oh dear, I knew the good vibes couldn't last for long. My mother had been looking for an excuse to bring up the whole issue of childcare, something of which she thoroughly disapproved. Unless a baby was cared for by an ancient nanny-figure who'd been in the family for generations, it had to be mother and mother alone looking after the little one. I couldn't bear to explain to her that modern childminders were usually just mums themselves who needed a bit of extra cash. I could tell she was revving up for one of her speeches.

'You see, when we were growing up at Little Goring,' she started, 'Nanny Dora was just part of the furniture. Like a marvellous dependable old footstool!'

Mum shouted all of this information from across the room while the Latvians dismantled my food mixer.

'Nanny Dora was nearly eighty when she looked after me. Wonderful woman,' she barked. Mum had a tendency to pronounce the word 'nanny' something like 'nyeh-nyeh' which always made me chuckle. I was determined to cheer myself up and get her to say it again.

'Who was Dora again, Mum?'

'Our nyeh-nyeh.'

I could feel laughter beginning to well up.

'Sorry?'

'Our nyeh-nyeh!' she screeched.

There, the day was looking up already.

'Such a shame that she died,' continued Mum. 'The wisteria just couldn't break her fall,' she shouted wistfully, which struck me as rather a feat.

I left a respectful pause, then asked, 'What did you call her again?'

'Who, Nyeh-nyeh Dora?' bellowed my mum.

'Yes, her!' I shouted with glee.

'Why, we called her Nyeh-nyeh Dora, you silly girl.'

'Oh yes, four-nil!' I shouted with delight, punching the air.

'Are your hormones quite all right?' asked my mother, looking at me blankly.

I couldn't reply, because the kitchen seemed to be filled with what can only be described as a wall of smell. It wasn't pleasant, and brought to mind offal. Both Latvians were hunched over a wok and were frying the life out of something. There was a heady cloud of soya sauce and burning blood. My mother reached into her Burberry for a hanky, I felt the need to stand up and hold my temples and Jo started to bellow, roused from her slumbers by these malodorous nymphs.

'Good God,' were my mother's words as she piled out of the kitchen and into her new suede jacket. 'I'll telephone soon, darling. Kiss Littly for me,' and she was gone.

I covered my mouth with my hand so as not to breathe in the stink, and plunged into the living room to rescue Jo. Dan poked his head round the back door.

'Blimey! Is that the Latvian national dish you're cooking there?'

Ruta turned to him and gave him a simpering smile. 'Hi, Dan.'

It annoyed me the way she called him Dan. I know it was his name, it was just the way she used it in such an offhand, intimate way somehow, as if it were her own private name for him.

'A really big subtitling job's come through!' announced Dan to the group.

'Congratulations, Dan,' said Ruta. The bitch was in there like a flash. 'You – how do you say? In German it's *verdienen*.'

'Deserve,' said Dan, smiling rather coquettishly at her.

'You deserve this. I know how you wanted big job.'

How many bloody cigarettes were these two smoking together? Enough for my husband to tell this Latvian witch his life story, by the sounds of it.

'That's great, darling,' I said pointedly in Ruta's direction. 'Will you fill me in later? When we're alone?'

'Sure. It's a bit different from the stuff that I normally do.'

'I'd better go. I'm dropping Jo off at Marcia's. I'm going into town to do a voice-test for an advert.'

'Good luck,' said Dan.

'Thank you, sweetheart,' and I gave Dan a lingering kiss on the lips right in front of Ruta. I was just leaving the kitchen when I turned and said to them coldly, 'Clean the kitchen after you, please.'

I marched along the street with the buggy, turning over the facts in my head. Dan and Ruta had the German thing in common, that was clear. They went out into the garden of an evening for a cigarette and that seemed to be that. Yet their relationship had clearly progressed to a more intimate level. The way she called him 'Dan'. The way she turned to look at him to congratulate him on his job. My womanly wiles were telling me that we had reached Amber Alert. I would have to keep eyes and ears fully open from now on. I stopped the buggy. A thought had suddenly occurred to me. Dan had taken to sleeping on the sofa sometimes. His snoring was starting to get to me, and I was finding it nigh-on impossible to sleep anyway. Was there just a possibility that the two of them were sharing a little late-night rendezvous downstairs when everyone else was asleep? I laughed out loud. It was absurd to be having these thoughts. I was chronically overtired – five weeks of insomnia brought on by having strangers in the house were starting to take their toll. I was imagining stuff. My Dan wouldn't do anything like that. This was the man who had gallantly offered me his cupped hands to be sick into at a Gary Numan gig. This is the man who'd gone and punched one of my French lecturers when his lecturing got lecherous. This was the man whose eyes had filled with tears at the altar when he saw me walk down the aisle on my dad's arm. I smiled to myself and carried on walking.

Then I stopped. Hang on a minute. This was also the man with whom I was having a platonic relationship at the moment.

Jo was delighted to see Marcia, and said her favourite word, 'Haddock! Haddock!', which made Marcia crease with laughter.

My grim mood lifted almost immediately, and I sighed and went inside. Marcia's little charges Vicky and Nathan were there too, and Jo was instantly absorbed into the gang. It was great to see her with her pals, gaining independence and enjoying herself. Marcia was a godsend. There she was, in a lovely fringed Indian skirt with her grey hair all swept back into a big leather clip, her gentle grey eyes smiling at the corners.

'She'll be walking any day now,' she said proudly.

'I know.' I smiled.

'Would you mind hanging on a tick, Mel?' she asked. 'I've just got to go to the loo. Would you mind sitting with the kids?'

'Of course, Marcia,' I said, delighted to watch them all playing. 'Take your time.'

I sat down in her charcoal-coloured sofa and felt immediately relaxed. Everything about her was tasteful and inviting – the shelves were filled with books about spiritual journeys and the lives of sculptors. There was a chessboard on a low Moroccan table and wonderful paintings on every wall – probably the work of artist friends. The kids were all playing on her lovely Persian rug with a set of African-looking wooden bowls and spoons. It was such a relief to be out of the Angie's Action atmosphere with its overhyped jollity and high-pitched voices. There wasn't a whiff of a primary colour in this house, and the kids loved it.

Vicky was a sweet little thing with blonde plaits and dungarees.

'Hello, Vicky,' I said, as she brought a bowl over for me to look at.

'Do you like Jo?' she asked me in that brilliantly direct way that children have.

'I do, Vicky. I'm Jo's mummy and I love her.'

'Marcia's gone to the big loo,' she told me.

'I know,' I said, giving her tummy a tickle, 'and what do you think she's doing in there? A big wee or a stinky poo?'

She giggled and then said, 'No. Marcia doesn't do pees and poos at the big loo.'

'Really?' I asked in mock surprise.

'No, because she does go in there with something silver.'

'Something silver? And what do you think that is? Is it treasure?' I asked her, continuing to indulge this little fantasy.

'No, it's not treasure. It's silver, like when my mum puts my daddy's sandwiches in his pack lunch box for big school.'

I laughed. 'You mean silver foil, Vicky.'

'Yes, silver foywill,' she said. 'Marcia does have silver foywill and she does go like this.'

Whereupon Vicky bent over and did a very big puff, as if she was blowing out several hundred candles on a birthday cake.

Marcia came back into the room serenely, and laughed.

'What are you doing, sausage?' she said and picked Vicky up for a hug, which Vicky was more than happy to give. 'Hey, shall we make those cup-cakes?'

'Yeah yeah yeah yeah!' squealed Vicky and off they all went into Marcia's homely Aga-warmed kitchen.

·I went into town and did the test voiceover for some ridiculous air-fresheners that had been tailored towards the Christmas market.

'Mmmmm. Mulled wine and minced pies. Mmmm. Turkey and cranberry stuffing. Mmmmm. Christmas pud and brandy butter. Bring home the smells of Christmas. In candle, spray or plug.'

I said this statement with a varying range of emotions in front of a group of diabolical stick-thin advertising women. I hated them all with their silly little furry moon-boots and parka jackets, pretend-scruffy hairdos and overly applied lipstick.

I arrived home, having collected Jo, to find a rather terse message on the answering machine.

'Hi, Mel. It's Judy.'

I hadn't heard much from her these last few weeks, apart from an information pack she'd sent me about the Christmas Fair. I think that's what it was about. I'd read the first sentence of her anal handwriting and got bored. And surely there'd be a mums' group coming up soon? Like a period, they were monthly and just as painful. What delights would they have in store this time? Probably a trip to the Good Parenting Roadshow at Earl's Court, followed by soup and a sandwich in a nearby brasserie. With some godawful quiz thrown in.

I was convinced that Judy was still peeved that I'd been the one to find Marcia for the two of us. She simply didn't like relinquishing control.

'Just phoning to remind you that the Christmas Fair's tomorrow,' she continued in a dry voice. 'Maybe we can get the Wonder Marcia to help out with the girls while we man the stall.' She over-enunciated the words 'Wonder Marcia' as if she were spitting them out crossly. 'The collection's looking fab. Call me. Bye.'

Right. Time to face up to the fact that tomorrow I would be on the stall with Judy and her bleak selection of childrenswear. This would be the last time I would ever do anything like this for her. After this our relationship would be even stevens and I wouldn't have to feel guilty about her having saved my daughter's life. I would then ease my way gently out of the friendship. It was ridiculous to suppose that Judy and I could ever be really close friends. I'd realized that, way back at the mums' night out. I'd just refused to admit it to myself. You couldn't make new friends when you were over the age of thirty. I knew that now. 'A Hundred Things To Do Before You're Thirty' had been a big slogan of late, with the media extolling the virtues of climbing Mount Fuji, trying three-way and drinking goat's urine to all of the *Guardian*-reading young fogies worried that life's great adventure was slipping through their fingers. There should be a list of 'A Hundred Things Not To Do When You've Reached Thirty', and from number one right up to a hundred would be written the same piece of advice: DON'T MAKE ANY NEW FRIENDS.

Mum had also left a message on the answering machine.

'Hello, this is Mrs Parkinson. I'd like to leave a message for my daughter Melanie, please. Right, here we go. I've done some research into brothels, dear. If your house is being used for such a purpose, it is not the "ladies of the night", let us call them, who will come under the hammer of the law should the brothel be discovered. No, dear, it is the house owners. That's you and Dan. Think about that very carefully. Thank you.'

At least the house was blissfully empty. No sign of the Latvians, although there was a whiff of kidneys about the place, half masked beneath the extraordinary combination of cheap perfume and scented candles.

Mmmmm, bring home the smell of lodgers this Christmas, I thought to myself grimly. Cat's piss perfume, a stranger's wet tights hanging over your bathtub, the fragrance of grilling spleen. Mmmm. Available in candle, spray or stick.

I was going to have to draw up a new list of house rules and at the top of it this time, even before 'Try to enter the house without sounding like a Morris dancer wearing iron-clad boots' would be: 'DO NOT FLIRT WITH LADY OF THE HOUSE'S HUSBAND.' I rubbed my eyes. I felt dog-tired.

Jo was finicky and hungry and starting to whinge. God I'd never felt so tired in all my life. This was a tiredness worse than the first few weeks after the birth even. I suppose then I'd been allowed to slump and indulge. This was different. The novelty had gone, Jo was nearly a year old and the tiredness I was experiencing now was the tiredness that was going to last for the rest of my life. That was the reality. No wonder my mother was dancing into her retirement on high-heeled boots.

I fed Jo, plopped her in the bath and tucked her up in her cot. She smiled at me and said 'haddock' a few times – she sensed that I was feeling terrible. I sang in a rather tense, warbling voice like a novice nun – 'Lavender's Blue Diddle Diddle', 'Mary Mary Quite Contrary' and then her absolute favourite – 'I Surrender' by Rainbow. I bent down into her cot and she licked my face. I stroked her soft hair and looked into her eyes – cornflower-blue and almond-shaped like Dan's – and told her that I loved her more than anything in the world. She responded with an enormous fart. I set her music box going, crept backwards out of the room and listened at the door for a minute. I was very pleased to hear her attempt a version of 'I Surrender' on her own, which sounded something like 'Asender Asender'. God I was proud of her.

I sloped around the corridor upstairs, peeked over the banisters to check nobody was coming, and then I just couldn't resist going into the lodgers' room.

The bed seemed to have even more cuddly toys on it. There was a rather sinister addition – a doll that was Red Riding Hood at one end, and when you flipped over her skirt she became the wolf at the other. How apt, I thought, picking it up and looking at it.

There was a lot of talcum powder on the floor, and reams of miniscule thongs and rolled-up tights everywhere. Piles of sweet wrappers filled the bin, and newly bought hardware – a camera, video camera, roller-blades – sat in boxes under the sink, untouched.

On the bedside table were various bits of paper. A letter, payslips from Sonata's restaurant, a mobile phone bill. I crept to the door and stuck my head round it, just to check. The house was totally silent. I prowled back into the room and started to sift through the papers by the bed.

There was a letter in Latvian that I couldn't decipher a word of, apart from the words 'Bryan Adams' written in pink capitals. Then I picked up the phone bill. All the calls and texts made from Ms Ruta Vitauta's phone were laid out in sequence. A lot of calls to a foreign country, presumably Latvia. One mobile number cropped up again and again, at all times of day and night – probably Sonata's – and then I saw it. Twice. She'd rung this number, let me see, twice, no, three times over the last two weeks. It was a number I knew as well as the wrinkles on my hand: Dan's mobile phone number. That tart had been phoning my husband, and the bastard hadn't even TOLD me about it. I didn't know at that point who I was more angry with – him or her. I couldn't make sense of anything at the moment – I could barely register if I was wearing any clothes. My heart was bumping so hard I felt I was going to pass out.

This is not actual proof, I told myself again and again as I went slowly down the stairs.

Of course it wasn't proof, but it was weird. Why had she phoned Dan's mobile number rather than phoning our house number? She'd obviously wanted to speak specifically to him, the crafty little minx. Why had Dan given her his mobile number? Why had she phoned three times? I hadn't checked to see what the lengths of the calls had been. Damn. I wasn't going to risk going back in there – maybe I was scared to find out the truth.

I decided to phone Pen.

She was in a rush, on her way to Amsterdam to set up some trendy trance-weekend or something. I would have happily donated a limb at this point to be in Pen's shoes. If I'd donated a leg then I wouldn't be able to wear Pen's shoes so my plan rather fell apart. I would do anything to be off on some mission to a city far far away. Anything to get me out of this vice-filled house of lies.

'Hi, darling, I can't talk for long,' said Pen. 'Are you OK?'

'Pen, I'll cut to the chase. I think Dan's having an affair with one of our lodgers.'

There was a silence.

'What?' she said.

'I'm not sure, but I've got a feeling in my waters.'

'Now hang on, Mel. Your waters have let you down before.'

'My waters are continually letting me down. They make a regular appearance in my trousers, Pen, especially when I sneeze or jump on a trampoline.'

'Are you sure about this, Mel? This is your soul mate and best friend Dan we're talking about. Lovely Dan, who you love,' she added passionately.

'Lovely Dan has been a bit sex-starved, boo hoo poor him, and is clearly going crazy,' I said, trying not to cry.

'Oh. I see,' said Pen quietly. 'Listen, Mel, you know what blokes are like. You've got to get back on that pony, sweetheart.'

'I'm scared of the pony. And confused by the pony. And my flume just doesn't feel the way it used to, and I'm so bloody tired all the time, Pen, and my clothes are shit and I've got no work, and ...'

The tears were starting to flow now.

'Oh my darling,' she said. 'Listen, my bloody cab's beeping outside. I've seriously got to catch this flight. I'm going to phone you from my mobile, hon, OK?'

'OK,' I said, sniffing. 'Have a great time in Amsterdam.'

'I hate Amsterdam,' she said.

'Oh come on,' I said, still sniffing. 'We used to have a great time there. Remember all those jazz cigarettes we used to smoke?'

'It's not jazz cigarettes any more, Mel. It's crack alleys with junkies hunched over silver foil. Listen, I'm going to phone you in a few minutes from the cab, OK?' and then she hung up.

Silver foil. I wiped my tears away and smiled as I remembered Vicky saying 'silver foywill'.

Hearing Pen's voice had calmed me right down. I was going to be like her. Cool, logical, focused. I'd found something resembling a clue in Ruta's room. It was time to have a snoop in Dan's shed.

The garden was pitch-black as I opened up the back door. I'd put on a large woolly hat and gloves. I didn't want to leave any fingerprints.

'So why are you wearing a hat?' my new logical self asked the old befuddled self.

'It makes me feel like a detective,' answered my old befuddled self, strangely in an American accent.

I'd also put on the nearest thing I could find to keep warm: Dan's towelling dressing gown. It smelt of him, warm, familiar, half BO, half male hair conditioner. I put it on over my clothes and bundled into the garden. If someone chanced to look over our garden fence at this moment, they'd have sworn that Worzel Gummidge was alive and well.

The shed was dark. Good. I knew where Dan kept a torch, so I'd be able to do this thing properly. I stopped suddenly. There was some kind of light coming from Dan's shed. It was a flickering one, but it was definitely there. Was Dan in there? Maybe he was. I'd sort of lost track of his movements today, and to be honest, his movements over these last few weeks. What he was doing, where he was going. We didn't seem to talk that much any more, and when we did it was usually about Jo. It was funny – in some ways having a baby had driven a wedge between us rather than knitted us more closely together.

If somebody were in the shed I'd have to go very very quietly. I'd have to practise what I'd preached to the Latvians. I must be silent, gliding, prowling. I slid across the garden like a shadow. I was about two metres away from the shed window when I heard it. A sort of low male grunting. Followed by a female teasing little giggle.

I could feel every blood vessel in my face about to explode. My whole chest was thumping.

The grunting got more insistent, louder. Then I heard the female voice squeak to a high pitch. Then there was a silence.

Then I heard Dan laugh. The bastard laughed. My Dan who had held up my skirt chivalrously in a lay-by on the A3, so that I wouldn't pee on it. My Dan who told me once that I was more beautiful than Juliette Binoche. My Dan who cried when Jo had emerged from the bloodstained madness of that delivery room, and told me that I was still more beautiful than Juliette Binoche. Tears started to prick at my eyes. No, this was simply not the time for tears. There would be time for tears later.

My heart jumped as I heard a piece of furniture moving in the shed. Quick as a flash, I raced back into the house, ripped off his odious dressing gown and went upstairs to the darkened landing. I hunched by the window so that I could scan the garden, and waited. I could hear my pulse in my ears. Feel it behind my eyeballs. I didn't feel tired any more.

I breathed. Maybe, just maybe, I was overreacting and in some way misconstruing the situation. I was exhausted and people did mad things when they were exhausted. I had a brief revelation that everything was going to be all right, that life would be normal once again. There would be some perfectly obvious explanation for this. But then the shed door opened and out stepped Dan. He was smiling. He pulled out a packet of fags from his pocket. Several moments later, Ruta walked out of their darkened love-nest, still in her pyjamas but with a jacket over the top, the cheap little slattern. Dan offered her a cigarette, she ran her hands through her hair, accepted it and cupped her hands round his as she dipped her cigarette into his flame. Not the first time she'd dipped into his flame, and I was going to make bloody sure that his flame was going to be extinguished for ever. Feasibly with a pair of garden shears, which I would borrow from Frank and Cheryl.

The two of them laughed conspiratorially down there in our garden, and sucked deeply on their post-coital fags, the bitching bollocking bastarding bastards.

The phone rang, extra loudly, it seemed, in the darkness. I came back downstairs.

'Mel, it's me, love.'

It was Pen.

'Hello.'

'Mel, what's going on? You sound totally weird.'

'I'll tell you what's going on. I heard them shagging in his shed, and have just seen them emerge for a cigarette.'

'Mel, are you absolutely sure?' Pen sounded serious.

'Utterly. I heard everything.'

'Are you sure you heard everything?'

'Yes.'

'Oh my God, you poor thing. I wish I was there to hug you.'

'Yes.'

'Have a brandy and get into bed.'

'Yes.'

'It's funny,' Pen said, laughing grimly, 'I was going to send you that sex-survey thing in the post. But there's a lot of stuff about infidelity so I won't.'

'Yes.'

'Oh and by the way. I got it wrong. Remember the swingers thing I told you about? It wasn't pampas grass. It was bamboo grass. Mel? Mel? Are you still there?'

There was a pause of about ten seconds.

'Yes,' I said.

Chapter Twelve

It was time for action. I felt adrenalin start to pump through my body, like a boxer preparing for a big fight. My eyeballs weren't itchy any more, but felt as if they'd been taken out and given a good polish. I hadn't had this much energy in two years. I actually jogged up the stairs. I wrote Dan a note, which I left on the stairs: 'Knackered. Gone to bed. Do you mind sleeping on the sofa? See you in the morning. M.' I was going to buy myself some hours to work out my next move. I checked Jo, who was rasping gently on her back. I eased my way down the corridor to our bedroom like a Ninja.

I sat up in bed and waited. I still had the woolly hat and gloves on for security. I heard the back door open, and Dan and Ruta come into the kitchen. I couldn't hear what they were saying but they were talking in German. I felt like something out of the Resistance, and briefly imagined myself called Delphine, in a rain-coat and beret. I heard Ruta come upstairs and go into her bedroom, while Dan clanked around with the dishwasher down-stairs. Then he came up the stairs and I heard a rustle of paper – he was reading my note. There was a pause, then I heard him walk along the corridor. Hang on, this wasn't part of the plan. I dived under the duvet and held my breath. Our bedroom door squeaked open and he whispered, 'Mel. Mel? Are you awake?'

Judas. What did he want to know that for? So that he could sit at the end of our marriage bed and tell me about his exploits with the Latvian slut in the shed? I kept as still as a tortoise. There was a dreadful silence that seemed to last for ever, but then he finally receded into the corridor and went downstairs once again.

I watched the hours flick by on our big green digital clock – a wedding present from Jim and Shorty. 2 a.m., 3 a.m., 4 a.m. went by. I didn't feel like crying at all, which was odd considering the amount of tears I had shed over the last year. I'd cried when the Mori poll woman came round to the house, simply because she was the first adult I'd spoken to in days. I'd cried watching breakfast television when an old man was presented with a special award for all he'd done for The Year Of The Labrador. I'd cried at the Trooping of the Colour – motherhood had made me feel fond of the Queen. I had cried reservoirs of tears since Jo'd been born, but not tonight. Tonight, the ducts were dry.

I needed something to focus on. When I was a little girl I used to lie in bed and imagine what my future house would look like when I became a grown-up. I basically saw it as a big doll's house whose whole front opened up. And this is what I started doing. I lay in bed planning a new house for myself and my daughter, a big safe doll's house with food made from plaster of Paris, and unchangeable views out of the windows made from postcards. Life would be fixed, everything safe. We'd have Clacton-on-Sea out of the kitchen window, Cricket St Thomas wildlife park out of the bathroom, Rome by night from my bedroom, and Jo could have Paris by night from hers.

As I lay there designing the soft furnishings, a visitor entered my fantasy in the form of Ivana Trump. There she was in my bedroom in a purple satin trouser-suit and her trademark blonde beehive. She'd famously said after her husband cheated on her, 'Don't get mad, get everything', and I took comfort from these words as I lay huddled in the darkness. I'd always thought of her as a faintly ridiculous character, but now she came to me through the shadows like Boadicea. Ivana perched her bony behind at the end of my bed, and raising an exquisitely manicured nail purred: 'Everything, darling. Get everything.'

'But, Ivana,' I replied, with a wobbly voice, 'when you say "everything", what exactly do you mean?'

'Properties, darling. Jewellery, clothes, cars. Hell, even try to get your hands on his portfolio.'

'OK, Ivana. Property-wise I think there's a strong chance that I might get his shed.'

'Good, darling,' Ivana said, lighting up a pink Sobranie.

'I think I can lay a claim to the big green digital clock, the board games, the collection of Whimsies, because strictly speaking they're already mine, possibly the bicycle helmets, definitely the hairdryer, and there's a very strong chance I could get my daughter as well.'

'Fabulous,' said Ivana.

'But he can keep the record collection. It's full of Steely Dan and 10CC.'

'Eeeuurgh,' she said, pulling a disgusted face. Ivana was fading, drifting slowly back towards the door. 'Remember. Everything,' she said. I was sad to see her go.

'Goodbye, Ivana, and thanks for everything.' I waved with one woollen hand. She was gone; the last thing to leave the room was her beehive.

Right, that was it. I would lose at least two stone with the stress of our split and would emerge, butterfly-like, from my fat-suit. Jo and I would move to a gentle all-woman commune in the countryside. I'd seen one in a Sunday supplement; it looked so peaceful and nurturing. Everyone helped collect fresh water from a well, and then washed their clothes together in a courtyard smothered with jasmine. They looked so serene. My manless existence would be blissfully free from hearing how we'd nearly beaten the All Blacks, how red wine is best left to breathe at room temperature and how Jeff Beck was the greatest guitarist that ever lived. My life would be tranquil, uncluttered; never again would I have to suffer the droplets of urine splashed all round the loo. I was starting to look forward to the commune, and planned a whole range of kaftans, ponchos and moulded leather pumps in my head. Jo would grow up as a sort of wood nymph, far away from male-dominated, aggressive city-life. She'd be able to recite the poetry of Elizabeth Barrett Browning by heart, and would be a dab hand at milking goats. We'd need some sturdy waterproof boots. I'd pick them up in the morning.

I looked at the big green digital clock. It was morning: 5.30 a.m. already. Jo would be awake in an hour. I spent the next forty minutes planning tofu-based meals for the commune, and then drifted off to sleep. The baby woke me twenty minutes later.

I heard the front door shut, and peeked out of the window to see Dan heading down the street with his briefcase. I had some vague memory of a conference in Brighton. Perfect. I'd have the whole day to formalize my plans.

I could still taste the adrenalin in my throat, but my muscles were starting to ache. I looked briefly in the bathroom mirror and saw two eye-bags looking back at me. It was like looking at a blood-hound. I changed Jo's nappy and took her downstairs. Everything was functioning normally. I was even humming the theme tune to the *Fimbles* and making her laugh by sticking out my tongue. Ostensibly all was as it should be. Unless you were to come very close to my face and see an enormous pulse flickering under my right eye.

I made breakfast for myself and the baby and started to make a shopping list.

2 pairs of waterproof boots
10 metres of calico (good fabric for commune-life)
Complete works of Virginia Woolf
Pulses
Fruit
Vegetables
Compass
Guitar

There. Everything we'd need for our new life. There was no sign of the lodgers, but I did hear them giggling in their bedroom. Ruta was probably regaling her sister with the events of the night before. Latvian hussies. I'd never go near the Baltic as long as I lived, and neither would my daughter.

I hadn't yet worked out what I was going to say to Ruta, but I knew it would be loud and full of swear words. I would speak to Pen about that first. Out of everyone I knew, she had the most experience in jiltings, passionate affairs gone wrong, and everything that marriage had protected me from these last six years. Dan had seemed like such a safe bet. Dan, who on our first date at college had turned up with a scrunched-up copy of Nietzsche sticking out of his pocket, and I'd been so impressed. What a bloody mug.

Jo and I left the house to walk to Marcia's. It was freezing, the sort of weather that makes you grin with cold. On seeing Marcia's kind, gentle face at her door, and the tender way in which she scooped up Jo and took her inside, I wanted to crumple on the doorstep and clutch at Marcia's soft tassled skirt. I bit back the tears and left them.

As I walked home with the empty buggy, I passed a mother pushing a double-buggy, smiling and talking to her kids. She glanced at my empty one and gave me a pitying look. She probably assumed I was one of those sad childless women who walk empty buggies around, sometimes with a doll strapped inside.

I fished out my mobile and phoned Pen in Amsterdam.

'Pen, it's me.'

'Mel, how the hell are you today?'

'OK.'

'Have you confronted Dan yet?'

'No. Any advice?'

There was a pause as she sipped at something, probably a skinny latte. 'Right, this is the deal,' she said, completely business like. 'You want him to feel like the scum of the earth, and her to feel scared and totally humiliated, right?'

'Yes.'

'OK. Confront them separately. Make sure you look fantastic. She'll feel intimidated by that, and he'll realize what an idiot he is cheating on such a sex goddess.'

'OK,' I said uncertainly. Looking 'fantastic' might pose a few problems.

'Don't, I repeat, don't lose your cool, and for God's sake don't drink.'

'Oh come off it, Pen.' It always slightly annoyed me the way Pen assumed I couldn't hold my drink.

'Mel, who had to pull you down off the Christmas tree in Bicester marketplace?'

She had a point.

'All right. I won't drink a drop.'

'And you must do it tonight, Mel. You have to nip these things in the bud straight away. Are you clear? Tonight!' and she hung up dramatically.

I felt like I'd just been given instructions by MI5. My secret mission, henceforth to be known as Operation Trump. And I held all the trump cards. 'Ha ha ha haa ha ha haa ha!' I laughed out loud, but had to stop when an elderly couple crossed the road to get away from me and my empty buggy.

The phone was ringing as I opened the front door, so I rushed to answer it. I was hoping it would be Pen with more secret instructions. Things like 'strap a knife to your bra' and 'leave the microfilm in Finsbury Park'.

It was Judy.

'Hello, Mel, have you got a minute?'

She sounded frosty. I hadn't returned her call of yesterday. Oh God, the Christmas Fair.

Through the kitchen door I saw Ruta swish down the stairs and slip her feet into a pair of pompommed moon boots. Her legs looked slim even in those. Bitch. She left the house quickly. That was fine. I would bide my time before I confronted her. Operation Trump was all about waiting for the right moment.

'Sorry, Judy, of course I've got time to chat.' I sat down in a kitchen chair.

'Are you sitting down?' she asked.

'Yes, I've just sat down in a kitchen chair.'

'Good. I've got something extremely serious to tell you.'

Maybe she'd seen the light and decided that her collection of children's fishermen's clothes was actually rubbish. Leaving me well and truly off the hook.

'What is it?' I asked with undisguised glee creeping into my voice.

'It's Marcia, Mel. The Wonder Marcia.'

Suddenly I realized what this was about. She was finally going to give vent to her annoyance that she hadn't found Marcia, but that I had. Of all the petty, small-minded, ungrateful people. I really didn't have time for this.

'What about her?' I sighed.

'She's a heroin addict, Mel.'

'Excuse me?'

'She is addicted to the Class A drug heroin, Mel. She's a junkie.'

'Judy, is this a joke?'

'I wish it were, Mel. I wish it were. I wish that you had found us a childminder who was wholesome and fit to look after our precious babies. But I'm afraid you didn't, Mel. You found us a dragon-chasing lowlife who could easily have harmed or even killed them. So thanks for that, Mel.'

I stood up out of the chair, and had a queasy feeling as the kitchen seemed to rotate around me very slowly.

'I don't believe it,' I said.

'I had Vicky's mum on the phone this morning. Excuse me one second – Oliver, put my bicycle light down, you naughty boy. Straight into the Naughty Nook, IMMEDIATELY. Where was I? Yes, Vicky told her mum very explicitly that she saw Marcia sniffing over some silver foil in the bathroom. She was immediately suspicious and so didn't leave Vicky or Nathan there this morning. And I've got Minnie here with me.'

'But when Vicky told me about silver foil I thought she was just talking about treasure or something,' I said lamely. I felt a dryness in my throat. 'Jo's there now.'

'Well, we'd better go and get her. I'll be round in five minutes. I'd like a word with that bloody Marcia woman anyway.'

I put the phone back on its hook, and my mobile rang almost immediately. It was Dan. I paced round the kitchen while it bleated its silly White Stripes ringtone. On and on it rang. The words 'DAN MOBILE' looked strange. And then it stopped. I was glad I hadn't answered – Dan was no longer worthy to be involved in issues facing our daughter. He'd have to get used to that feeling.

Five agonizing minutes and two largish brandies later, Judy was outside my house parking her people-carrier. I raced straight out and she opened the passenger door for me to get inside. These were movements worthy of the A-Team. I half expected some motivational 1970s funk to strike up as we drove.

'Can I suggest something to you, Mel?'

'That I hand in my resignation, and leave the job of being a mother to somebody with qualifications?' I said flatly.

'No. Research, Mel. When you took this Marcia woman on, did you do your research?'

'I spoke to one of her previous employers ...' I said quietly.

'One employer?'

'Yes.'

She tutted. 'When I embarked on my fishermen's clothes project, do you know how much research I did, Mel? Fabrics – would they be breathable? How washable? The design – was it authentic enough? You know, I even went out with fishermen on a boat in Suffolk to get a real feel for the clothes. I didn't just bumble into it willy-nilly.'

I wish the boat had sunk, I thought to myself.

'Marcia loves those kids,' I said quietly. 'She may be on drugs, but she's a bloody good childminder.'

'Are you mad, Mel? What's to say she wouldn't suddenly turn on them, shout at them or smack them?'

'She's clearly not interested in that type of smack,' I replied dryly. I heaved an enormous sigh. This was rapidly turning into the worst day of my life. Judy looked at me.

'Are you OK?' she said briskly.

I thought about this question before answering her. Should I tell her about Dan's betrayal and our imminent split? Was she a true friend?

I replied, 'I'm fine, thanks. A bit tired.'

'You're tired. I've got the whole of my Christmas Fair stall piled up at home waiting to go to the town hall this afternoon. I should be there now sorting it all out. I take it you can still help me?'

'Of course I'll be there. Of course.'

I'd rather spend the afternoon back at the piles clinic. I looked out of the window gloomily as we swung into Marcia's street. Judy parked the car, and turned to face me.

'We'll creep round to the side window and see if we can see anything untoward. I'll go in front, you bring up the rear, Mel. Keep quiet and just do as I say, OK?'

Judy was obviously loving every minute of this. It gave her the chance to utilize those Duke of Edinburgh Award skills that had been lying dormant for so long. Operation Trump would have to wait. I felt like sulking and refusing to get out of the car, but Judy's sports-mistressy barking of orders got the better of me.

'Yes,' I replied weakly.

'Phones off,' she commanded.

I'd never noticed what a wide bum Judy had until now. It was impossible not to analyze it, two inches away from my face as we crept up front path. We followed the house round to the left and into her garden. She was probably in the living room with Jo at this very moment, so we'd be able to spy in through the window quite easily. I felt a sudden pang of foolishness.

'Judy, I'm not sure about this at all. All we're going on is some random comments made by a four-year-old. You know what a bunch of fantasists kids are.'

'What?' said Judy whispering so loudly that her nostrils flared like a horse. 'You, a mother, are saying that you're going to just leave this to chance? For all we know that woman could be in there now, having a hit. Your child could be lying there, breathing in the fumes.'

And for the hundredth time in Judy's company, I felt like the worst mother in the whole world.

'You're right,' I said.

'Now just be quiet and listen. We're going to look through the window and see what's going on. When I give the signal, I want you to duck down and do nothing. Just keep out of the way. I'll go up to the front door, confront Marcia and rescue Jo. Is that clear?'

'Yes, Judy,' I said meekly.

We inched up to the window, so that our noses were poking just over the sill. All looked completely normal in the living room. Marcia was with Jo on the rug, and they were sorting out wooden bricks and stacking them into some kind of tower. Jo was beaming and Marcia was smiling back at her encouragingly. As far as I could make out, there were no empty Jack Daniels bottles or overflowing ashtrays, and definitely no Brian Jones collapsed in the corner with his trousers off.

'I think we should wait,' I whispered.

Judy turned to face me, and I noticed a slightly sour breath coming off her, like someone who has drunk too much coffee. She crouched down and laughed a nasty little laugh.

'You just don't understand what being a mother's about, do you?' and she crept off along the side of the house.

I was genuinely stunned by that comment. My mouth fell open, and I felt my cheeks redden. My heart started thumping and new adrenalin surged through my blood, just as it had the night before. Why had I never accessed this most marvellous of hormones till now? It would have done wonders for me on the dance floors of late 1980s Leatherhead. I suddenly found myself following Judy's gargantuan bottom at great speed. So fast that I was overtaking her, and arrived on Marcia's front step in front of her.

'What do you think you're doing?' snapped Judy. 'Stay back like I told you to.'

'No, you listen to me, Judy,' I said. 'I am Jo's mother, do you understand?'

Judy was speechless.

I continued: 'I know you see yourself as some sort of über-mother who can swing in and take control of everyone around you, but I'm afraid that's not the case with me.'

She looked at me, horrified.

'I don't want you to "rescue" my daughter, thank you. If anyone's going to rescue her, it will be me.'

She folded her arms grumpily.

'I'm going to go in and talk to Marcia, Judy. I'd be grateful if you could go and wait in your people-carrier.'

I felt a burning sensation in my jowels, and my left knee was wobbling slightly. Judy let out a snort of indignation and marched down the path like a teenager who'd failed to make the netball team. I pulled myself upright and rang the doorbell.

Five minutes later I was sat on the sofa with Marcia, with my arm round her. She was sobbing into her camomile tea.

'I'm so sorry,' she said again. 'I'm just so so sorry.'

'There's been no harm done to any of the kids,' I said gently. 'Let's just focus on that for the moment.'

'You have to understand, Mel,' she said through the tears, 'I don't do it for recreation. It's my way of blotting out the pain. It's been my way of coping for six years since … since … he left me. You don't know what it feels like, the pain.'

'No, I don't,' I said, 'but I have an inkling as to what it might be like.'

'I just feel very alone. This job keeps me going. You know I'd never do anything to harm the children.'

'I know that,' I said, and then couldn't help adding, 'You look remarkably good on it, Marcia, considering you've been on it six years.'

She allowed herself a wry smile through the tears.

'I only use the good stuff.'

'Look, Judy's waiting for me outside. I'm going to have to take Jo and go.'

'There's a phone in the hallway if you want to call the police,' said Marcia sadly.

'I don't want to call the police, Marcia,' I said. 'I don't really know what I want to do about this. I need to get my head straight. Shall we talk about it tomorrow?' I said.

Marcia nodded, wiping her nose. 'Thank you,' she said, looking very drained.

'And thank you for looking after Jo so beautifully. She'll miss you.'

Judy had a face like thunder when we emerged. It felt good to have Jo's solid little frame in my arms. She was pulling at my fringe and laughing.

I clipped Jo into a baby-seat and then got into the front. Judy looked at her watch and sighed.

'Thanks for waiting for us,' I said to Judy, with a brief smile.

She sniffed.

'I hope you told that disgusting woman that we will be visiting the Council's Pre-School Development Unit first thing on Monday morning to lodge a complaint. I want that woman drummed out of town.'

'This isn't the Wild West, Judy. "We" are not going to do anything. I'm going to deal with this in my own way, thank you.' I was liking the new steely edge to my voice. 'I'm the one who found her, anyway. Go left here, please.'

We turned into Brook Grove and she parked the people-carrier outside my house. She looked straight ahead of her while I got Jo out.

'Do you still want me to help out at the Christmas Fair?' I said, trying to sound downbeat, praying that she wouldn't want me there. Surely after this she'd never want to see my face again?

I directed this question to her profile, which was still staring through the windscreen.

'Yes,' she replied, 'and please be there at twenty to, so that I can take you through the drill.'

I sighed very slightly to myself. 'OK. I'll be there at twenty to.'

The people-carrier moved away from the kerb and was gone.

I entered the house feeling suddenly exhausted. Last night's twenty minutes' sleep was taking its toll. I slumped down at the kitchen table feeling old and wretched. I toyed with the idea of blowing Judy out, but pride got the better of me. I was determined not to give her the upper hand by thinking that I couldn't handle her stupid Christmas Fair. But I did have the slight problem of child-care. With Marcia off the scene, I'd have to take Jo with me.

I was putting her lunch together when I heard the front door open. With the events of the morning, I'd completely forgotten about Operation Trump. If this was Ruta darkening my doors, I'd have to confront her immediately. As Pen had said, better to nip the whole thing in the bud. The door slammed shut. My jaw clenched involuntarily.

'Get mad. Get everything,' I whispered to myself.

The kitchen door opened and Sonata put her head round. 'Hello,' she said brightly, coming in and unpacking several jars of pickled dill cucumbers into my cupboard.

'Hello,' I replied in monotone.

'How are you?' she said, looking me up and down with pity. Everyone was giving me this look today. It was as if I was wearing a sweatshirt with 'MY HUSBAND'S HAVING AN AFFAIR' emblazoned on it.

'Oh you know, Sonata, things could be better at the moment.'

'It must be very difficult for you.'

I was taken aback by the candour of her comment. I felt tears spring to my eyes and had to open the biscuit tin and examine its contents very closely to avoid her looking at me.

'Can I help you with Baby perhaps?' she said. 'I have day off.'

'That'd be great, Sonata. Just have to check one thing. You're not on heroin, are you?' and I laughed loudly for a few seconds.

'Excuse me?' she answered.

Sonata agreed to look after Jo till Dan got home, leaving me free to tackle Judy and the Christmas Fair on my own. It was better that way – Jo'd have much more fun at home being spoiled rotten.

On the way to St Martin's church hall I popped into the local off licence and bought five miniature bottles of whisky. I hadn't done this for years, and suddenly felt sixteen again as I walked along the pavement swigging away. I definitely didn't look sixteen, however. I sought out my reflection in a shop window and thought: who's that old tramp with the care-in-the-community woolly hat? I walked on, then stopped in my tracks and backed up again. I checked the reflection once more. I was still wearing that ridiculous woolly condom on my head. That's why people had been giving me pitying looks all day. There was no way that I could take it off now.

My hair was so dirty underneath that it would have moulded itself into a mound of grease, and there was no way I was going to unleash that onto the Christmas Fair. The woolly hat was, unbelievably, the more attractive option of the two.

I sloped further along the street, and had a little bottle fully upended in my mouth when I heard a familiar voice in front of me.

'Mel.'

I gulped back the whisky a little too greedily, and started coughing and spluttering. Frank and Cheryl were standing there looking at me, and my hat, with concern.

'Not on the soft drinks today, I see,' said Frank, laughing loudly.

'Are you OK?' said Cheryl.

'I'm great,' I said, holding up the little empty bottle to show them. 'I'm drinking this because of an infection, you see.'

Frank and Cheryl continued to look at me like a pair of budgies.

'Yes,' I continued, 'whisky's the best thing for it.'

'Oh dear, what sort of infection is it?' asked Cheryl, all politeness.

'Heart,' I said immediately and nodded vigorously.

'A heart infection?' repeated Frank.

'Yes. The whole thing's infected. Up like a space hopper. Should be better soon, though. Doctor says it's nothing to worry about,' and I burped very gently. 'Well, super to see you both. You must come to us for drinkies next time.'

'Yes, dear, we'd like that,' said Cheryl.

'Bye then,' I said and started to lurch off.

'Look after your heart. That sounds nasty,' said Frank.

'Will do!' I called jovially behind me.

There was some jaunty red and green bunting up over the main entrance to the church hall, with 'CHRISTMAS FAIR TODAY!'

splashed across a large banner. A grey-haired lady in a Santa hat was giving out fliers. A spry lady with a white perm tried to charge me two quid to get in even though I told her repeatedly that I was helping out on a stall. She wasn't having any of it, and glanced at my woolly hat suspiciously. I wasn't going to give up on this without a fight. The nips of booze had given me courage, and I felt the spirit of Ivana at my side.

'Listen, greydy,' I said. I'd been meaning to say 'grey lady' but the whisky had somehow elided the two words together. 'A woman I know called Judy is running the fishermen's clothes stall and I'm helping her out.' I enunciated each word over-carefully, a sure sign I was in my cups.

'Oh, you mean Lovely Judy?' said Greydy, suddenly softening at the edges and twinkling behind her glasses on chains.

'Yes. "Lovely" Judy,' I said sourly. 'She's an extremely close friend of mine. We're like that.' At which point I tried to twist my fingers over each other to denote extremely close friendship, but somehow the manoeuvre was beyond me.

'Oh well, anyone who's with our Judy gets in for free,' said Greydy, waving me through as if she had just opened the portals to Paradise.

It was twenty past two, and the fair was in full swing. It seemed to be peopled by women. The odd bloke slunk around in the wake of some bossy wife or mother, but mainly the whole place had a female musk to it. Christmas carols were being piped through a sound system, and the overall feel of the place was tinsel, poinsettia and gingham. There were stalls for all of your Noel needs – chutneys and pickles, mince pies, quilts and Christmas cards, candles, wooden toys, sheepskins, decorations for the tree, hand-made jewellery, lavender bags, padded coat-hangers, drawer liners, hand knits, hand crochets, hand embroidery, tapestries, dog bootees and coats. There was an almost suffocating smell of spice. It was as if an enormous Smelly Tree, like you see hanging in minicabs, had been suspended from the ceiling. There was also not an open window in sight, and the large municipal room was stifling.

I spotted Judy's stall in the corner of the room, and was delighted to see that the mulled wine stall was right next door to it. I bought two cups straight away.

Judy didn't see me because she was talking to Alison and Bridget intently over the stall. Judy had her arms folded and looked as if she was telling them some story with a dire ending, because both women in her audience lifted their hands up to their mouths simultaneously once Judy had finished speaking. Bridget even patted Judy on the shoulder comfortingly. I bowled up and all three looked at me in silence. Judy coughed slightly and gave me a brittle smile. Bridget and Alison looked down at the stock on the stall and didn't even register that I was there.

'Hi there, groovers,' I said, with a little wink.

Bridget and Alison mumbled something and hurriedly left the stall.

'Sorry I'm late, Judy,' I said loudly and jovially. 'I was drinking some whisky on the way. Fancy a spot of ye olde mulled?'

'I'll have one when my work on the stall is finished, thank you,' said Judy tersely. 'Now that you're here, maybe I can take you through the stock, so that at least you can give some semblance of knowing what it is you're selling.'

'Judy, I'm putty in your hands,' I said, taking another enormous slug of mulled wine, which was going down very easily. 'This is super vino,' I added, licking my lips.

Judy took me through her collection. All the clothes were hewn from a very rough material and only came in two colours: navy or sludge green. They were the most un-child-friendly garments I had ever seen. There was nothing soft, jolly or giving about them. It was like handling a selection of industrial cleaning cloths. There were smocks that had one big pocket on the front. 'The pockets aren't in keeping with the original fisherfolk design, but I thought they'd be fun for children,' she explained.

The idea of a pocket being 'fun' depressed me, and I had to sluice down half of the second cup of mulled wine. I looked at my watch: quarter to three in the afternoon. I had to get through five more hours of this.

'Now, these are the trousers,' said Judy, holding aloft some very flared, cropped sailor trousers that were so stiff they could have stood up on the trestle table on their own. There was a mixture of tabards and smocks, some featuring the fun pocket, to go on top of the trousers, and there was an array of jerkins with specially unhemmed edges. The overall look of the clothes was poorly concocted sailor-outfit for the school production of *HMS Pinafore*. And talking of pinafores, my mother's Clothkits would have looked like a Dolce and Gabbana collection compared to this lot.

The stall on the other side of us was selling handmade items featuring cloves. Whole oranges studded with cloves with ribbon attached, little clove-stuffed pouches, bags and liners. The stall was heaving. Three women were running it, and they barely had a moment to gift-wrap and bag all the items from the clawing crowds. Judy's stall had precisely nobody looking at it, so I nipped off to fill up on mulled wine.

My hat was starting to feel itchy and my cheeks were scorching. Annoyingly I only had a bra and vest underneath my jumper, so was very wary about taking it off in case somebody mistook me for a road-digger, what with my woolly hat on the top.

Judy kept looking at her watch and nervously scanning the room. 'I'm sure it was busier last year. It was definitely busier, yes.

Carol cleared her stock and she was only selling stupid mice made from Cheddar.'

I didn't answer but glugged at my mulled wine. I was beginning to lose the feeling in my teeth, which was rather pleasant. I sat down in the one chair we had available on our stall.

'Aren't you going to take that hat off?' Judy whispered, although there was no need; John Lennon's 'Merry Merry Christmas' was cranked up to top volume.

'No, Judy, I like it,' I said so firmly that I managed to spill about half a cup of wine over my jumper.

The chair was starting to move underneath me, or maybe it was me that was moving on the chair. I really couldn't tell.

'Well, I wish you'd take it off. Nobody'll recognize you in it.'

Nobody stopped at our stall. Not surprising, really; it had about as much festive cheer as Chairman Mao's regime.

'What did you say, Judy?'

'I said you should get rid of that ridiculous woolly hat. Nobody's going to recognize you in it.'

My mulled brain was trying to pursue a thread of logic here. 'Why do you want me to be recognized, Judy?'

She looked away for a moment, and then said directly to my face: 'I thought we'd sell more clothes with somebody off the telly behind the stall, but it appears I've been proved wrong, doesn't it? It appears to have actually had the opposite effect. Not even one jerkin gone. Unbelievable.'

I was speechless.

'Now you stay here, Mel, and man the stall. Are you able to do that? I've got to go and buy some raffle tickets from my friend Laura.'

I slumped in the chair and shook my head from side to side. The bitch had got me here under false pretences. I'd stupidly thought that she'd asked me here as a friend, but no, she wanted to pimp me out like some performing monkey, with my Z-grade celebrity status, in an effort to shift her preposterous outfits. I was staring into the middle distance when my eyes alighted on a group of mothers laughing round a table at the far end of the room. Their children were all running around, playing tag with each other joyously. The mums were enjoying some shared anecdote and seemed totally at ease in each other's company. God I hated other mothers. I wanted to run over to them and tell them to wipe the collective grin off their cow-like faces. I wanted to go and shove an enormous quantity of home-made chutney into their smug grins and then crown them individually with poinsettias. The mulled wine was really starting to hit home. I suddenly imagined Dan and Ruta wandering into the Christmas Fair, hand in hand, strolling among the sheepskin slippers and the handmade basketry, picking out little mementoes for each other. Dan had phoned three times but I had ignored each and every call. I was going to enjoy speaking to him later.

I was aware of somebody actually looking at the goods on Judy's stall. I burped to myself and looked up, trying to assemble some sort of facial expression.

'Ooh, now what do we think of these lovely trousers, little man?'

'We like them, don't we, Mum?'

'Yes we do, and we're going to talk to the nice lady about buying some, aren't we?'

'Yes, Mummy, we are.'

It was my old friend the Ventriloquist Mum with her considerably larger son, now attached to a pair of reins but still being subjected to her falsetto madness. He looked as if his own mouth hadn't moved a muscle since his birth. He had a depressed Tony Hancock look about him. I was in half a mind to offer him some mulled wine.

'Hello there, we'd like to look at some of these lovely trousers,' said Ventriloquist Mum.

'Yes we would,' she said again, only higher.

'I wouldn't if I were you,' I said, moving closer to her in a rather unwieldy way, so that my fist plonked itself heavily into Judy's cashbox. 'I shouldn't be telling you this, madam, but these clothes are all made in child-labour camps.'

Her little eyes widened in horror.

'Child-labour camps? We don't like that, do we, little man?'

'No, we don't, Mummy' she said right back to herself.

'They're also dipped in a toxic material to keep their stiffness. Look at that flare – that's not natural, is it?' and I grabbed a pair of trousers for Ventro Mum to have a good sniff at, and pushed them rather roughly into her face. I could see Judy heading back through the throng towards her stall.

'They also cost three hundred pounds,' I said.

'Three hundred pounds? Did you hear that, little man?'

'Yes I did, Mummy. That's my holiday at Center Parcs,' she squeaked.

'Right, well, I think I'll leave those, thank you,' and with that she was off, pulling her little man in reins behind her.

'She looked interested,' said Judy as she asserted herself behind her stall.

'Not really,' I said, swinging round to look at her. My hat was now super-itchy and my face could be used to guide ships into a port. The song going round the room was Pinky and Perky's 'I Saw Mummy Kissing Santa Claus'. I crushed an empty cup in my fist and then swayed over to the mulled-wine stall again.

'I think you've drunk enough, Mel,' said Judy coldly.

'I haven't drunk nearly enough, Judy,' I said loudly.

'I think you're completely out of control,' said Judy, as yet another group of mums passed by the stall. 'This is all your fault,' she said, lowering her voice so that only I could hear.

The mulled wine stopped swilling around my head, but suddenly focused behind my eyeballs. All at once, I realized what the phrase 'seeing red' really meant. I had mulled-wine vision, and my optical nerve was broiling in it.

'No, Judy. The fault is with this crappy merchandise.' She opened her mouth in horror, but I continued. 'These cack clothes that you have the audacity to call a "collection", which have been cobbled together in about five minutes, are rubbish, Judy. No, they are worse than that, they are pretentious rubbish. Why would a child in its right mind want to wear authentic Suffolk fishermen's gear in London? London's landlocked, you dozy cow. The nearest sea is Southend. Oh and I'd love to see a child survive five minutes in Southend wearing one of these bloody jerkins.'

My voice had got progressively louder, and I was aware of a small group gathering round the stall.

'You're drunk, Mel,' said Judy through her teeth.

'You think I'm drunk, do you? You think this is the drink talking?' I said, so sibilant with the mulled wine that big clots of spit were beginning to form round my mouth. Judy backed away looking genuinely worried; maybe she feared getting rabies.

'Don't you dare lay a finger on me,' she said.

I was then aware of my boot making sharp contact with what must have been the main leg of the trestle, which was slightly shy of the tabletop. It tipped my balance, and to redress this I put both arms heavily onto one side of the trestle, which had the effect of a seesaw. Within seconds the whole stall had collapsed round our ears. It was like at school when a plate was broken in the canteen. A hush fell upon the room, apart from George Michael valiantly singing 'Last Christmas'. The most terrible outcome of all was that my woolly hat was knocked off its purchase by a flying smock. I put my hand up to my head. It was worse than I'd feared.

'Happy Christmas, Judy. And many more Happy Christmases for the rest of your life.'

I picked up my hat, shoved it back onto my head, picked up my tepid mulled wine, which had miraculously survived the blast, and walked through the throng of grey ladies and mothers, who parted to let me pass.

Once outside, the cold air hit me like an angry woman's handbag. It didn't register as cold, strangely enough. I didn't feel anything at all. I fumbled around for the mobile phone in my coat pocket and scrolled through my list of contacts. Who could offer me the solace I needed in this terrible hour of crisis? Dan? Sadly not. Pen? Answering machine. Mum and Dad? Out with Nancy. And then I fell on it, a name that said clarity and simplicity. Not besmirched with betrayal or muddied with the attendant problems of an old friendship. Robin. The name sang out to me like a chorister. I dialled his number eagerly. Robin, our dear Relationship Manager, would keep a cool head when he'd heard my story. How Judy had turned out to be a false friend, Marcia a heroin addict, and my husband a lying, cheating hound.

'This number has not been recognized.' The telephone lady's posh calmness only served to taunt me further. I tried Robin's number three more times with the same devastating result. He had changed his number without telling me. We had met in inauspicious circumstances but we had bonded, and now he had betrayed me too. I thought about going home via his bank – there was an outside chance he would be there, but then I remembered. I had Operation Trump to see through to its bitter end.

The effects of seven polystyrene cups of mulled wine, two miniature bottles of whisky plus the brandies from earlier on were various, but the most pressing concern was my bladder. Like a homing pigeon, I'd gone home the long way, via our old flat, and was standing outside it, looking up wistfully at the friendly plant-filled windows adorned with somebody else's curtains. I was just thinking that this was the place where Dan and I had been so much in love with each other. We had written each other silly notes on the stairs in that flat, things like 'follow this piece of string', and then Dan had followed the string all around the flat till he found it attached to me at the other end. I grimaced slightly at that memory.

I was now in danger of exploding if I didn't have a pee. I jogged down the road, turned the corner and got to the little park. It was pitch dark but still open so I hared inside and, like a dog, found the nearest tree. The Playhut was still open and I could see various gurning figures within it trying to entertain their toddlers. I pulled down my trousers unsteadily. It seemed like an age, but eventually relief came to me and it went on for ever and for ever, slashing into the ground like an old horse. Just as it was starting to ebb, I felt a presence behind the tree.

'May I ask what you're doing there?' said a voice emanating from a fluorescent yellow jacket.

'Fertilizing the grass with my own special brand of mulled-wine-infused urine,' I replied quickly.

'Did you know that it's an offence to do that in public?' he said.

'No, but I'm six months pregnant,' I lied, 'and did you know that it's an offence to prevent a pregnant lady from relieving herself? Indeed, she is allowed, nay encouraged, to relieve herself in a policeman's helmet, an upturned builder's hard-hat or in the boot of a Justice of the Peace's car.'

I pulled my trousers up, and myself up to my highest possible height from my crouching position.

'Oh yes. So you are,' he replied rather mortifyingly. 'Sorry, I didn't see your bulge. Sorry, miss.'

'Mrs,' I said sourly. 'For the moment anyway.'

He looked at me suspiciously. 'Do I know you from somewhere?' he said, narrowing his eyes. 'Have I seen you in this park before?'

I pulled down my woolly hat so that it all but covered my eyes.

'Excuse me, my good man, I have Operation Trump to conclude,' and swept past him, giving his fluorescent jacket a little pat.

I made it home. I stood outside our front gate, feeling curiously like a cowboy. The house was warm and silent. I looked at my watch. Quarter past seven. Where had all that time gone? Then I felt something greasy in my pocket. I pulled out a fish 'n' chips wrapper. I had the blurry recollection of sitting in a café and talking to a tramp about love gone bad and betrayal. That's where the time had gone.

I crept up to Jo's bedroom and checked her. Nothing from her but little regular snuffles. I stroked her head, but hastily withdrew my hand when I realized I was plastering her head with fish grease. I blundered out of the room and tried to breathe deeply. I could hear a muffled television coming from the lodgers' room. It was time. Operation Trump Phase One was about to be accomplished.

I knocked on the door. There was a bit of giggling and then someone said, 'Hello?'

And I entered the vipers' den.

'Good evening, girls, and before I go any further I'd like to thank you, Sonata, for looking after Jo this afternoon. It's very kind of you.'

'No problem,' she said softly.

'Now I suppose you know why I'm here, so I'm going to keep it very brief,' I said, hardly able to look at the witch-faced Ruta. 'Things in this house have reached a bit of a ... head. Haven't they, Ruta? You and my husband Dan have, I realized, become intimate through a shared love of nicotine and the German language. But I didn't realize that you had become such a ... a – ' and my eye alighted on her Red Riding Hood doll – 'wolf,' I concluded.

'Wolf?' said Ruta.

'Yes, you are a wolf in sheep's clothing, Ruta. A snide little animal who preys upon other people's husbands and traps them into your filthy lair, you Jezebel.' My voice had dropped to a low growl by this point, and I was aware of the rabid spittle rearing up again in my throat. 'I know why you come to this country. You don't come to steal our jobs and all of that frankly racist nonsense. You come to steal our men. You bewitch them with your long legs and your short skirts and your glacial eyes the colour of the Baltic. You ensnare them with your pretend lack of English and your musky perfume, you hoary old fox.'

'Fox?' she enquired, with a sardonic lift of the eyebrow.

I stopped for breath, and also to reflect briefly about my disappointing mix-up of the wolf and fox analogies. It weakened the speech somewhat. The pause also gave me the time to think that there was something different about the room. The layout was different, maybe. I looked at Sonata and Ruta, who were in bed together. Nothing strange about that. They were sisters and had shared double beds before. It was just that they didn't have any clothes on. That's what was different about the room. It was candle-lit and the air was heavy with the smell of Fruits of the Forest, so I hadn't quite noticed till now.

I looked at them again. Maybe both their pyjamas were in the wash? Then Ruta kissed Sonata's neck.

'We are not sisters,' she said, almost defiantly.

I clapped my hands together, and like the wife at a cricket match who stands behind the cakes table, I smiled around the room with a matronly air. 'OK then, I'm going to go downstairs and adjust the thermostat. Is it me or does anyone feel very very hot in here? Lovely to talk, girls, there's extra loo paper in the bathroom cupboard, do help yourselves, and I'll see you tomorrow, I'm sure. I'm just going now. Just backing away slowly.'

And I literally backed out of the door.

What the hell was going on in my house? My mother was right. It was rapidly turning into some sort of brothel, and I was its madam. It seemed that bloody everybody was at it except for me. Right. Time for Phase Two. I marched down the stairs, the mulled wine now starting to ferment in my head. I no longer felt roaring drunk and full of tiger-like bravery. I felt pissed. Proper pissed and up for a brawl.

Shed-wards it was, then. I crept across the garden again and stopped about a metre away from its door. I cocked my ear so that I could listen better. I couldn't believe this. I heard Dan's male grunting followed by some German and then a woman's squeals of pleasure. Who the hell was in there with him this time? Everything was clear to me now. He'd probably enjoyed sessions with both Latvian lodgers, probably at the same time. And they weren't the only ones. I was sickened. I burped up some mulled wine and tasted allspice deep in my gizzard. I almost threw up on the spot. I breathed deeply, wrenched the door open and saw Dan hunched rather surreptitiously over his small TV screen.

'Right, where the hell is she?' I demanded.

'What?'

'Where's your floozy this time? Last night it was Ruta. Which lucky lady is it going to be tonight? Eh? Cheryl, is it? It'd be convenient, I suppose, she's only next door. Any time you fancy a quick one you only have to whistle over the garden fence.'

'Whoah whoa, slow down, Mel. I can't keep up. What do you mean, Ruta last night?'

'That's exactly what you did, Dan. Root her last night.'

'What?'

'Oh don't play the innocent with me, Dan. I heard you both in the shed and then saw you come out together.'

'She was helping me with some translation, Mel. I'm doing subtitling for some German films and I wanted her advice.'

'I heard grunting and squealing, Dan. There was some nookie going on in here and don't try and deny it.'

'I've been trying to tell you, Mel.'

Finally I was going to get the truth from him. He stood up. Goodness, I'd forgotten how tall he was. My heart sank; he was about to confess his infidelity, and for some reason I was overcome by how much I fancied him.

He moved aside so that I could see the TV screen, which featured some semi-nude Germans coupling on a supermarket deli counter.

'I'm subtitling some German porn films. Embarrassing but true – we need the money.'

I was transfixed by the leering faces on the screen.

'But you don't need subtitles for this, do you?'

I blushed suddenly as I thought of my mother being present in the shed.

Dan laughed. 'German pornos do have a bit of story to them, actually. Anyway, I'll turn this off, it's absolute rubbish.'

I sat down on the floor heavily. I didn't feel drunk any more; just heavy.

'I was all set to go and live in an all-women commune,' I said, deflated. 'Jo would have learned the flute and everything.'

'We haven't been communicating very well, have we?' said Dan, taking off the woolly hat and stroking the grease sculpture.

'I was supposed to look fantastic for this confrontation,' I laughed.

'You do,' said Dan, kissing me. 'It's really nice to see you.'

'I'm sorry I've been distant. I've been going slightly mad,' I said.

'And I haven't helped,' he said, and kissed me again. I was transported back to our old flat for a moment. We were carefree once more.

'Admit it, Dan, you did have a bit of a crush on Ruta, didn't you?'

Dan smiled and didn't say anything.

'Come on,' I said, tickling him. 'Admit it.'

'OK, I did fancy her a bit.'

'Well, bad luck, she's a lesbian,' I said and cackled long and loud. Dan started laughing too.

'Fancy trying out my new sofa?' he said cheekily, before quietly closing the shed door.

Epilogue

It was Christmas Eve and the streets were full of last-minute shoppers buying presents way more expensive than they would normally buy. A man was running round Boots with a really half-cocked pile of gifts filling his basket – hair tongs, overpriced perfume, hot-water-bottle cover – anything just to fill the space under the tree. I gave him a pitying smile – I had finished all of my Christmas preparations days ago. The devils on horseback were in the freezer, the turkey was in the shed, the presents were wrapped and hiding under my desk, and the tree, looking like an overweight ballerina, tottered in the living room under a mass of lights, tinsel, trinkets and baubles. Since the departure of the Latvian lodgers, I was sleeping again and I felt like a woman reborn. My old nativity music box was installed on the hall table, ready to be wound up and play its 'Silent Night' tune at an ever-decreasing pace.

'Looks like Santa's grotto in here,' mumbled Dan that morning.

I just laughed. Since our shed encounter several weeks before, Dan and I found it easier to laugh at pretty much everything.

I went past the bank and my thoughts turned wistfully to my dear friend Robin Jones. He'd been promoted to the Kingston branch, which might mean I'd never see him again. I'd sent him a Christmas card but hadn't received anything back yet. I wheeled Jo into the shopping centre, a hive of activity since the arrival of several live deer, which had been drafted in for an hour to perk up the festive display in the central atrium. Jo was entranced by them and jiggled around in the buggy, growling with delight.

Outside the shopping centre the traffic was insane, everybody desperate to pack in their last-minute errands. A green people-carrier stopped to let us go over the zebra crossing, and I smiled at the driver briefly in acknowledgement. She was a cross-faced woman with curly blonde hair, shouting at a young boy strapped into the seat beside her. Poor lad, on Christmas Eve too. She looked up and caught my eye. It was Judy. I gave her a brief smile; she looked at me quizzically for a moment, and then turned her head to look out of the side window. I was glad. That movement said everything I needed to know. I hurried over the crossing and then heard the White Stripes alerting me that a caller was trying to get through.

'Hi, Pen!' I shouted excitedly. 'What time are you all coming?'

'I'll be there with Jim and Shorty at about seven, and then the rest of the gang are coming about seven thirty.'

'Brilliant. The beers are in the fridge already.'

'Can't wait. See you later, hon. Oh by the way, I've just bought Jo the most superb present.'

'Oh yes?' I asked.

'She's coming with me to an evening with Camille Paglia and the Royal Philharmonic Orchestra. Christmas and first birthday combined. It's high time she was exposed to something inspiring. I've just bought the tickets.'

I was speechless.

'Feminism and classical music?'

'It's the future. See you later.'

I was turning into our street when the phone went again.

'Happy Christmas, dear.'

'Hi, Mum. Happy Christmas to you and Dad.'

'Now, what time are we going to see you tomorrow?'

'Around eleven OK for you?'

'Fine. So I'll expect you at noon. Now is Littly all right with bacon and prune stuffing?'

'Yes, Mum,' I said.

'I've invited Nancy too so that she can give you some makeover tips after lunch. Is that all right?'

'Yes, Mum.'

'She's chosen me the most fabulous outfit for tomorrow – red suede waistcoat, green boots and big black belt.'

'Yes, Mum,' I said, starting to chuckle.

'What are you laughing for, dear?'

'Nothing, Mum,' I said, but in my head I was imagining a sixty-five-year-old Jack and the Beanstalk.

I turned the key in the lock and there was Dan, on a ladder tying up the last of our decorations. He kissed me and unstrapped Jo from her buggy for a big hug.

'Just going to the loo,' I said cheerily. 'Be down in a minute.'

I came down three minutes later and handed Dan a plastic white stick with a blue line running through the square in the middle of it.

'Happy Christmas, Dan,' I said, beaming.

'What's this?' he said, looking at the white stick curiously. Then it dawned on him. 'Here we go again,' he said, smiling.